THE KINGDOM OF THE BRIDE

A Book on the Last Days

Martin R. Bachicha

Prescott Press

Prescott Press, Inc.
P.O. Box 53777
Lafayette, Louisiana 70505

Library of Congress Card Catalog Number:
94-068881
ISBN:933451-31-8

CONTENTS

ACKNOWLEDGMENTS

Many thanks to:

—David H. England, for taking a chance on *Kingdom of the Bride* when nobody else would;

—Linden Ritchie, for his many long hours of proofreading and whose objective criticism has made this a much better book;

—my dad, who took me to the library those many Saturdays when I was a child, and to my mom, who first taught me how to write;

—Tom Stipe, for his vision of Christian discipleship;

—Gary Greenwald, for his vision of a reigning Bride;

—Gary Larson for his wonderful painting for the cover;

—to the Bride, may she adorn herself in bright apparel and make herself ready; and most of all to the Bridegroom.

INTRODUCTION

This book is a story on the end times. As an exposition on the last days of our planet and the Second Coming of Christ, it represents a blending of the old and the new. The intermingling of the traditional and the novel is what I believe makes this book unique amongst all others on the subject of prophecy.

Much of the confusion that I believe pervades other books on *eschatology—the study of the end times*—most of which reflect the present day evangelical teaching on Christ's return, stems from a misunderstanding of two things: first, from what is actually meant by the term *the Consummation* (which literally interpreted means "completion"), and second, from what is meant by the term the *day of the Lord*. The prophetic view presented in this book is quite simple. *The Kingdom of the Bride* takes the elementary historical view that *the Consummation*, or the climax of human history, will be brought about on a literal, final day, referred to as the *day of the Lord*, in which the Lord Jesus Himself will return from Heaven to rescue those who believe in Him.

Resultantly, Christ's Second Coming is presented as a single, stupendous event. Coincident with His return on that day, also called the Last Day, will be the resurrection of the dead, the rapture or translation of living believers, the final judgment of the living and the dead, the ultimate victory of life over death, the destruction of our present world and universe, and the creation of a new heaven and a new earth in which righteousness dwells. Any prophetic system that teaches otherwise ignores the Scriptures. This view, called Amillennialism (meaning no millennium), pervaded the church for well over a thousand years after being established as doctrine by the renowned early church father Augustine. It was also vigorously defended against the premillennialists (those who teach of a thousand year earthly reign of Christ after His Second Coming) by the Protestant reformers Martin Luther and John Calvin. Amillennialism still is a central tenet of the Roman Catholic Church and many of the mainline Protestant denominations.

With regard to the new, this book introduces a revolutionary new paradigm on end time eschatology, one I call "Kingdom Amillennialism," which builds upon the basic amillennial thought of Augustine, Luther, and Calvin. Kingdom Amillennialism says there will be an appointed season of time after the great tribulation and the destruction of the Antichrist and *before* Christ's Second Coming and the end of the world. During this epoch Christ's Bride, the church, will reign upon the earth, for it is written of her, "then the sovereignty, the dominion, and the greatness of all the kingdoms under the whole heaven will be given to the people of the saints of the Highest One" (Dan. 7:27a). Henceforth, the Kingdom of the Bride represents a monumental paradigm shift from the premillennial, and particularly from the pretribulational, teachings that pervade the evangelical Church today. It is my desire that all who read this book will gain fresh new insights into the prophetic Scriptures and the drama that is presently unfolding before them, a drama that will climax with the soon return of the Son of God for His beloved Bride. I sincerely hope this will likewise serve to inspire all to a new level of devotion in serving their Master, the beautiful Bridegroom, the Lord Jesus Christ.

1
THE BRIDEGROOM IS COMING ... BUT IS THE BRIDE READY?

The *Bride of Christ* is a prophetic term. In the nineteenth chapter of the Book of Revelation, the apostle John writes, *"Let us rejoice and be glad and give glory to Him, for the marriage of [Jesus] the Lamb has come and His bride has made herself ready."*

Yet just who is the Bride of Christ? The simple truth is that most people, including Christians, don't know. Today if you mention the term "Bride of Christ" many people may be reminded of one of the 1980s most controversial films, *The Last Temptation of Christ*, and its offensive dream sequence where Jesus fantasized of forsaking the cross to marry an enticing Mary Magdalene. The world will ask, "If Jesus was truly human, wouldn't he have desired what most men desire—a beautiful, elegant bride?" The answer to this question is *yes*. Even so, the Bride for which Jesus yearned and still yearns is not a beautiful woman but a glorious Bride composed of his very body, the Church of his people (Eph. 5:25-32).

What a joyous reunion it will be when the Bridegroom at last returns for His Bride. In America this imagery seems inconsequential. Today, engaged couples spend time with each other right up until the wedding. Only on their wedding days is it still traditional for an American bride and bridegroom not to see each other prior to the marriage ceremony. However, if we were to examine the Hebrew wedding custom of Jesus' day, we would better appreciate the significance in comparing Jesus Christ's coming for His church to a bridegroom returning for his bride.

In those days the Jewish bridegroom would return to his father's house after the betrothal and would remain separate from the bride-to-be for an extended period, usually around twelve months. Only after this long year of isolation would he return to receive her. Doing so consummated the wedding. If the couple loved each other (which wasn't usually the case since most marriages were prearranged), you can imagine how this prolonged parting must have intensified their desire for one another. So it is with Christ and His Church. Christ longs to receive His Bride and His Bride longs for His return, the moment when they will be forever joined. For nearly to 2000 years, she has anticipated their reunion. And judging from the signs He told her to expect prior to His return, she now knows the moment is near.

Two Thousand Years of Waiting

Notwithstanding, when the subject of Christ's second coming is brought up we usually don't think about a reunion of a bride and a bridegroom. Instead, grim visions of an apocalypse come to mind; glimpses of Armageddon and the end of the world. Many of us have heard the doomsday preachers proclaim how the signs of this age signify how ours is the generation that soon will witness Christ's return. The infamous David Koresh built his cultic following by teaching he was Christ—the Lamb of Revelation who alone could break the seven seals of the apocalypse (Rev. 5-7) and usher in a fiery end on earth. Tragically for the misguided disciples and innocent children of his Branch Davidian cult, his destructive prophecy came to pass during the fiery calamity at their Waco, Texas, compound. This "last-days consciousness" explains not only why some people now flock to groups like Koresh's, but also why others—even those who don't believe in Christ—sometimes wonder whether the earth's chaos will one day lead to its destruction.

So what distinguishes our generation from prior ones? Hasn't turmoil from the beginning of time always covered the earth? What is it that makes the twentieth century an apocalyptic century? Indeed many could argue that ever since Jesus of Nazareth lived, the world itself has been a swirling apocalypse. When we read the passage in the Book of Revelation describing the breaking of the Lamb's first four seals, which unleashed the four horsemen of the apocalypse, it seems we are reading a history of the world from the first century onward. And still, Christ has not returned. In describing the loosing of the first dreaded horseman, the one who conquers, the Apostle John writes:

> *I watched as the Lamb opened the first of the seven seals. Then I heard one of the four living creatures say in a voice like thunder, "Come!"*
>
> *I looked, and there before me was a white horse! Its rider held a bow, and he was given a crown, and he rode out as a conqueror bent on conquest.* (Rev. 6:1-2, NIV)

The pounding hooves of the first horseman's steed have been galloping over the earth since the time of Christ. His first horrific conquest occurred when the Roman General Titus reduced Jerusalem to rubble in 70 A.D., thirty-seven years after Christ. And his appetite has not abated since.

Down through the centuries, noble and ignoble names of conquerors have filled the pages of our history books: Attila and his malevolent Huns, the "Scourge of God" who ravaged Europe during the fifth century; Mohammed and his conquering armies of Islam; Genghis Khan and his Mongol hordes who conquered Asia while threatening the gates of Europe; Suleyman the Magnificent and his fearless Turks who marched on Christendom; the Spanish conquistadors, the first conquerors of the New World; the British, who spanned an empire across the farthest oceans; Napoleon and Hitler, whose marches on Moscow met the disaster of the dreaded Russian winter; and finally the United States and the Soviet Union, once diametrical opponents in the most urgent chess game for world power and dominance. These are but a sampling of the conquerors the white horse has borne.

Following in the hoofbeats of the conquering horsemen, John sees a second horseman. This one wields a sword and straddles a red horse. In his trail lie the slain of all who litter the first horseman's countless battlefields.

> *When the Lamb opened the second seal, I heard the second living creature say, "Come!"*
>
> *Then another horse came out, a fiery red one. Its rider was given power to take peace from the earth and to make men slay each other. To him was given a large sword.* (Rev. 6:3, 4, NIV)

It is not just the conquering white horseman and the warmongering red horsemen who have ravaged our earth. For snorting in the dust of the first two horsemen rides a third. This one is black. He brings hunger to the world.

> *When the Lamb opened the third seal, I heard the third living creature say, "Come!" I looked, and there before me was a black horse! Its rider was holding a pair of scales in his hand.*
>
> *Then I heard what sounded like a voice among the four living creatures, saying, "A quart of wheat for a day's wages [a denarius], and three quarts of barley for a day's wages, and do not damage the oil and the wine!"* (Rev. 6:5, 6, NIV)

In ancient Rome a denarius was a typical worker's daily wage. We could paraphrase verse six as "a few loaves of bread for a day's pay." This implies a drastic decrease in the sustenance people need to feed their families. How prophetic! For the shortage of food has plagued mankind since its creation, particularly in the last two thousand years. In A.D. 1337, the black horseman starved four million victims during China's "Great Famine." He claimed ten million more in India's terrible (Bengal) famine of 1769-70. During the great potato blight of Ireland (1846-47) he killed nearly three million more innocents, while famine spread by drought in Northern China (1876-79) resulted in the deaths of nearly thirteen million people. All told, upwards of sixty million humans have died from famine in the last 1000 years, with most of them perishing during times when the earth's population was much less than what it is today.

After all this, is there any wonder why bringing up the rear behind the conquering, sword-wielding, and famine-inducing horsemen comes the fourth and most dreaded horseman of all: one named Death!

> *When the Lamb opened the fourth seal, I heard the voice of the fourth living creature say, "Come!"*
>
> *I looked, and there before me was a pale horse! Its rider was named Death, and Hades was following close behind him. They were given power over a fourth of the earth to kill by sword, famine and plague, and by the wild beasts of the earth.* (Rev. 6:7, 8, NIV)

The Pale Horseman kills mankind with his own weapon, the weapon of plague. In centuries past, the Pale Horseman has spewed plague over the earth in its most ghastly of forms: the feared bubonic and pneumonic plagues. Transported by parasitic fleas that lived on rats that infested the many filthy quarters of the medieval world, these plagues have claimed more than 200 million victims in three separate pandemics (A.D. 541-767, A.D. 1347-1771, and A.D. 1855 to present). The plague during the second pandemic had by 1352 killed twenty-five million people in Europe alone. So devastating was the scourge that it became known as the Black Death. The fear that accompanied the plague led a chronicler during a plague outbreak in Siena, Italy, to write, "Father abandoned child, wife husband, one brother another. . . . And I, Agnolo di Tura . . . buried my five children with my own hands. . . . So many died that all believed that it was the end of the world."[1]

The Pale Horseman's weapon of plague was thwarted temporarily when sulfa drugs and antibiotics were found to treat the diseases in the 1930s and 40s. Nevertheless, this horseman's ability to strew death and destruction by other means has not ceased. If we were able to calculate the portion of civilization that has perished over the centuries as the result of war, famine, disease, infant mortality, and the beastly cruelty of man, I'm sure a fourth of humankind (Rev. 6:8) would be a conservative estimate. Yes, the Four Horsemen of the Apocalypse have ravaged mankind for nearly two thousand years. They still ravage as the Bride continues to await her Bridegroom.

The Signs Preceding Christ's Coming

Why then are Jesus' descriptions of the signs He said would appear on the earth prior to His second coming so pertinent to our present age? What is unique about the world today? What could make us think Jesus was talking about the days in which we live? He vividly described the future turmoil while sitting on the Mount of Olives:

> *And as He sat on the Mount of Olives, the disciples came to Him privately, saying, "Tell us, when will these things be? And what will be the sign of Your coming, and of the end of the age?"*
>
> *And Jesus answered and said to them, "Take heed that no one deceives you."*
>
> *For many will come in My name, saying, "I am the Christ," and will deceive many.*
>
> *And you will hear of wars and rumors of wars. See that you are not troubled; for all these things must come to pass, but the end is not yet.*
>
> *For nation will rise against nation, and kingdom against kingdom. And there will be famines, pestilences, and earthquakes in various places.*
>
> *All these are the beginning of sorrows [or birth pangs, NASB].*
>
> *Then they will deliver you up to tribulation and kill you, and you will be hated by all nations for My name's sake. . . .*
>
> *But he who endures to the end will be saved.*
>
> *And this gospel of the kingdom will be preached in all the world as a witness to all the nations, and then the end will come.*
> (Matt. 24:3-9, 13-14, NKJV)

The Sign of Religious Deception

The deception of false religion; this was the first sign Jesus warned His disciples to watch for in the last days. Undoubtedly, this phenomenon is leaving its mark on our generation. Still, Jesus was talking about more than false religion, for false religions always have been in our world, and were even more prominent in Jesus' day when paganism and idol worship were the accepted civil practice outside of the Jewish worship of Yahweh. Paganism, with its worship of Caesar, was the state religion of the Roman empire. Its darkness cloaked the entire gentile world, separating it from God at the time of Christ's birth.

Jesus' exact words regarding the great religious deception of the last days were, *"See to it that no one misleads you. For many will come in My name, saying, 'I am the Christ,' and will mislead many."* Jesus was warning His disciples about false Christianity. He was warning them about a different Christianity with a different gospel and Messiah than the gospel He and His apostles had preached—a Christianity in which Jesus of Nazareth is not solely exalted as Lord and worshipped with the Father.

One doesn't need to envision David Koresh and his deceived Branch Davidians burning to death at Camp Apocalypse to realize that religious cults are sprouting up everywhere. Many of them profess a belief in Jesus or in "the Christ." The problem is, they profess a Christ totally different from the one the Bible proclaims. In *Approaching Hoofbeats*, a book reflecting on the Four Horsemen of the Apocalypse, Billy Graham writes,

> Many cults claim to have a high view of Christ, but deny that He rose again from the dead, or that He was the unique and divine Son of God, or that we are saved only through His atoning death on the cross. But Jesus declared, *"I am the way and the truth and the life. No one comes to the Father except through me"* (John 14:6). The apostle Peter summarized the consistent message of the New Testament from beginning to end: *"Salvation is found in no one else, for there is no other name under heaven given to men by which we must be saved"* (Acts 4:12).[2]

Yes, religious deception with its twisted gospel has greatly blinded the hearts and minds of its followers. It has filtered its message into our society, just as Jesus predicted, and has become a screen against the true Gospel of our Lord. Howbeit, this present darkness portends the forthcoming of the true Messiah, Jesus Christ.

The Birth Pangs of the 20th Century:
Earthquakes, Volcanoes and Other Natural Disasters

For nation will rise against nation, and kingdom against kingdom. And there will be famines, pestilences, and earthquakes in various places.

All these are the beginning of sorrows [or birth pangs, NASB]. (Matt. 24:7, 8, NKJV)

The twentieth century is a time of birth pangs. Cataclysmic spasms have shaken our globe continually. Wars and rumors of wars, nation rising against nation, famines, pestilences, and earthquakes have been unceasing. The earth travails, it is erupting and taking vengeance upon its inhabitants. Everywhere we gaze, we see its outbursts.

This generation of Americans observed nature's enormous destructive power firsthand in May 1980 when Mount Saint Helens violently erupted. Who can also forget the devastation wrought by the October, 1989, Bay Area earthquake that registered 7.1 on the Richter scale?

The increase in volcanic activity and earthquakes the world over is the subject of many recent books. In the book *Pole Shift*, John Warren White reports that recent data taken on the major volcanoes of Etna, Vesuvius, Pelee, and Soufriere points to a marked increase in these volcanoes' frequency of eruption over the past 200 years. Volcanic eruptions made the news as recently as June 1991 when the Philippines' Mount Pinatubo and Japan's Mount Unzen erupted simultaneously. Earthquake activity is likewise on the increase, especially in recent decades. Twenty-five of the forty-nine largest most destructive earthquakes in recorded history occurred from 1960 to 1980. In fact, in the last five years of the 1970s, more people in the world were killed by earthquakes than in the entire seventy-five years preceding![3] A July, 1976, earthquake that devastated the city of Tangshan, China, for instance, claimed between 240,000 and 750,000 lives.

The same trend has been seen in the 1980s and 90s. During the last decade and a half, major earthquakes and volcanoes resulting in substantial losses of life have occurred in Iran, Colombia, Mexico, Italy, Turkey, the Soviet Union, Indonesia and the United States. In the interim between Mount Saint Helens and "Bay Quake 89," the Mexico City earthquake of September 1985 killed between 10,000 and 20,000 people. An earthquake in El Salvador in October, 1986, killed 1200 more, injured 10,000, and left 200,000 homeless. A volcanic eruption in November of 1985 killed 20,000 people and destroyed the town of

Armero, Colombia. Tidal waves caused by earthquakes and monsoons in the Bay of Bengal struck Bangladesh in June of 1985 (and again in 1991), claiming thousands of lives. A deadly cloud of lethal gas released from Cameroon's volcanic Lake Nios killed at least 1,700 people in September of 1986. And in December, 1988, initial estimates of an earthquake centered in Soviet Armenia put the loss of life between 50,000 and 200,000 people.

The increase in earthquakes and volcanic eruptions the world over is a phenomenon that continues to puzzle scientists. Nevertheless, these occurrences coincide with predictions Jesus Christ made 2,000 years ago. Jesus said these things are merely the beginning of birth pangs. And as with a women in labor, whose birth pangs become more frequent as the moment of childbirth nears, so also will these calamities increase over the earth as the day of His return approaches.

The Birthpang of Famine

Earlier in the chapter we saw the grisly activity of the Black Horseman of the Apocalypse, the rider who brings famine to the world. The black horseman has not bridled his steed in this century, for the pains of hunger continue to gnaw at our earth's malnourished. How prophetic it was that 190 years ago the English clergyman and economist Thomas Mathus wrote, "The power of population is so superior to the power of the earth to provide subsistence," that man will succumb to "gigantic inevitable famine." Could Mathus possibly have known that one-and-a-half centuries later, experts in the 1970s would predict that famine would claim between 50 to 200 million lives around the globe within a decade?[4] Paul R. Ehrlich, a Stanford University biologist, went so far as to say, "The race between population growth and food production has already been lost. Before 1985 the world will undergo vast famines—hundreds of thousands of people are going to starve to death . . . unless plague, thermonuclear war, or some other agent kills them first."

Today the birthpang of famine is relentlessly striking Somalia, Ethiopia, and Central Africa. Today more than 150 million people on the African Continent alone are being threatened by starvation. Over the past two decades, severe famines likewise have ravaged Bangladesh and the countries of Latin America. The United States also has suffered famine's merciless pains. Nearly three million homeless in the United States go to sleep hungry every night. Yes, famine, with all of its hunger and heartache, is another of the drastic signs Jesus said would precede the Bridegroom's coming for His Bride.

The Birthpangs of Plague and Pestilence

The evolution of technology, while providing cures for such killers as the bubonic and pneumonic plagues, has introduced other woes into our society. The industrial revolution has brought with it a whole slew of new pestilences to torment humankind. Coupled with the world's exploding population, technological growth is enormously stressing the planet's ecosystem. Along with every new modern product man introduces to the world's marketplace, he produces also some poisonous and wasteful byproduct. A ghastly example of human-induced pestilence was the 1984 Union Carbide plant disaster in Bhopal, India, where poisonous vapors escaped from a leaking tank of methyl isocyanate. The deadly pesticide killed more than 2,500 people and left 3,000 critically ill. With tears running down his face, an Indian farmer who survived the calamity exclaimed, "I thought it was a plague." Others thought it was a nuclear bomb or the end of the world.[5]

A far more dangerous threat is that posed by nuclear radiation. The April, 1986, accident at the Soviet Union's Chernobyl nuclear power plant killed thirty-one Ukrainian citizens and sent clouds of radiation spewing over the European continent. Dan Beninson, chairman of the International Commission on Radiological Protection, initially predicted that radiation from the disaster would cause as many as 24,000 cancer deaths over the next seventy years.[6]

And still man continues to pollute the air he breathes and the rivers, lakes, and oceans of the world. What a tragic example was the March, 1989, Exxon Valdez oil spill off Alaska's southern coast, an ecocatastrophe that dumped eleven million gallons of petroleum into the Prince William Sound and contaminated 1100 miles of pristine Alaskan shoreline. The wreck was quickly dubbed the greatest environmental disaster in American history!

The pressures from world population and industrial evolution are depleting our globe's natural resources and wildlife also. For the first time in history thousands of wild animals are endangered species. We are also destroying our world's vegetation. While watching a recent documentary, I heard it said that if we continue to fell our world's rain forests—the providers of more than fifty percent of the world's plant and animal species, and suppliers of much of the world's fresh water and oxygen—at the present rate, in eighty-five years there will be none left. If the plants and the animals no longer survive, how much longer will man survive?

If all these pestilences were not enough, the Pale Horseman of death has introduced a new plague into our world, one called AIDS, which in time could prove to be the greatest killer ever of mankind. Through 1988, this deadly disease had claimed 45,000 victims in the United States and infected up to two million more. Former Surgeon General C. Everett Koop projected that AIDS would kill 180,000 Americans by 1991.[7] In Africa the situation is even grimmer; nearly five million Africans were carriers of the dreaded virus through 1986. This could translate to as many as 1.5 million dead Africans just from the 1986 level of infection. AIDS is making the birthpangs of plague and pestilence one of the most horrible birthpangs of all.

The Birthpang of War

> *And you will be hearing of wars and rumors of wars; see that you are not frightened, for those things must take place, but that is not yet the end.*
>
> *For nation will rise against nation, and kingdom against kingdom . . .* (Matt. 24:6, 7)

War is the most catastrophic of all the birthpangs predicted of the last days by Jesus and the Book of Revelation. We all have heard, and some of us have experienced, that "war is hell." The flames of war continue to blaze across the earth's surface. They are an inherent part of man's fallen nature, raging uncontrollably within his members. Wars always have been fought and undoubtedly always will.

Still, the warring Red Horseman of the Apocalypse has exacted his greatest vengeance on the twentieth century. So great has his recent lust for war been that more people have died from wars and related acts of genocide in our century than in all prior centuries combined. Never before in history has the red horseman fought wars of such enormous magnitude as the twentieth century's two world wars. Never before has he unleashed greater weapons of destruction for brother to annihilate brother. World War I claimed ten million military casualties alone. World War II claimed up to forty million military and civilian lives, while pitting nearly every nation of the world against the sadistic regime of an Austrian madman. The wars in this century truly have fulfilled Jesus' prophecy of "nation rising against nation," and John's admonition of the red horse: *"Its rider was given power to take peace from the earth and to make men slay each other"* (Rev. 6:4, NIV).

In addition, the wars in this century have brought with them some of the most heinous and genocidal crimes ever committed by man. Crimes against humanity unequaled from the world's foundation have occurred in most of our lifetimes. The great despot Joseph Stalin exterminated between thirty-five and forty-five million people during his twenty-five-year reign of terror over Soviet Russia. A U.S. Senate Internal Security Subcommittee report estimates that Chinese communists have killed between 34 and 62.5 million Chinese since they took power.[8] During the Second World War, Adolf Hitler butchered six million Jews in Nazi death camps, not to mention several million Russian POWs, Poles, Gypsies, and other "undesirables," as he attempted to exercise his "final solution." During World War I, more than one million Armenians died at the hands of the Ottoman Turks while on forced marches into exile in Syria. In the mid 1970s, the ruthless communist Khmer Rouge under the wicked Pol Pot annihilated three million of their own Cambodian people as they tried to create a society where love was no longer a word, much less a virtue. These are but a sampling of the holocausts that wars in our century have brought.

In the 1980s and into the 90s, we continue to witness nation rising against nation and kingdom against kingdom. The news headlines of the past two decades have displayed an immensity of armed struggles throughout the globe: Afghanistan, Lebanon, the Falkland Islands, El Salvador, Nicaragua, Northern Ireland, Angola, Iran and Iraq, Kuwait, and Rwanda. We've seen the crushing of China's pro-democracy movement, and the overthrow of Communist regimes in Eastern Europe. We witnessed Palestinians revolting on the West Bank and South Africans rebelling to overthrow apartheid. We stood aghast as Serbs slaughtered Muslims in Bosnia. Ironically, World War I was supposed to have been "the war to end all wars." But war and the suffering it brings continue to take man along a road to destruction.

Peace in a Nuclear World?

World War II, despite destroying Hitler's Germany and Imperial Japan, helped spawn nuclear weapons of mass destruction. From it also emerged two of history's greatest superpowers, the United States and the Soviet Union. America emerged from the war as the strongest military and economic power ever. Not to be ignored, within five years of the war's end, the Soviet Union had installed communist regimes in every country of Eastern Europe.

The ensuing "Cold War" between capitalism and communism brought the world's two new superpowers to the brink of war. As nuclear and biochemical weapons were developed and deployed on both sides, a "nuclear fear" gripped the hearts and minds of our world's inhabitants. We were a generation without parallel in human history. Man now possessed the power to destroy all life on planet earth. The prospect of a nuclear holocaust led Chinese premier Deng Xiaping in 1980 to expound on the inevitability of World War III: "War will burst [out] sooner or later. And whoever believes the contrary makes a tragic mistake."[9]

To the world's amazement, however, historic arms-reduction treaties between the United States and Russia, the Soviet Union's new policy of glasnost (openness) under Soviet President Mikhail Gorbachev, and most astonishingly, the crumbling of the Berlin Wall and the collapse of Communism in Eastern Europe brought about the long-hoped-for thaw in the world's Cold War as the 1980s drew to a close. By the end of the decade, the world for the first time in most our of lives appeared to be on the brink of a permanent and lasting peace.

War in the Persian Gulf

This specter of peace was shattered in August of 1990 when Iraqi strongman Saddam Hussein ordered his massive half-a-million-man army to invade defenseless Kuwait. The final United States troop concentration of more than 400,000 American soldiers ordered to the Persian Gulf was to become the largest U.S. troop buildup since the Vietnam War. Once again the world teetered on the brink.

The ultimate, lighting-quick victory of the Allied Coalition over Iraq was itself almost biblical in its proportions. Some 100 thousand Iraqi soldiers were killed by Coalition Forces who themselves suffered fewer than two-hundred dead, a rout commensurate to Gideon and his band of Israelites who smote 120,000 Midianites on a single night, with help from the angel of the Lord (Judg. 7 and 8). Nonetheless, by attempting to draw Israel into the war with his Scud missile attacks, Saddam Hussein demonstrated once again that the Middle East is a powder keg waiting to explode—a powder keg that, despite the recent Israeli-Palestinian peace plan, could someday ignite an Armageddon. The massive environmental damage caused by Saddam's dumping of oil into the Persian Gulf and his burning of Kuwaiti oil fields is eerily reminiscent of predictions in Revelation, which prophesy of the sea being turned to blood (Rev. 8:8), the earth being burned with fire (Rev. 8:7), and the sun being blackened (Rev. 8:12). The United States victory in the Persian Gulf war likely will produce unknown repercussions for the quagmire of the Middle East in the years to come.

The Persian Gulf War also all but overshadowed the massive upheaval that took place inside the Soviet Union. Gorbachev's policy of *perestroika* (restructuring), along with events such as the emergence of

Russian President Boris Yeltsin, ethnic strife in the republics of Armenia and Azerbaijan, the independence movements of the Baltic states, and the grim state of the Soviet economy brought about the ultimate downfall of the Soviet Union's Communist Party. Prior to its collapse, former Soviet Foreign Minister Eduard Shevardnadze resigned, predicting that if perestroika failed a dictator would come to power. As early as March 1990 *Time* magazine reported that a fragmenting giant with an immense nuclear arsenal like the former U.S.S.R. must be carefully watched for signs of instability, especially if it unraveled to a point where a Russian nationalist republic gained control of it. At that time, William Webster former director of the CIA, even testified that Gorbachev's enemies would one day try to oust him. True to his word, hard-line Russian Stalinists attempted to overthrow Gorbachev in an August, 1991, coup—an action that for the moment again instilled fear in the inhabitants of the free world. Despite its failure, the coup hammered the final nail into Gorbachev's political coffin and paved the way for the ultimate dissolution of the USSR by the end of 1991.

All but forgotten during the breakup of the Soviet Union, the Persian Gulf War, and the liberation of Eastern Europe, is the question of China. How can anyone forget the pictures of the Red Army's bloody squelching of China's pro-democracy movement in Beijing's Tiananmen Square in the spring of 1989? No one knows how China's quest for democracy will affect world peace.

In view of these vexing realities, is there truly peace in our world? Or are we as those in the Bible who cry out, " *'Peace! Peace!' but there is no peace!*" (Jer. 8:11)? Contrasting our superficial yearnings for peace, Jesus warned of coming inevitable conflict when he announced:

> *For then there will be great tribulation, such as has not occurred since the beginning of the world until now, nor ever shall.*
>
> *And unless those days had been cut short, no life would have been saved. . . .* (Matt. 24:21, 22a)

Jesus predicted our world would come to a gruesome climax. Days are coming, He warns, which if they are not cut short, no flesh will survive.

Speaking to the Pharisees and the Sadducees, the religious people of His day, Jesus also said:

> *When it is evening, you say, "It will be fair weather, for the sky is red."*

And in the morning, "There will be a storm today, for the sky is red and threatening." Do you know how to discern the appearance of the sky, but cannot discern the signs of the times? (Matt. 16:2b, 3)

The same can be said of this generation. It discerns the appearance of the sky when predicting a storm. But it fails to discern the signs of these stormy times. Even though it observes them, it fails to grasp what they point to: the soon return of the Bridegroom, Jesus Christ.

A Bride Without Spot, Wrinkle, or Blemish

Judging from the many ominous signs occurring throughout the earth, the time seems ripe for the Lord's return. So what is Jesus waiting on? What is keeping Him from coming for His beloved Bride? Could it be the Bride herself? The one sign Christians have failed to observe when making predictions about the Lord's return is the condition of Christ's Bride, the Church. The Bible says Jesus will return for a glorious, mature Bride—a Bride without spot or blemish; a Bride who is spreading the good news of Jesus Christ. The Apostle Paul spoke of the glorious Bride Christ will return for when he wrote to the Ephesians:

Husbands, love your wives, just as Christ also loved the church and gave Himself up for her; that He might sanctify her, having cleansed her by the washing of water with the word,

that He might present to Himself the church in all her glory, having no spot or wrinkle or any such thing; but that she should be holy and blameless. (Eph. 5:25-27)

The Apostle John in Revelation also described the resplendence of the Bride that Jesus will take for Himself when he wrote:

Let us rejoice and be glad and give the glory to Him, for the marriage of the Lamb has come and His bride has made herself ready.

And it was given to her to clothe herself in fine linen, bright and clean; for the fine linen is the righteous acts of the saints. (Rev. 19:7-8)

Finally, the Song of Songs, long thought to be a story of the love affair between Christ and His church, describes the Bride this way:

There are sixty queens and eighty concubines, And maidens without number; But my dove, my perfect one, is unique: She is

*her mother's only daughter; She is the pure child of the one who
bore her. The maidens saw her and called her blessed, The queens
and the concubines also, and they praised her, saying, Who is this
that grows like the dawn,*

> *As beautiful as the full moon,*
> *As pure as the sun,*
> *As awesome as an army with banners?* (Song of Sol. 6:8-12)

How marvelous it is for Christ to view us as a beautiful virgin adorned in splendor—His beautiful one, His perfect one—a Bride who is unique, even as He is unique. A Bride sharing in His glory and partaking in His holiness, which He made possible by dying on the cross for our sins.

Is the Bride Ready?

Yes, Jesus is coming for a magnificent, holy, and mature Bride—a Bride without spot, wrinkle, or blemish, who is boldly taking the gospel message to the world. He will not settle for less. And why should He? After all, He is the Father's only begotten Son, the most glorious of Bridegrooms.

But do the wonderful portrayals that we've just read describe the Church as she is in America and the world today? Is she indeed as perfect and unique as the Song of Songs says?—"but my dove, my perfect one, is unique." The word for "unique" here comes from the Hebrew word *echad*, which means "united" or more simply, "one." Is the Church truly united? Is she truly one? If we realize that some 22,000 denominations have formed the Church since the Reformation, some 9,000 of which still exist, this question isn't difficult to answer. The truth is, the Church today is not united. She is divided. She is splintered as she has never been since the Lord founded her. Nonetheless, Christians continually observe the signs of our times, hoping for the Lord to come back, yet wondering why He doesn't. He hasn't because we are not yet His perfect one—His unique and united one.

A late-1980 broadcast of Pat Robertson's 700 Club showed an interview with a young charismatic Catholic priest from India. This young priest related how God had begun the mighty work of bringing together the body of Christ's many elements in his country. Prior to this move of God, he explained, he often had asked God why the gospel of Jesus had met such stiff opposition and had experienced such little success in his predominantly Hindu and Muslim homeland. At the right time God answered him. God's reply was that even though religious and social tensions run higher between Muslims, Hindus, and Sikhs in India than they do between these groups and Christians, the Muslims, Hindus, and Sikhs view each other as united rivals: Muslims united with Muslims, Hindus united with Hindus, and Sikhs with Sikhs. Yet, all three look at their country's Christians and see them divided and segmented along denominational lines. They don't see Christians as they are described in the book of Acts: *"And all those who had believed were together, and had all things in common"* (Acts 2:44).

The unity of these early believers is a far cry from the continuing cycle of fragmentation and church splitting we see throughout the world today. The Church has not sought to remain united. She has not listened to Jesus's petition to the Father on the night before He was crucified where He prayed that:

> . . . *they may all be one; even as Thou, Father, art in Me, and I in Thee, that they also may be in Us; that the world may believe that Thou didst send Me.* (John 17:17, 20-21)

Jesus prayed that the Father would make us one. By this unity, the world would believe that the Father sent Jesus. And yet the Church has split over disagreements on matters such as when and how we are to be baptized, on what day of the week we are supposed to worship, on whether or not spiritual gifts are for today, and on whether or not the communion sacraments become the actual body and blood of Christ. I'm not saying there can't be such disagreements. But they should never be greater than the love we should have for each other as children of the same Father. And since we haven't loved one another and have not remained united, the world has not come to know that the Father sent Jesus.

The problem of divisiveness in the Body of Christ has other ramifications in addition to creating doctrinal differences and new denominations: every time a church splits, it leaves in its wake damaged relationships and hurt people. Often times these people abandon fellowship with the body of Christ altogether and never seek another church home.

America's Church in Decline?

The Reverend Tom Stipe, pastor of Crossroads Christian Fellowship of Denver, Colorado, has taught on the recent decline of the Church in the United States. During a sermon in early 1985, citing data presented at the International Conference of the Evangelical Association in Nairobi, Kenya, Stipe stated: "Christianity in the United States is on the decline. . . . in Southeast Asia, 34 million people came to the Lord in 1979, while in the United States . . . just less than a million people turned from Christianity to either atheism, agnosticism, or a non-Christian cult. . . . People are leaving the church in the United States by the millions. . . . That's why many missionaries from Southeast Asia are coming to the United States. I'm telling you . . . when I talk about the church needing to repent before we call the nation to repentance, the church has something to repent about."[10]

The essence of the problem, Stipe argues, is that of discipleship. Discipleship has been altered to such a degree that Christianity has become a self-improvement program. The church has become something we measure according to what we gain by joining—"what is it going to do for me?" This kind of self-centered attitude toward the church ("it wasn't meeting my needs") often causes a person to drop out of active involvement.

The Church today is calling people to believe, but it is not making disciples. The Church is not relating the whole cost of following Jesus. Much has been related about the benefits and the abundant life we receive when we give our lives to Christ, but little has been said about the costs and the sacrifices involved. The reality is that we are called by Christ. Every Christian is called to do the ministry of the Son of God. We are called to fill the role He filled while He was here on earth. We are called to follow the model and pattern he set for us.

According to Stipe, the problem is that the Church today doesn't look anything like Christ's second cousin, much less like His righteous bride. The Church has strayed from the model of what Christians are supposed to be. Stipe also said, "In Antioch they got the title 'Christian' for behaving Christlike. Christlike means they were doing the things Jesus did: preaching the gospel, raising the dead, healing the sick, feeding the poor, giving sight to the blind and casting out demons. Today we get the title when we have been to camp, . . . [been] baptized, prayed the sinners prayer, and [shown] other forms of proving that we have been born again."[11] We have the foundation, but we are missing the building. We have strayed from the model for discipleship that Jesus and His apostles established for us. In simple words, it is doing the works of Jesus. Of this model, the Apostle Paul exhorts us: *"Brethren, join in following my example, and observe those who walk according to the pattern you have in us."* (Phil. 3:17).

Jesus established the pattern. He set the example for us during His ministry on earth. Once the Church starts doing His works, she will see the fulfillment of Jesus' words: *"Truly, Truly, I say to you, he who believes in Me, the works that I do shall he do also; and greater works than these shall he do; because I go to the Father"* (John 14:12).

The Problem of Materialism and Worldliness

It has been said that the American church is the epitome of the Laodicean church in our world. The church of Laodicea was the lukewarm church of the Book of Revelation. She said of herself, *"I am rich, and have become wealthy, and have need of nothing."* But the Lord saw her and said, *"yet you do not know that you are wretched and miserable and poor and blind and naked,"* (Rev. 3:17). The Church in America has been blessed like no other church in history. Christians here should be extremely grateful for living in a country where they can practice their faith without the fear of being persecuted or killed. Beyond freedom, many in America's Church have experienced the blessings of enormous wealth and prosperity. But materialism has brought about spiritual hunger as Americans everywhere cry out for meaning in life beyond what material blessings can bring.

Added to materialism is the American notion that individual happiness and fulfillment is the grand purpose of life. "I did it my way," "do your own thing," and "if it feels good do it" are attitudes that have caused a rapid moral decline in America over the past twenty-five years. It is happening to our country just as the Apostle Paul predicted, *"But realize this, that in the last days difficult times will come. For men will be lovers of self, lovers of money, boastful, arrogant. . . , lovers of pleasure rather than lovers of God"* (2 Tim. 3:1-4). Christians, too, have been caught up in this worldliness. Need we emphasize how much the sex and money scandals of certain televangelists have damaged the reputation of the body of Christ? When one person in the body sins, the whole body is labeled guilty.

We need to realize that when the Lord spoke the following, He was not speaking to unbelievers, but He was speaking to the Church:

> *I know your deeds, that you are neither cold nor hot; I would that you were cold or hot.*

> *So because you are lukewarm, and neither hot nor cold, I will spit you out of My mouth.* (Rev. 3:15-16)

These are awfully harsh words. Fortunately, the Lord offers us His grace by calling us to repentance:

> *Those whom I love, I reprove and discipline; be zealous therefore, and repent.*

> *Behold, I stand at the door and knock; if anyone hears My*
> *voice and opens the door, I will come in to him, and will dine*
> *with him, and he with Me.* (Rev. 3:19, 20)

The Bride For Whom Jesus Returns

In the Song of Solomon the chorus sings of a little girl who has no breasts:

> *We have a little sister,*
> *And she has no breasts;*
> *What shall we do for our sister*
> *On the day when she is spoken for?*
> *If she is a wall,*
> *We shall build on her a battlement of silver;*
> *But if she is a door,*
> *We shall barricade her with planks of cedar.* (Song 8:8, 9)

Gary Greenwald, pastor of the Eagle's Nest of Santa Ana, California, explains this parable: "this little sister is going to grow up some day . . . to become . . . either . . . a wall against sin, standing up for righteousness . . . and putting up the holy standard of God, or . . . a door . . . [letting] worldliness come . . . into her to prostitute it. If she be a wall standing for righteousness, we will build on her a battlement of silver. And if she be a door open to all immorality, we will enclose her with boards of cedar. We are going to board her up and let no one into her."[12]

Then the little sister speaks and says, *"I was a wall, and my breasts were like towers; Then I became in his eyes as one who finds peace"* (Song of Sol. 8:10). Only when the Church grows up to be a mature, developed, and united Bride, standing against evil and delivering the gospel's saving news to the world, will she be as one who finds favor in the Bridegroom's eyes. Only then will she be ready to be taken by Him to spend eternity at His side, living and reigning together with Him for time everlasting.

Notes

1. Nicole Duplaix, "Fleas: The Lethal Leapers," *National Geographic*, 173 no. 5 (May 1988), 676-682, 690.

2. Billy Graham, *Approaching Hoofbeats* (Minneapolis: Grason, 1983), 89.

3. John Wesley White, *The Coming World Dictator* (Minneapolis: Bethany Fellowship Inc., 1981), 104-106.

4. Thomas Canby, "Can the World Feed its People?" *National Geographic*, 148 no. 1 (July 1975), 5.

5. Pico Iyer, "India's Night of Death," *Time* (17 December 1984), 22. Used by permission.

6. Michael S. Serrill, "We Are Still Not Satisfied," *Time*, Sept. 8, 1986, 46. Used by permission.

7. "A Dose of Straight Talk on AIDS," *U.S. News & World Report* (3 November 1986), 8.

8. Dr. Fred C. Schwarz, *Why Communism Kills: The Legacy of Karl Marx* (Long Beach, CA: Christian Anti-Communism Crusade, n.d.), 2.

9. *The Los Angeles Times*, 2 September 1980, quoted in Graham, *Approaching Hoofbeats*, 127.

10. Tape of Tom Stipe's Bible study entitled *Call to Discipleship: Servanthood Renewal*, no. 3326, Crossroads Christian Fellowship, Wheatridge, CO.

11. Tape of Tom Stipe's Bible study entitled *Being the Church Outside the Building*, no. 5111.

12. Tape of Gary Greenwald's Bible study entitled *The Reigning Bride*, no. 201, The Eagle's Nest, P.O. Box 19038 Irvine, CA 92714.

2
DANIEL'S FOUR
WILD BEASTS

We saw in chapter 1 how the events taking place in the twentieth century remarkably portray the predictions Jesus Christ made about events leading up to the end of the world. In this chapter we will look at vital Old Testament prophecies being fulfilled in our generation, occurrences that the prophet Daniel predicted in his apocalypse which, likewise, predict the soon return of Jesus for His Bride.

The prophecies we will look at deal with the rise of the twentieth century's superpowers and with how their ascent is foreboded by the four wild beasts of Daniel, chapter 7. Daniel, in his apocalypse, sees these four great beasts rising out of the sea, a prophetic symbol of the Gentile world. The prophet describes them as being wild, vicious, and cruel. Their identities have baffled generations of Bible scholars. Most recent scholars believe the first three beasts symbolize the three ancient kingdoms of Babylon, Medo-Persia, and Greece, while the fourth, and most dreadful, represents some kind of latter-day Roman Empire. The true identities of these four beasts not only are crucial for interpreting prophecy, they are critical to the end-times believer. For if these beasts are not the ancient realms just mentioned, but instead are latter-day empires, Christians can be even more assured they are living in the last days. In the following pages we will identify these symbolic beasts, seeing how each relates to modern history and the onset of the Great Tribulation, the time of the greatest testing man ever will know.

Daniel and the Four Beasts

Daniel's vision of the four beasts is as follows:

> In the first year of Belshazzar king of Babylon . . . I was looking in my vision by night, and behold, the four winds of heaven were stirring up the great sea.
>
> And four great beasts were coming up from the sea, different from one another.

The first was like a lion and had the wings of an eagle. I kept looking until its wings were plucked, and it was lifted up from the ground and made to stand on two feet like a man; a human mind also was given to it.

And behold, another beast, a second one, resembling a bear. And it was raised up on one side, and three ribs were in its mouth between its teeth; and thus they said to it, "Arise, devour much meat!"

After this I kept looking, and behold, another one, like a leopard, which had on its back four wings of a bird; the beast also had four heads, and dominion was given to it.

After this I kept looking in the night visions, and behold, a fourth beast, dreadful and terrifying and extremely strong; and it had large iron teeth. It devoured and crushed, and trampled down the remainder with its feet; and it was different from all the beasts that were before it, and it had ten horns. (Dan. 7:1-7)

As I previously mentioned, most biblical scholars believe the first three beasts Daniel saw were the three, powerful, ancient kingdoms of Babylon, Medo-Persia, and Greece. Without meaning to downplay the roles each of those great empires played in history, there are two main reasons the first three beasts cannot symbolize them. Before stating them, however, note that Daniel previously identifies Babylon, Medo-Persia, and Greece as parts of the statue Babylonian King Nebuchadnezzar saw in his "statue vision" (Dan. 2:31-45). (We will study Nebuchadnezzar's Statue Vision later in chapter 3.) In addition, the prophet portrays Medo-Persia and Greece as the wild ram and wild goat of Daniel, chapter 8. Daniel uses different imageries to identify Medo-Persia and Greece, first as parts of a statue representing their inherent idolatries, and then as two overpowering beasts (the ram and the goat) that symbolize their warring, conquering armies. There is no clear reason why he would symbolize them again as the bear and the leopard of Daniel 7. If the bear and the leopard of chapter 7 were meant to represent Medo-Persia and Greece, then these two empires would be symbolized three times in the book of Daniel. We must ask if the importance of two empires that existed well over two thousand years ago warrants such attention by Daniel, the foundational book on the end times.[1]

In sharp contrast to the statue vision and to the one of the ram and the goat, both of which he boldly interprets, the vision of the four wild beasts perplexes Daniel, implying these beasts had identities different than any he could have known. Regarding the vision's meaning and the time when it will occur, Daniel writes:

> *As for me, Daniel, my spirit was distressed within me, and the visions in my mind kept alarming me.*

> *I approached one of those who were standing by and began asking him the exact meaning of all this. So he told me and made known to me the interpretation of these things:*

> *These great beasts, which are four in number, are four kings who will arise from the earth.* (Dan. 7:15-17)

Verse 17 provides the vital clue why the first three beasts Daniel saw cannot symbolize the past realms of Babylon, Medo-Persia, and Greece. Here the angel is speaking to Daniel of the future: *"These great beasts . . . are four kings who will arise."* From this it becomes clear that ancient Babylon cannot possibly symbolize the first beast. At the time of Daniel's vision, Babylon was not a future kingdom, it had already reached its pinnacle and was in a state of decline under Belshazzar. Thus, the angel is speaking of a power that will arise in the future after Babylon. If the first beast was not Babylon, we can only conclude the second and third beasts were not Medo-Persia and Greece.

Also, look at Daniel 7:11 and 12:

> *Then I kept looking because of the sound of the boastful words which the horn was speaking; I kept looking until the [fourth] beast was slain, and its body was destroyed and given to the burning fire.*

> *As for the rest of the beasts [the first three], their dominion was taken away, but an extension of life was granted to them for an appointed period of time.* (Dan. 7:11,12)

These verses show that after the destruction of the fourth beast, which every Bible scholar identifies with the Antichrist's future end-times kingdom, there will be remnants of the first three beasts still present on the earth, howbeit in some incapacitated form. Babylon, Medo-Persia, and Ancient Greece cannot leave such a remnant, for none of them exist today. Even though it might be argued that traces of Nebuchadnezzar's Babylon, Cyrus' Medo-Persia, and Alexander's Greece still exist in the present-day countries of Iraq, Iran, and Greece, we must recall from verse 17 that Daniel is looking into the distant future. Thus, to provide a viable remnant in these last days, the first three beasts in Daniel's vision must be three end-time Gentile kingdoms. Let us now identify them.

The Winged Lion: The British Empire

The first was like a lion and had the wings of an eagle. I kept looking until its wings were plucked, and it was lifted up from the ground and made to stand on two feet like a man; a human mind also was given to it. (Dan. 7:4)

The first great beast Daniel sees arising from the sea has to be the British Empire, which reached its pinnacle of power from the late sixteenth, through the early twentieth centuries.

The turning point in this first great beast's rise to world power came in the summer of 1588 when the English navy defeated the powerful Spanish armada off the British coast. This event established England as the world's premier power and opened a door for her to colonize the globe. Via her powerful navy, the British Empire subjugated much of the known world throughout the next three-and-a-half centuries. Countries and entire continents, including India, Australia, America, Canada, much of Africa, and even China, paid homage and tribute to her ruling monarch. It is no coincidence the stately lion, which throughout history has symbolized kingly rule and authority is the beast Daniel saw rising up from the sea. Today it still is the proud symbol of the British Commonwealth.

When spread, the lion's wings of eagles symbolize how British dominion covered the earth. As an eagle's wings soar with the wind, so also did British canvas sail the ocean's tempests while establishing its providence. Despite being imperial, British rule had its positive side. No nation of its day contributed more toward spreading the gospel by sending missionaries out into the world than did England. Since the eagle is a symbol of God, the eagle wings also represent how the British Empire once covered the earth with the Gospel of Jesus Christ.

The plucking of its wings, however, symbolizes the wane of the lion's worldly empire and its decline as a major herald of the gospel. Being lifted up from the ground and made to stand on two feet like a man represents the beast having to fend for itself on its own two feet, no longer the ruling lion that devoured the material resources of its former colonies. The human mind given to it represents the secular, humanistic mindset that has swept over this once God-fearing country in years past.

Yes, the winged lion that became like a man is the once-powerful British Empire. Having identified the first beast, who is the second?

The Bear: Russia

> *And behold, another beast, a second one, resembling a bear.*
> *And it was raised up on one side, and three ribs were in its mouth*
> *between its teeth; and thus they said to it, "Arise, devour much*
> *meat!"* (Dan. 7:5)

Can there be any doubt about the identity of this second great beast? If the first beast is the British Empire, then the second has to be Russia— or the former USSR. The beast's form, "resembling a bear," is clearly the symbol of the former Soviet Union and present day Russia.

According to Paul Carell, author of the book *Hitler Moves East*, 1941-1943, the main event in Russia's rise to world power occurred at the Battle of Poltava near Kiev where "Tsar Peter the Great inflicted a crushing defeat on the Swedes in 1709. The battle was the death-blow to Sweden's Nordic empire, and marked the emergence of Russia as a modern great power in history."[2] The Bear being raised up on one side symbolizes how the Soviet Union's populace and its military and industrial prowess historically have been more heavily weighted towards its European frontier.

In order to interpret the meaning of the three ribs between the beast's teeth, one needs to know the locale of the Bear's head and mouth. Quoting the Russian poet Alexander Pushkin, Carell writes: "Novgorod the father, Kiev the mother, Moscow the heart, and St. Petersburg the head of the Russian empire." The Bolshevik revolution did not alter this. Communism's mind evolved in the shipyards of St. Petersburg. Lenin spawned his revolution there, and to honor him the Bolsheviks changed the city's name to Leningrad (it has since changed back). For this, Carell calls Leningrad "the conscience of the Red Empire."[3]

Not only is Leningrad-St. Petersburg the ideological head and conscience of the Russian empire, but its port located on the Gulf of Finland (an arm of the Baltic Sea) is the largest in Russia. During his reign, one of Peter the Great's prime objectives was to obtain a major seaport for his empire. Tsar Peter believed the new city would provide a port for trade through the Baltic Sea, giving Russia a "window on Europe." For years millions of tons of imported raw materials and foodstuffs, in particular U.S. wheat, have flowed through Leningrad. In retrospect, the Baltic Sea route to the "head" Leningrad-St. Petersburg is the mouth of the Soviet Union.

If the Baltic sea is the Bear's mouth, then the three ribs clenched between its teeth must undoubtedly be the three recently independent Baltic Republics of Lithuania, Latvia, and Estonia, countries annexed by the Soviet Union in 1940, and recaptured from the Nazi's during World War II. Being themselves victims of Soviet repression, the phrase "devour much meat" appropriately symbolizes the violation the Bear inflicted upon them over nearly fifty years of totalitarian rule.

The Bear is Russia. Now who is the third beast?

The Leopard: The United States of America

> *After this I kept looking, and behold, another one, like a leopard, which had on its back four wings of a bird; the beast also had four heads, and dominion was given to it.* (Dan. 7:6)

The third beast's identity should be harder to establish, partly because God hasn't portrayed it as the eagle we symbolically use for her. Howbeit, if the first two beasts are the British Empire and the Soviet Union, then almost by default the third beast coming up from the sea must be the United States of America. Even as you examine this beast's features, that of a leopard with four heads and four wings, you will begin to see the parallels with our great nation.

The U.S.A is not the largest country in the world, either in area or population. It is without a doubt though, one of the strongest, swiftest, and most powerful, just like a prowling leopard. Likewise, the leopard in its jungle habitat is a solitary beast, completely concerned with its own interests. In the same way the United States, despite its enormous might, was strongly isolationist prior to Pearl Harbor; a trait that initially kept it out of the first two world wars. Today the mindset developed by this long history of solitude still influences the United States in its dealings with other nations of the world.

In order to understand the meaning of the leopard's four heads and four wings, we must look at Ezekiel, chapter 1, wherein the prophet Ezekiel also sees a vision of four beasts, each having four faces and four wings (v. 6). In Ezekiel's vision each face of each beast gazes toward one of the earth's four directions. Because of its similarities, the same is likely true for Daniel's beast.

The leopard's four heads face toward each direction—north, south, east, and west—symbolizing how its eyes gaze over all the earth. Isn't this like the United States, whose intelligence networks and strategic spy satellites allow nothing to take place on the earth that it doesn't know about? The leopard's four wings symbolize how it spreads its dominion over the whole earth, exercising its strategic interests in every corner of the globe, north (Canada), south (Latin America), east (the Middle East and the Orient) and west (Western Europe). The winged leopard's speed signifies how swiftly the United States is capable of responding to a national crisis in any of these four strategic directions (witness the massive military buildup in the Persian Gulf). Since dominion is given to it, this beast is more influential and powerful than the first two beasts.

Yes, the leopard with four heads and four wings is the United States. Are you surprised the Bible actually talks about America? Later you will discover Daniel 7 is not the only place it is mentioned.

The First Three Beasts in Retrospect

Even though they arise in order, the first three beasts in Daniel 7 do not successively destroy each other as history tells us is the case with the ancient kingdoms of Babylon, Medo-Persia, and Greece.[4] Their rise to power—the British Empire in 1588, Russia in 1709, and the United States in 1776 (the year of her independence)—corresponds to the order in which Daniel saw them: the lion coming up first, then the bear, then the leopard. But consistent with Daniel's vision, Great Britain, the Soviet Union and the United States, the three main victors and the most powerful countries in the world after World War II, never have fought a war amongst themselves that has resulted in one of the three being severely weakened or destroyed.

Based on these observations, and on the scriptures themselves, we must conclude the first three wild beasts in Daniel's frightening, end-times vision are three world empires that have risen to power in the last four hundred years: the British Empire, Russia, and the United States of America. This makes it even likelier that the return of our blessed hope, Jesus Christ, is right at the door.

The Fall of the First Two Beasts

No one can contend that Great Britain is but a shell of its former greatness. The end of World War II brought about the dismantling of its empire. The lion's demise already has happened, as Daniel 7:4 predicts.

But what about the bear and the leopard? Before glasnost and the fall of the Berlin Wall, either of their declines would have been difficult to contemplate. It seemed nothing short of an all out nuclear war between the Soviet Union and the United States would prevent one of the two world superpowers from gaining a dominant position over the other. But today the Berlin Wall has fallen, the Cold War is over, and the Soviet Union, after being torn apart by internal strife and economic ruin, is no more. The Baltic republics of Lithuania, Latvia, and Estonia are now independent. Gorbachev, once hailed as the Man of the Century by admiring Americans, has resigned, overwhelmed by the events that dismantled his country. The United States, via its overwhelming victory in the Persian Gulf War, has now entrenched itself as the world's sole military superpower. The hungry Bear Russia has fallen and no longer appears to be a threat to world peace.

Nevertheless, there is one key event that still must take place—an event that in the end must kill the great Bear. This event, which the Bible predicts, will bring about Russia's utter destruction. It is the future war prophetically known as the Battle of Gog and Magog.[5] The following passage from the Book of Ezekiel describes the participants in this great battle:

> *Son of man, set your face toward Gog of the land of Magog, the prince of Rosh, Meshech, and Tubal, and prophecy against him, and say, "Thus says the Lord God," Behold, I am against you, O Gog, prince of Rosh, Meshech, and Tubal.*
>
> *And I will turn you about, and put hooks into your jaws, and I will bring you out, and all your army, . . .*
>
> *Persia, Ethiopia, and Put with them, all of them with shield and helmet;*
>
> *Gomer with all its troops; Beth-togarmah from the remote parts of the north with all its troops—many peoples with you. . . .*
>
> *After many days you will be summoned; in the latter years you will come into the land that is restored from the sword, whose inhabitants have been gathered from many nations to the mountains of Israel which had been a continual waste; but its people were brought out from the nations, and they are living securely, all of them.*
>
> *And you will go up, you will come like a storm; you will be like a cloud covering the land, you and all your troops, and many peoples with you.* (Ezek. 38:2-6, 8-9)

Continuing in the next chapter, the prophet writes:

> *And you, son of man, prophesy against Gog, and say, "Thus says the Lord God," Behold, I am against you, O Gog, prince of Rosh, Meshech, and Tubal;*
>
> *and I shall turn you around, drive you on, take you up from the remotest parts of the north, and bring you against the mountains of Israel."* (Ezek. 39:1-2)

These verses predict the future invasion of Israel, after she is restored to the promised land, by a confederacy of nations headed by a prince named Gog, whose homeland is found in the uttermost north in a land called Magog. Gog is also referred to as the chief prince of Rosh, Meshech, and Tubal. As to the identity of Gog, nearly all Bible scholars concur: by viewing a world map, it is the only nation that lies to the remote north of the land of Israel—it is Russia.

A future Russian invasion of Israel seemed inevitable when the Communist Party possessed the full reins of power in the 1980s. In view of recent events, such an invasion now seems unlikely to some people. At the very least, the motives for such an attack will be different.

Perhaps a future invasion of Israel will be one last desperate act by hard-line, pro-Stalinist Russian Nationalists, a grassroots movement motivated by fierce anti-Semitism that grows deeper than the top layer of hard-line ousted communists. The invasion could soon become reality if some future Russian dictator comes to power, such as rising right-wing, extremist politician Vladimir Zhirinovsky—feared by some as the next Hitler. Fiercely anti-Semitic, Zhirinovsky likely would use the easiest scapegoat he could find to instigate his military aggression. Throughout European history, Jews have been that scapegoat. The presence of Gomer—the Hebrew word for Germany—in the invasion force substantiates this. Especially when one considers the recent rise in Germany of right-wing, Neo-Nazi ultranationalists and the fact Zhirinovsky is vigorously lobbying their support. He also advocates dividing up Poland and the Baltic states in a German-Russian alliance. Pure hatred of the Jews likely will prove to be the prime motive for Russia's invasion.

Whatever the motive, there is abundant prophetic and historical evidence that predicts Russia will instigate such an attack. First, Arno C. Gaebelein in his book *The Prophet Ezekiel* writes:

> We know from Genesis 10:2 that Magog was the second son of Japheth. . . . Magog's land was located in, what is called today, the Caucasus and the adjoining steppes. . . . Rosh,

Meshech and Tubal were called by the ancients Scythians. They roamed as nomads in the country around and north of the Black Sea and the Caspian Sea, and were known as the wildest barbarians. . . .[6]

In addition, Hal Lindsey in *The Late Great Planet Earth* quotes Herodotus, a fifth century B.C. Greek philosopher, as mentioning Meshech and Tubal, identifying them with "a people named the Samaritans and Muschovites who lived at that time in the ancient province of Pontus in northern Asia Minor."[7] Lindsey quotes Josephus, a Jewish historian of the first century, who wrote "that the people of his day known as the Moschevi and Thobelites were founded by Meshech and Tubal respectively. . . . these people lived in the northern regions above the Caucasus mountains."[8]

Quoting Pliny, a noted Roman writer of early Christian times, Lindsey writes, "Hierapolis, taken by the Scythians, was afterward called Magog."[9] He also says "any good history book of ancient times traces the Scythians to be a principal part of the people who make up modern Russia" (p. 53).

Lindsey quotes Wilhelm Gesenius, a great Hebrew scholar of the early nineteenth century, from his unsurpassed *Hebrew Lexicon:*

> "Meshech . . . was founder of the Moschi, a barbarous people, who dwelt in the Moschian mountains."[10] . . . the Greek name, "Moschi," derived from the Hebrew name Meshech is the source name for the city of Moscow. In discussing Tubal he [Gesenius] said, "Tubal is the son of Rapheth, founder of the Tibereni, a people dwelling on the Black Sea to the west of the Moschi." Gesenius concludes by saying that these people undoubtedly make up the modern Russian people (p. 53).

Speaking of Rosh, the German scholar Dr. Keil says, "The Byzantine and Arabic writers frequently mention a people called Ros and Rus, dwelling in the country of Taurus, and reckoned among the Scythian tribes."[11] In addition, Lindsey quotes Gesenius from his *Lexicon* as saying, Rosh was a designation for the tribes then north of the Taurus mountains, dwelling in the neighborhood of the Volga.[12]

He concluded that in this name and tribe we have the first historical trace of the Russ or Russian nation (p. 54).

There can be no question regarding the identity of Gog, the chief prince of Rosh, Meshech, and Tubal. The abundance of historical evidence clearly points to it. It is Russia.

Following at Russia's heels when it invades Israel will be Iran, Libya, and Ethiopia (Ezek. 38:5), countries that are currently hostile towards Israel. Persia, as most know, is the ancient name for Iran. *Put* is the Hebrew word for Libya. What most people don't know is that parts of ancient Persia encompassed much of what is now modern day Iraq. In fact, Baghdad has been the capital of the Persian Empire several times throughout past centuries. One can only speculate what effect Iraq's defeat in the Persian Gulf War will have on future courses of events. Here are two possible scenarios. First, since it has been a traditional Soviet ally and adversary of Israel, Iraq might attempt to align itself with a future anti-Semitic Kremlin regime in order to reestablish itself as a dominant force in the Middle East. Such an alliance would pave the way for the Russian and Iraqi troops to march through Iraq toward Jerusalem. Another possibility is that Iraq will remain so severely weakened, it will be unable to resist any future onslaught of Russian armies across its borders when an invasion does begin.

Despite the great invasion force Israel will face, Ezekiel writes:

> *"And it will come about on that day, when Gog comes against the land of Israel," declares the Lord God, "that My fury will mount up in My anger. . . .*

> *"And I shall call for a sword against him on all My mountains," declares the Lord God. "Every man's sword will be against his brother.*

> *"And with pestilence and with blood I shall enter into judgment with him; and I shall rain on him, and on his troops, and on the many peoples who are with him, a torrential rain, with hailstones, fire, and brimstone.* (Ezek. 38:18, 21-22)

These scriptures paint a vivid picture of how God will utterly destroy the armies of Russia and its allies when they invade Israel. Whether God will accomplish this through divine intervention or whether He will use the most powerful country on earth, the United States, to achieve His purpose remains to be seen. Since the United States is a staunch ally of Israel, it is likely the U. S. will become involved in the conflict. If the battle escalates into a limited nuclear war (note the fire in Ezek. 39:6), Russia will come out the loser.

As to its timing on the prophetic calendar, the first battle of Gog and Magog must occur at least seven years prior to the abomination of desolation, the event that will initiate the Great Tribulation (Matt. 24:15). It must occur then because Ezekiel says the inhabitants of Israel will consume the spoil and wreckage of the Gog/Magog war for seven full years (Ezek. 39:9, 10). Moreover, as we will see in chapter 7, Israel will desert the Holy Land after the abomination of desolation and throughout the Great Tribulation, leaving the land desolate. Thus, the seven years (after Gog/Magog) during which Israel lives off the spoil in the land must occur before she flees from it .

Russia's defeat at Gog/Magog will finally eliminate the bear from the stage of world power. But what about the third great beast Daniel saw—the leopard, the United States of America—what will bring about its demise? We will discuss this important topic in the next chapter, seeing how its decline will lead to the rise of the dreaded fourth beast, the Kingdom of the Antichrist.

Notes

1. We should also note that the leopard does not crush the bear in Daniel 7, as the goat (ancient Greece) crushes the ram (Medo-Persia) in Daniel, chapter 8. This further implies the bear and the leopard of Daniel 7 are different kingdoms.

2. Paul Carell, *Hitler Moves East* (New York: Ballentine Books, 1964), 124.

3. Carell, 233.

4. Medo-Persia under Darius the Mede conquered Babylon in 539 B.C. The Greeks under Alexander the Great conquered the Medo-Persian Empire in 331 B.C.

5. It should be noted this first Gog/Magog war is different from the one involving Gog and Magog in Revelation 20:8. That battle will take place at the end of the "millennium." This battle will take place sometime before the start of the tribulation.

6. (New York: Our Hope, 1918), 257-258, quoted in Steve Shearer, *The Beginning of the End* (Englewood, CO: Catalyst Publishing, Inc., 1985), 182. Used by permission.

7. Walter Chamberlein, *The National Resources and Conversion of Israel* (London: n.p., 1854), quoted in Hal Lindsey, *The Late Great Planet Earth* (New York: Bantam Books Inc., 1981), 53.

8. Louis Bauman, *Russian Events in the Light of Bible Prophecy* (Philadelphia: The Balkiston Co., 1952), quoted in Lindsey, *Planet Earth*, 53.

9. John Cumming, D.D., *The Destiny of the Nations* (London: Hurst & Blackette, 1864), quoted in Lindsey, *Planet Earth*, 53.

10. Wilhelm Gesenius, D.D., *Hebrew and English Lexicon*, quoted in Lindsey, *Planet Earth*, 53.

11. C.F. Keil, D.D. and F. Delitzch, D.D., *Biblical Commentary on the Old Testament* (Grand Rapids, MI: Eerdmans Publishing Co., n.d.), quoted in Lindsey, *Planet Earth*, 54.

12. Gesenius, op. cit., quoted in Lindsey, *Planet Earth*, 54.

3

THE FOURTH BEAST: THE KINGDOM OF THE ANTICHRIST

After this I kept looking in the night visions, and behold, a fourth beast, dreadful and terrifying and extremely strong; and it had large iron teeth. It devoured and crushed, and trampled down the remainder with its feet; and it was different from all the beasts that were before it, and it had ten horns.

While I was contemplating the horns, behold, another horn, a little one, came up among them, and three of the first horns were pulled out by the roots before it; and behold, this horn possessed eyes like the eyes of a man, and a mouth uttering great boasts. (Dan. 7:7, 8)

No one will disagree that the Fourth Beast in Daniel's vision, the beast with ten horns that "devoured and crushed, and trampled . . . the remainder with its feet," is the future kingdom of the Antichrist, the future evil world ruler who will attempt to destroy God's church and bring the entire earth under Satan's dominion. In fact, C. I. Scofield[1] and Hal Lindsey[2] directly identify the personage of the beast's "little horn" with the Antichrist himself.

But what are the characteristics of this fourth great beast? What kingdom will the last, great gentile empire encompass as it reigns and exercises dominion in the earth? Reading further into Daniel's vision provides a better understanding of this beast's nature, because an angel later describes to Daniel the meaning behind the beast's ten horns and the little horn that rises up among them.

Then I desired to know the exact meaning of the fourth beast, which was different from all the others, exceedingly dreadful, with its teeth of iron and its claws of bronze, and which devoured, crushed, and trampled down the remainder with its feet, and the meaning of the ten horns that were on its head, and the other horn which came up, and before which three of them fell, namely, that horn which had eyes and a mouth uttering great boasts, and which was larger in appearance than its associates. . . .

Thus he said: The fourth beast will be a fourth kingdom on the earth, which will be different from all the other kingdoms, and it will devour the whole earth and tread it down and crush it.

As for the ten horns, out of this kingdom ten kings will arise; and another will arise after them, and he will be different from the previous ones and will subdue three kings. (Dan. 7:19-20, 23-24)

As these verses show, the Antichrist will rise to power as the head of a coalition originally formed by ten kingdoms, of which the Antichrist will uproot three. When I first started writing this book, I believed what most prophetic writers teach today—that the ten horns represent ten nations that will one day form a latter-day Roman empire; an empire that will be territorially (and in the eyes of God) equivalent to the Roman Empire of old. An important verse that led me to believe this was Daniel 9:26. Prophesying of Jerusalem's destruction in 70 A.D. by the Roman general Titus, Daniel writes, "and the people of the prince who is to come will destroy the city and the sanctuary." Since it was the Romans; i.e., the people of the prince who is to come, who destroyed the holy city and the temple in Titus's time, this verse implies the prince who is to come—the Antichrist—will come out of a latter-day version of Rome.

The most popular scenario supporting this theory is that the ten countries likely to form this modern-day Roman Empire will be members of the European Economic Community (EEC). Coincidentally, the EEC comprised ten nations over much of its twenty-year existence. A monkey wrench was thrown into this theory in December of 1985, when the addition of Spain and Portugal raised the EEC's membership to twelve. Still, just considering the locale of the EEC's member nations (Italy and Greece among them) was enough to give the common market theory credibility.

It wasn't until I began reconsidering the identity of the vision's first three beasts that I started realizing how little scriptural support there is for teaching Daniel's Fourth Beast is the Roman Empire. To begin with, if the first three beasts in Daniel Seven are not Babylon, Medo-Persia, and Greece, then the fourth beast does not have to be Rome (as it would if they were[3]). In addition, there is nothing in Revelation, chapters 13 or 17, which further discuss the ten-horned beast, that suggests the Antichrist's kingdom will be a reinstitutionalized Roman Empire. Look for yourself. There is simply nothing there.

Daniel and Nebuchadnezzar's Statue Vision

Most importantly, the more we look at the other common passage used to support the latter-day Roman Empire theory—King Nebuchadnezzar's Statue Vision of Daniel 2:31-45—the less support we see for the final, gentile world kingdom being Rome. The memory of this ancient Babylonian king was resurrected recently during the Persian Gulf Crisis when it was reported that Saddam Hussein viewed himself as a latter-day Nebuchadnezzar who would restore to Iraq the past glory of ancient Babylon. In his vision, Nebuchadnezzar saw a statue that represents four powerful, ancient kingdoms that were to reign over the earth. The statue's head of gold, symbolizing the first kingdom, is Babylon, for Daniel interpreted it as so (Dan. 2:38). Consequently, the statue's breast and arms of silver represent Medo-Persia, which arose after Babylon, while its bronze belly and thighs symbolize Greece under Alexander the Great. The fourth kingdom—represented by the legs of iron and the feet partly of iron and partly of clay—the kingdom that crushed and broke all the others in pieces, is ancient Rome, which arose as a world power after Greece, crushing and subjugating Greece in the process.

It is the fourth kingdom's description, however, that fails to show any connection between ancient Rome and a reinstitutionalized Roman Empire of our day. The following verses will make this clear:

> *Then there will be a fourth kingdom as strong as iron; inasmuch as iron crushes and shatters all things, so, like iron that breaks in pieces, it will crush and break all these in pieces.*

> *And in that you saw the feet and toes, partly of potter's clay and partly of iron, it will be a divided kingdom; but it will have in it the toughness of iron, inasmuch as you saw the iron mixed with common clay.*

> *And as the toes of the feet were partly of iron and partly of pottery, so some of the kingdom will be strong and part of it will be brittle.*

> *And in that you saw the iron mixed with common clay, they will combine with one another in the seed of men; but they will not adhere to one another, even as iron does not combine with pottery.* (Dan. 2:40-43)

Those who teach the revived, latter-day Roman Empire theory try to make a connection between the statue's ten toes and the ten horns on the fourth end-times beast of Daniel 7, saying they will represent the ten-nation, end-time confederation that will make up the Antichrist's kingdom. Since they believe the fourth Kingdom of Iron will exist in the end-times, they also teach that Daniel 2:34-35 refers to the Second Coming of Christ. These verses describe a stone that, after being cut out of rock without hands, crushes the statue and becomes a great mountain that fills the whole earth.

Notice, however, that verses 40-43 refer to only one kingdom: ancient Rome. They make no reference to a time lapse between ancient Rome and some modern-day resurrection of it. It is pure conjecture to read a time lapse into these verses. On top of this, those who equate Rome's ancient empire with a confederacy of nations from the EEC are as Jim McKeever says, "ignoring a bit of history." McKeever writes in *The Coming Climax of History,* "The Roman empire was not primarily a European empire . . . it included parts of Africa, the Middle East, Turkey, Armenia, and even a part of Russia. . . . Some of the members of OPEC; [i.e. their geographic area] were included in the old Roman empire. Thus, OPEC could be the re-establishment of the Roman empire as easily as the EEC, . . ."[4]

Like McKeever, we should identify the fourth kingdom with ancient Rome only, a kingdom of many provinces where native unrest like that in Palestine during Christ's time was a thorn in the side to the local Roman magistrates, causing great divisiveness throughout the empire (v. 41). Even the Romans intermarrying with their provincial subjects—"in that you saw the iron mixed with common clay, they will combine with one another in the seed of men"—was not enough to assimilate the peoples in outlying regions of their empire into Roman culture and civilization—"but they will not adhere to one another, even as iron does not combine with pottery." The toes of iron and clay also symbolize how Rome fell by fragmentation.

It was also during the time of Rome that God established, through His death on the cross and by His resurrection from the dead, the everlasting kingdom of His Son, Jesus Christ. Just as Daniel wrote:

> *And in the days of those kings the God of heaven will set up*
> *a kingdom which will never be destroyed, and that kingdom will*
> *not be left for another people; it will crush and put an end to all*
> *these kingdoms, but it will itself endure forever.* (Dan. 2:44)

What kings does Daniel talk about when he says: "And in the days of those kings . . . God . . . will set up a kingdom which will never be destroyed"? The answer is given in the rest of verse 44 and in verse 45. He is not referring to ten end-time kings represented by the ten toes of the statue, but to the kings represented by the iron, the bronze, the silver, and the gold. For "it [Christ's Kingdom] will crush and put an end to these kingdoms, . . ."

> *Inasmuch as you saw that a stone was cut out of the mountain without hands, and that it crushed the iron, the bronze, the clay, the silver, and the gold, the great God has made known to the king what will take place in the future; so the dream is true, and its interpretation is trustworthy.* (Dan. 2:45)

That the kingdom of our Lord Jesus was established at his first coming, we need only read from the Apostle Paul's letter to the Colossians:

> *For He delivered us from the domain of darkness, and transferred us to the kingdom of His beloved Son, in whom we have redemption, the forgiveness of sins.* (Col. 1:13, 14)

Here then is the greater meaning of Nebuchadnezzar's statue vision: God's destruction of Gentile pagan idolatry and idol worship; the end of reverencing gods sculpted by human hands. Even though idols of different sorts exist today, such as material possessions, wealth, power, and passion, history clearly teaches us that the advent of Christianity contributed more to the fall of ancient Rome and the world's institutionalized system of paganism and polytheism than any other event. In addition, Christianity birthed among the Gentiles the monotheistic belief in the one true and invisible God; a God not made by human hands. The first coming of Jesus Christ, who is the stone cut out of the mountain without hands, crushed and brought about the eventual death of pagan idolatry, which is symbolized by the great statue of iron, bronze, silver, and gold. This same stone became a great mountain that filled the earth, a reference to the Church much like Paul's where he states that *"the whole building being fitted together is growing into a holy temple in the Lord"* (Eph. 2:21). The downfall of paganism and the rise of Christianity is the significance behind Nebuchadnezzar's statue vision, the symbology is too great not to be. And history tells us the first coming of Jesus Christ brought it about.

If the fourth beast Daniel saw rising out of the sea is not a revised Roman Empire, what is it? And how do we now interpret Daniel's reference to *"the people of the prince [the Antichrist] who is to come"* (Dan. 9:26)? Before answering these questions, let's lay a foundation for them by looking at an emerging phenomenon in our society that is affecting every aspect of our lives—the rise of a world economic system.

A World Economic System

A major phenomenon today that signals the ascent of the Antichrist's kingdom is the rapid emergence the world over of ultra-high-speed computers with their vast, linked systems of hierarchical networks and integrated hardware.[5] Today's high-speed computer networks can perform every function that a world monetary system and cashless society requires. The advent of such computers, along with products like the "smart card" (a credit card with a built-in microprocessor) and the laser bar code scanner, brings to our generation new meaning from John's words of Revelation 13, which says *"no one should be able to buy or sell, except the one who has the mark, either the name of the beast or the number of his name."*

> *And he causes all, the small and the great, and the rich and the poor, and the free men and the slaves, to be given a mark on their right hand, or on their forehead, and he provides that no one should be able to buy or to sell, except the one who has the mark, either the name of the beast or the number of his name.*

> *Here is wisdom. Let him who has understanding calculate the number of the beast, for the number is that of a man; and his number is six hundred and sixty-six.* (Rev. 13:16-18)

With today's computer technology, a person can make a fully automated, cashless transaction for any purchase he or she desires. Describing this buying potential, the 11 August 1986, issue of *Forbes* magazine states, "Another opportunity should be 'smart credit cards,' with a chip embedded in the plastic. Stores will be able to check their customer's current credit limit and then debit their bank accounts when a sale is rung up. MasterCard is test-marketing such a card with a Motorola microcontroller chip."[6] And they will work in a matter of seconds. Now, what if such a computer chip were imbedded in the buyer's body, say on his hand or forehead? One more flaw in the system would be eliminated. Nobody would have to worry about lost or stolen credit cards!

Today the major computer companies already possess the technology for a new device that will do just this. A codable, cosmetically undetectable computer chip, which can be read by a special scanner, that when surgically implanted on a person's body will contain all data pertinent to the buyer. The only thing this invention needs to make it the mark of the beast is the prefix 666.

The Nature of the Fourth Beast

Consider the following assertion from Alvin Toffler's intriguing futuristic work, *The Third Wave*.[7] Speaking of civilization's "third wave" that is now engulfing the earth—the information wave—he writes:

> The Third Wave brings new problems, a new structure of communications, and new actors on the world stage—all of which drastically shrink the power of the individual nation-state. (p. 317)

Who are these new actors on the world stage, these new players in the drama of the latter days? Toffler tells us:

> The best-publicized and most powerful of these new forces is the transnational or, more commonly, the multinational corporation. (p. 319)

No one can question the enormous impact the transnational corporation (or TNC) has on today's society. As the providers of almost all the goods and services we consume and require, these huge multinational conglomerates affect every aspect of our daily lives. In fact, there are corporations today that possess more wealth and wield more power and influence on the global scene than most countries. Because of this, they are tremendously impacting the role the nation-state plays in the world. On this, Toffler writes:

> For the past few centuries, Lester Brown has written, "the world has been neatly divided into a set of independent, sovereign nation-states. . . . With the emergence of literally hundreds of multinational or global corporations, this organization of the world into mutually exclusive entities is now being overlaid by a network of economic institutions."[8]

> In this matrix, the power that once belonged exclusively to the nation-state when it was the only major force operating on the world scene is, at least in relative terms, sharply reduced.

> Indeed, transnationals have already grown so large that they have taken on some of the features of the nation-state itself—including their own corps of quasi-diplomats and their own highly effective intelligence agencies. . . .

Sometimes cooperating with their "home" nation, sometimes exploiting it, sometimes executing its policies, sometimes using it to execute their own, the TNCs are neither all good nor all bad. But with their ability to shunt billions back and forth instantly across national boundaries, their power to deploy technology and to move relatively quickly, they have often outflanked and outrun national governments. (pp. 321-322)

The growing power we see transnational corporations exercising on the global stage should make us believe that the Fourth Beast Daniel saw—the kingdom of the Antichrist—will be a united, corporate kingdom.

Several things point to this. First, Daniel said this kingdom would be different from all the beasts preceding it. The *King James Bible* translates Daniel's words as diverse, which means it will be unlike all the other beasts. Certainly, a ten-nation confederacy comprising countries from the European Common Market is not vastly different from, say, the Soviet Union, which itself was formerly a composite of multiple republics (the Soviet Republics of Georgia, Armenia, the Ukraine, Estonia, Latvia, and Lithuania among them), each with its own language and culture. Even ancient Rome, as I mentioned earlier, was made up of hundreds of different provinces. Each would have been a separate country with its own distinct nationality had it not been under Roman dominion. A transnational, multicorporate kingdom that spans national boundaries, however, will be vastly different from any kingdom that has ever exercised dominion on our planet.

Second, and most important, such a kingdom will need to possess a sheer economic nature with purely financial motives if it is to support a one-world economic system—a system in which "*no one could buy or sell except they have the mark of the beast.*" The primal motive of any corporate entity is the monetary one—the profit. This base, corporate motive fits right into a one-world monetary system.

Furthermore, the vast, integrated, hierarchical computer networks that would underlie such an economic system, the very ones that are being developed and implemented by corporations and other institutions today, are of themselves nothing more than support systems for the flow of information up, down, and across a company's organizational hierarchy. The "computer hierarchy" is inherently designed to support the corporate hierarchy. The corporate hierarchy uses the "computer hierarchy" to assist it in data management and decision making, and in planning, controlling, and implementing corporate goals and objectives. Without the corporate hierarchy it supports, there would be no need for the computer hierarchy.

Surely massive computer support systems are also being used by national governments. But as Toffler's remarks show, the multinational corporation will continue to grow stronger as the influence of the nation-state on the global scene continues to diminish. Remember also that a transnational corporation's organizational structure and computer hierarchy spans national boundaries, a definite prerequisite for a one-world government, while that of the nation-state does not.

Moreover, if the trend of corporate acquisitions and mergers—as well as the growing number of partnerships and joint financial ventures between corporate mainstays—such as IBM and Apple—continues, there very well could be only ten dominant, multinational corporations in the world at the turn of the century; all in some kind of alliance with each other, all controlling smaller corporations and institutions, and all directing the entire spectrum of financial, production, and marketing resources in the whole western world.

Yes, the Fourth Beast Daniel saw rising out of the sea will at its onset be a ten-member corporate kingdom—a kingdom that will attempt to financially dominate the entire world and from which the Antichrist, the beast who opposes and exalts himself above all that is called God, will rise to world power!

But with the third of Daniel's four beasts, the United States of America, still dominating the world scene, how will this be possible? Read on and find out.

The Assault from Below

Toffler in *The Third Wave* writes:

> In terms of the global power system, the rise of the great transnationals has reduced, rather than strengthened, the role of the nation-state at precisely the time when centrifugal pressures from below threaten to part it at the seams. (p. 322)

What pressures is he talking about? The word *centrifugal* means to tend away from centralization. These are precisely the kinds of forces tearing at the United States and every other industrialized nation in the world today. They are the forces that ultimately dismantled the Soviet Union. Even the giant multinationals are not immune to their grips, as witnessed by the breakup and restructuring of IBM in late 1991. These forces take on a multitude of forms. On the domestic front, they are special interest groups of differing racial, social, religious, and sexual backgrounds, some leaning politically left, others right, all fighting to transfer political power into their own particular arenas by ripping it away from the central, national government. Toffler says this phenomenon typifies the rapid demise of Second Wave Industrial Society and describes it as a necessary prelude to the coming of the Third Wave, the Information Age. Along with the transnational corporations' assault from above, it threatens to strip away the power of our national government.

Also, what will the world's mood be after the destruction of a hostile Russia and its threat to world peace after the earth reels from another such immense outbreak of war? If "Gog/Magog" involves a nuclear escalation, it is obvious. The world will demand immediate global nuclear disarmament, especially in Europe, where today the anti-nuclear movement is still in full swing. With the threat of a hostile Russia destroyed, the disarmament movement in Europe and the United States will burgeon without opposition.

The nations of the Far East might not greet a decrease in American military power with such enthusiasm. Asia's economic powers of Japan, Taiwan, South Korea, and Singapore, still facing the threat of Red China, might possibly oppose such a drastic reduction in American military might. Feeling abandoned, their opposition could possibly start the rift between the kingdom of the Antichrist and the "Kings of the East" in the Book of Revelation (Rev. 16:12).

Nevertheless, unable to withstand the "vise-like pressures" from above and below, the United States will go through a drastic disarmament in both nuclear and conventional forces, much like it did after World War II. The strength of its armed service (compared to its peak after victory in the Persian Gulf War) will be drastically reduced. With a national budget deficit running in the billions of dollars, the United States government will go bankrupt.

When I first started writing this book, I believed Russia's defeat at "Gog/Magog" would be the event that would bring down the Berlin Wall. Since then God has proved otherwise. The liberation of Eastern Europe from Communism will ultimately provide capitalism with huge new markets that will spawn tremendous corporate growth. *Business Week* magazine writes, "as the world's last such industrial market up for grabs, Europe is likely to become the fulcrum of the world's economic power balance for the new century. It's a booming base from which multinationals will consolidate the financial strength and the economies of scale essential to compete around the world."[9] At the forefront of the battle for these new commercial frontiers are the American and

European corporations, along with the Japanese, to whom they are losing dominance of the world marketplace. *Business Week* continues by saying, "a three-way fight is now shaping up among the Americans, Japanese, and the Europeans . . . to determine who will reap these benefits. (pp. 44-45). Striving to take advantage of the European transnational corporations' proximity to these new markets, American transnationals are answering the Japanese threat by forming alliances with the European multinationals. Writes *Business Week*, ". . . Europeans, including [former French] Prime Minister Cresson, are preaching alliances with American companies to resist Japan. . . . they are eager to team up with U.S. companies, with which they feel most comfortable culturally" (p. 46). These powerful American and European corporate alliances will form the basis for the future, ten-horned beast of Daniel 7. Its first goal will be to move and establish its main centers of production throughout a reunited Europe.

Recent developments involving the European Economic Community will only enhance this transfer of power to the TNCs. Even though the EEC is not destined to become a latter-day Roman Empire, it will nonetheless make a global impact in these last days. The 12-nation group achieved complete political and economic unity at year end 1992. This unity brought about by the EEC, the liberation of the Iron Curtain countries, and cast in concrete by the democratic liberation of Russia, will allow the European- and American-based Transnational Corporations to entrench themselves across the European continent after the Gog/Magog war.

Revelation: The Final Form of the Beast

The final form of Daniel's fourth, end-times beast is taking shape. In the book of Revelation, an elderly Apostle John exiled on the Greek Island of Patmos saw in his apocalyptic vision this same terrible beast rising out of the sea. The beast he envisioned had more detail than Daniel's; nevertheless, there is no question they are one and the same. John describes Revelation's beast—which symbolizes both the Antichrist and his kingdom—when he writes:

> *And I saw a beast coming up out of the sea, having ten horns and seven heads, and on his horns were ten diadems, and on his heads were blasphemous names.*
>
> *And the beast which I saw was like a leopard, and his feet were like those of a bear, and his mouth like the mouth of a lion. And the dragon gave him his power and his throne and great authority.*

> *. . . And the whole earth was amazed and followed after the beast; and they worshipped the dragon, because he gave his authority to the beast; and they worshipped the beast, saying, "Who is like the beast and who is able to wage war with him?"* (Rev. 13:2-3, 4b-5)

The beast John sees has seven heads, something not seen by Daniel. These seven heads symbolize the seven foundational TNCs that will remain after the Antichrist, the "little horn" of Daniel 7, rises to power. Daniel saw them as the seven horns that remained after the little horn on his beast uprooted three of the original ten (Dan. 7:8). Regarding these remaining kingdoms, or TNCs, John writes in Revelation 17, *"Here is the mind which has wisdom. The seven heads are seven mountains . . . and they are seven kings; . . ."* It must be noted the ten horns on John's beast are different from the ten horns on Daniel's. The ten horns John saw represent ten distinct, future kings (Rev. 17:12) who we will discuss in chapter 8.[10]

Next, John states, *"And the beast which I saw was like a leopard, and his feet were like those of a bear, and his mouth like the mouth of a lion."* Revelation's beast, in symbolizing the last great gentile world empire, retains characteristics of the first three beasts Daniel saw: the United States, the Soviet Union, and Great Britain.

The beast will have the form of a leopard. This is hardly surprising, for during this transformation of power, the United States will in no way disappear as a country, people, or society. Rather, the axis of its power will transfer from the leopard, the United States government, to the fourth beast—the Antichrist's alliance of transnational corporations.[11] Since the fourth beast also has the form of a leopard, we can conclude the American TNCs will form the strength and backbone of this future alliance.

John's beast had the feet of a bear. Daniel, likewise, was vivid in describing how the fourth beast *"trampled down the remainder* [of the first three beasts] *with its feet."* Its having feet like a bear depicts how the beast will inherit its ideal of world domination from the Bear, the Soviet Union. As for its "mouth like a lion," Revelation's beast will speak with a Lion's mouth—with kingly authority and in the language of the British Empire: English.

Thus, the Antichrist's future corporate kingdom, with its computer tentacles networking across the borders of Europe and America, will be a world power deeply rooted in Western civilization. It will be deeply rooted in a civilization influenced by, and passed down from ancient

Rome—the pinnacle of Western civilization in the ancient world. Hal Lindsey claims, "the Roman influence upon the world is so extensive that it touches Western civilization in every aspect of life" (p. 82). Steve Shearer in his book, *The Beginning of the End,* is very specific when he claims gentile world power will find its final form in Western civilization (pp. 133-135). This is what Daniel meant when he referred to the Romans as *"the people of the prince who is to come"* (Dan. 9:26). Looking six hundred years into the future, Daniel saw Titus' army of Rome, men out of Western civilization, and identified them with "the prince who is to come"—the Antichrist, who himself will head Western civilization in its final form of world power.

Notes

1. C. I. Scofield, *The New Scofield Reference Bible* (New York: Oxford University Press Inc., 1967), 908.

2. Hal Lindsey, *The Rapture* (New York, NY: Bantam Books Inc., 1983), 126-127.

3. If the first three beasts were Babylon, Medo-Persia and Greece, then the fourth beast would have to be Rome. Rome uprooted Greece as the dominant world power.

4. Jim McKeever, *The Coming Climax of History* (Medford, OR: Omega Publications, 1982), 89-91.

5. A good example is the automatic teller machine, ATM.

6. Barry Stavro, "Back in the Chips," *Forbes* Magazine, 11 August 1986, 36.

7. From *The Third Wave* by Alvin Toffler. Copyright © 1980 by Alvin Toffler. Used by permission of Bantam Books, a division of Bantam Doubleday Dell Publishing Group, Inc.

8. Lester R. Brown, *World Without Borders* (New York: Random House, 1972), p. 222, quoted in Toffler, 321.

9. Stewart Toy and Jonathan B. Levine, et al., "The Battle for Europe," *Business Week,* 3 June 1991, 44.

10. Whereas the ten horns on Daniel's beast and the seven heads on John's represent "kingdoms," the ten horns in John's vision represent ten future individuals who will rise to power.

11. With this transfer of power will come a new phenomenon: the build-up of the Corporate War Machine—the army of the Antichrist.

4
THE MAN OF SIN AND THE GREAT GUARDIAN

The Spiritual Nature of the Beast

The Apostle Paul, in writing to the Thessalonians, linked Jesus Christ's second coming to the unveiling of the Antichrist, whom he referred to as the "man of lawlessness" or the "man of sin." By taking up his seat in the temple of God and boasting to be God, this figure will achieve his ultimate goal: to be proclaimed and worshipped as Deity. In this chapter we will examine the final progression of our world toward this devious event—an event that Paul explicitly portrays when he writes:

> Now we request you, brethren, with regard to the coming of our Lord Jesus Christ, and our gathering together to Him, that you may not be quickly shaken from your composure or be disturbed either by a spirit or a message or a letter as if from us, to the effect that the day of the Lord has come.
>
> Let no one in any way deceive you, for it will not come unless the apostasy comes first, and the man of lawlessness is revealed, the son of destruction, who opposes and exalts himself above every so-called god or object of worship, so that he takes his seat in the temple of God, displaying himself as being God.
>
> Do you not remember that while I was with you, I was telling you these things?
>
> And you know what restrains him now, so that in his time he may be revealed.
>
> For the mystery of lawlessness is already at work; only he who now restrains will do so until he is taken out of the way.
>
> And then that lawless one will be revealed whom the Lord will slay with the breath of His mouth and bring to an end by the appearance of His coming; that is, the one whose coming is in accord with the activity of Satan, with all power and signs and

*false wonders, and with all the deception of wickedness for those
who perish, because they did not receive the love of the truth so
as to be saved.* (2 Thess. 2:5-10)

As described in the last chapter, this "man of sin" will rise to world
power as the head of a ruling alliance of transnational corporations.
Consequently, the Antichrist will be a tremendously powerful political
and economic figure. Yet, since he will be regarded by his followers as
God, he will be a spiritual leader as well. John in the apocalypse wrote:
"And the dragon [Satan] *gave him his power and his throne and great
authority"* (Rev. 13:2). The devil's power is spiritual, a power in the
universe second only to God's. Such satanic power will signify the
religious aspect of the Antichrist's future kingdom. What then are some
omens in today's society that portend this counterfeit spirituality?

The Rise of the Cults

The most obvious sign is the outbreak in this country and the world
over of countless new cults and religions, most with their own unique,
self-appointed messiah. Over the last twenty-five years the deviant
personalities of Charles Manson, Jim Jones, and most recently, David
Koresh, all of whom claimed to be Christ, have shocked the American
public by the unquestioned control they exercised over their flocks—
control to such extent their devotees killed and committed suicide at
their very command.

All of this is in fulfillment of what Jesus said would occur prior to
His return. For He warns us:

> *See to it that no one misleads you. . . .*

> *For false Christs and false prophets will arise and will show
> great signs and wonders, so as to mislead, if possible, even the
> elect.* (Matt. 24:4b, 24)

Satan's deception through radical cults and false religions such as
David Koresh's Branch Davidians is on a marked increase. Where will
it end?

False Signs and Wonders: The Occult

The growing amount of occultist activity in America is another
omen signifying Satan is fast preparing to bring Antichrist on the scene.
Satan worship, witchcraft, and sorcery are on the increase throughout
the world. The use of horoscopes, astrology, tarot cards, Ouija boards,
and demonic board games such as Dungeons and Dragons is becoming

commonplace in our society. In addition, we have seen a wide increase in hard-core occultist activities such as black magic, seances, and the black mass.

The demonic power released during occultist sessions is the reason for this renewed interest in the occult. Satan places a counterfeit anointing on his works of darkness to entice people into following him. These blinded to the truth of Jesus Christ are lured into its subtle trap.

Satan's strategy will reach its climax during the Great Tribulation, the time of Antichrist's reign, for accompanying the Antichrist into power will be a second beast, the false prophet, who will perform great signs in the presence of the first beast, deceiving those who dwell upon the earth into making an image of the Antichrist and into worshipping it (Rev. 13:14, 15). As the devil's antithesis of John the Baptist, the false prophet will go before the Antichrist, preparing his path and bearing witness to him by the miracles he performs in his presence:

> *And I saw another beast coming up out of the earth; and he had two horns like a lamb, and he spoke as a dragon.*
>
> *And he [the False Prophet] exercises all the authority of the first beast in his presence. And he makes the earth and those who dwell in it to worship the first beast, whose fatal wound was healed.*
>
> *And he performs great signs, so that he even makes fire come down out of heaven to the earth in the presence of men.*
>
> *And he deceives those who dwell on the earth because of the signs which it was given him to perform in the presence of the beast, telling those who dwell on the earth to make an image to the beast who had the wound of the sword and has come to life.*
> (Rev. 13:11-14)

While they are good indicators, the increase in the number of religious cults and the rise of Satanism are only pieces of the puzzle. Next, we will look at what many Christian leaders believe is the most crucial development in the rise of Antichrist's false religious system—the advent of the New Age movement.

The Lie of the New Age

If today you still have not heard of the New Age movement, just look at the newsstand. The New Age is spreading onto the American scene like a rampant weed. It is a mixture of ancient Hinduism and Buddhism, spirituality and superstition, earth religion and cosmic consciousness. It encompasses the belief in reincarnation, UFOs, extra-terrestrial life, higher powers and the "oneness" of all life. None of these phenomena are new. Grafted together, however, they represent a movement that is sweeping over America, which is known as the New Age. If you think this is just a crazy fad followed by a few "quacks" you are wrong. Internationally recognized cult expert, Dave Hunt, makes this clear in his work *Peace Prosperity and the Coming Holocaust,*[1] a book about the New Age movement in prophecy. Quoting New Ager Marilyn Ferguson, author of *The Aquarian Conspiracy*, Hunt writes:

> The Aquarian Conspirators [New Agers] range across all levels of income and education . . . schoolteachers and office workers, famous scientists, government officials and law-makers, artists and millionaires, taxi drivers and celebrities, leaders in medicine, education, law, psychology . . .
>
> There are legions of conspirators . . . in corporations, uni-versities and hospitals, on the faculties of public schools, . . . in virtually all arenas of policy-making in the country.[2]

As can be seen, the New Age movement is infiltrating every avenue of American life—and its influence is growing. For further proof, read the following excerpt from *Time*:

> Bantam Books says its New Age titles have increased tenfold in the past decade. The number of New Age bookstores has doubled in the past five years, to about 2,500. New Age radio is spreading. . . . Fledgling magazines with names like *New Age, Body Mind Spirit* and *Brain/Mind Bulletin* are full of odd ads: "Healing yourself with crystals," . . . [and] "Use numer-ology to win the lottery."[3]

Yes, New Age mania is being stirred up everywhere, with capitalist marketers doing much of the agitating. But why is it so dangerous? And how does it have anything to do with the rise of the Antichrist?

Gods of the New Age

The New Age movement is inherently related to the Antichrist's false religious system because the basic tenet of New Age thought is that every man and woman is God, a co-creator of the universe. The New Age publication, *The Next Whole Earth Catalog*, declares: "We are as Gods and might as well get good at it. . . ."[4] New Ager Beverly Galyean, in explaining the basis for her philosophy of New Age education, states:

Once we begin to see that we are all God, that we all have the attributes of God, then . . . the whole purpose of human life is to reown the Godlikeness within us; the perfect love, the perfect wisdom, . . . the perfect intelligence, . . . that essential oneness, which is consciousness.[5]

Perhaps the renowned Hindu philosopher Jiddu Krishnamurti best expresses the essence of the New Age when he writes in his poem "The Immortal Friend:"

My search is at an end.
In Thee I behold all things.
I, myself, am God.[6]

As Hunt says, this philosophy is "either the most important truth, the greatest discovery one can make, or else it is the most cruel hoax, the most blatant and destructive lie in the universe!" (p. 83). Like Hunt, I believe it is the latter, for it was the promise of godhood that Satan, through the serpent, presented to Eve in the beginning. And it was Eve's believing of the lie that brought about the fall of mankind. It was through her and Adam's acceptance of what is false that sin, death, and destruction entered creation, being passed down through Adam's seed to future generations. Hunt claims:

this lie will be at the heart of the Antichrist's religion that he will use to unite the world . . . before all hell breaks loose on planet Earth. (p.83).

It is not surprising that New Age aspirants will ignore this warning, for in their rejection of the Judeo-Christian faith, they believe the exact opposite of what the Bible teaches. Take for instance the New Age treatment of Lucifer. The Bible describes Lucifer as the fallen angel who led the angelic rebellion against God (Is. 14:12-15). He is Satan, the serpent in the garden who deceived Eve, archenemy of God and man. Notwithstanding, David Spangler, Planetary Initiative Board of Directors member, and a New Age leader, writes:

Lucifer prepares man . . . for the experience of Christhood. . . . The light that reveals to us the path to Christ comes from Lucifer . . . the great initiator. . . .

. . . many people in the days ahead will be facing [it], for it is an initiation into the New Age.[7]

By exalting Lucifer, the New Age movement has become Satan's own handiwork, containing in it the very spirit of Antichrist. For New

Age teaching denies that Jesus is the one and only Christ. It denies He is the complete embodiment of all truth and the only way to God. New Agers instead speak of the "Christ Spirit" or the "Christ consciousness" that Jesus attained between the time of His baptism and the crucifixion. According to New Age thinking, we all have the potential to attain this state and, thus, to become "Christed Ones." Yet, the apostle John wrote:

> *Who is the liar but the one who denies that Jesus is the [one and only] Christ? This is the antichrist, the one who denies the Father and the Son.* (1 John 2:22)

In an attempt to make the whole earth believe his lie, Satan is sowing the New Age movement into the very heart of the Antichrist's coming empire: the transnational corporate beast. And his sowing has already begun. For as the 4 May 1987 issue of *Time* magazine, states:

> The New Age Movement has gone corporate . . . Besides Pacific Bell, such corporate giants as Procter & Gamble, TRW, Ford Motor Co. and Polaroid have all signed on New Age consultants. By one estimate, their programs account for about $4 billion in corporate spending each year.[8]

Friedrich, in the "New Age Harmonies" article, states:

> One major engineering laboratory on the East Coast has established a program . . . that is using meditation, imaging techniques, and intuitive thought to instill more creativity and leadership in some 400 corporate managers and executives. (p. 69)

Indeed, the New Age is successfully infiltrating the power structures that eventually will form the basis for a "one world" government: the global, transnational corporations. In the process, it is planting in the hearts and minds of its followers the New Age ideal of the "perfect man," the god-man. Prophesying of this future personality, the New Age *Aquarian Gospel* predicts: "But in the ages to come, man will attain to greater heights . . . and at last, a mighty soul will come to earth to light the way up to the throne of perfect man."[9]

Perfect man—man in the seat of God—is the New Age ideal!

The Man of Sin

Just as the New Age gospel has its prophecy about a "mighty soul" who will rise up to the throne of "perfect man," so also does the Gospel of Jesus Christ. The Apostle Paul spoke of that time when:

> *. . . the man of lawlessness is revealed, the son of destruction,*
> *who opposes and exalts himself above every so-called god or object*
> *of worship, so that he takes his seat in the temple of God,*
> *displaying himself as being God.* (2 Thess. 2:3b, 4)

The true Gospel of the New Testament identifies this figure as "the man of lawlessness," "the beast," or the Antichrist. As the ultimate incarnation of deception and evil the world will ever know, he will operate in the full power of evil deception and false wonders; wonders that will begin when he astounds all of mankind by recovering from a mortal wound (Rev. 13:3, 14). He will ride to the crest of power via the tidal wave of New Age religious apostasy that states man is as God. This is the apostasy Paul was talking about: "for it will not come unless the apostasy comes first." Speaking of this, Douglas Groothuis, author of the book *Unmasking the New Age*, comments in the "Harmonies" article, "Once you've deified yourself, which is what the New Age is all about, there is no higher moral absolute. It's a recipe for ethical anarchy. I see it as a counterfeit religious claim. It's both messianic and millennial" (p. 72). Nonetheless, both men and women alike, via their scorn for the one true God, and their own desire to be as God, will wholeheartedly accept this apostasy's final revelation, the Antichrist. As the Apostle Paul warns us:

> *And for this reason God will send upon them a deluding*
> *influence so that they might believe what is false, in order that*
> *they all may be judged who did not believe the truth, but took*
> *pleasure in wickedness.* (2 Thess. 2:11, 12)

Admittedly, there are aspects of the New Age movement that seem admirable, such as its holistic approach to the mind and body. Indeed, there are nice people who are into the New Age. But had we been in Germany in 1936, we surely would have met many nice, sincere German folk who embraced Adolf Hitler. A lie once lived makes no distinctions between who's nice or sincere and who isn't. As witnessed by those who blindly followed Jim Jones and David Koresh to bitter doom, its pathway leads only to death. The truth is, the New Age movement is a lie—a dangerous lie that one day will sweep many people into a pit of destruction.

Israel and the Temple

The Apostle Paul clearly taught that before the Day of the Lord could come, Antichrist must come first. Christians today know that before Antichrist can come, the Jews must first rebuild their temple in the holy land. This is obvious because Paul said the Antichrist would set up his throne in the temple of God. Jesus meant the same thing when he prophesied that the Abomination of Desolation would stand in the holy place, the temple's Holy of Holies:

> *Therefore when you see the Abomination Of Desolation which was spoken of through Daniel the prophet, standing in the holy place (let the reader understand), then let those who are in Judea flee to the mountains; . . . for then there will be a great tribulation, such as has not occurred since the beginning of the world until now, nor ever shall. (Matt. 24:15, 16, 21)*

If Jesus and Paul's prophecies are to come to pass, a Jewish temple must be built in Jerusalem. Right now there is no temple for the Antichrist to make desolate. The last Jerusalem temple was razed to the ground with the entire city by the Romans under Titus in 70 A.D., with one million Jews being slain in its defense. With the city destroyed, Titus proceeded to expel the entire Jewish nation from Palestine, dispersing them among every nation in the ancient world. Jesus predicted this would occur, as did Daniel. As told in both Matthew and Luke:

> *And Jesus came out from the temple and was going away when His disciples came up to point out the temple buildings to Him.*
>
> *And He answered and said to them, "Do you not see all these things? Truly I say to you, not one stone here shall be left upon another, which will not be torn down." (Matt. 24:1, 2)*
>
> *But when you see Jerusalem surrounded by the armies, then recognize that her desolation is at hand.*
>
> *Then let those who are in Judea flee to the mountains, and let those who are in the midst of the city depart, and let not those who are in the country enter the city; because these are days of vengeance, in order that all things which are written may be fulfilled.*
>
> *. . . and they will fall by the edge of the sword, and will be led captive into all the nations; and Jerusalem will be trampled under foot by the Gentiles until the time of the Gentiles be fulfilled. (Luke 21:20-23, 24)*

The Seventy Weeks

Jesus was prophesying in reference to what is written in Daniel 9, the Bible chapter that describes the Jewish people's momentous "seventy weeks." In Daniel 9, each week represents seven years.[10] Daniel's prophecy of the seventy weeks not only predicts the destruction of Jerusalem and the last temple in Titus' time, but more importantly, it gives God's calendar for the salvation of the Jewish people, the timetable for the coming of the Messiah, and the events of the last, seventieth week—the time period of the tribulation and the reign of Antichrist;

> *Seventy weeks have been decreed for your people and your holy city, to finish the transgression, to make an end of sin, to make atonement for iniquity, to bring in everlasting righteousness, to seal up vision and prophecy, and to anoint the most holy place.*

> *So you are to know and discern that from the issuing of a decree to restore and rebuild Jerusalem until Messiah the Prince there will be seven weeks and sixty-two weeks; it will be built again, with plaza and moat, even in times of distress.*

> *Then after the sixty-two weeks the Messiah will be cut off and have nothing, and the people of the prince who is to come will destroy the city and the sanctuary. And its end will come with a flood; even to the end there will be war; desolations are determined.*

> *And he will make a firm covenant with the many for one week, but in the middle of the week he will put a stop to sacrifice and grain offering; and on the wing of abominations will come one who makes desolate, even until a complete destruction, one that is decreed, is poured out on the one who makes desolate.*
> (Dan. 9:24-27)

The seventy weeks of years (490 years) were foreordained to begin once a decree was issued to rebuild the city of Jerusalem, which was destroyed for the first time, along with Solomon's original temple, by Nebuchadnezzar prior to the Jews' Babylonian exile. From the issuing of this decree to the coming of the Messiah, there were to be sixty-nine (seven plus sixty-two) weeks of years, or 483 years.[11] (The years here are biblical or Jewish prophetic years and are 360 days long.) A precise decree was published by King Artaxerxes of Persia in 444 B.C. (Neh. 2:1-

9), approximately ninety-five years after the book of Daniel was written. Biblical and history scholars, having worked out the chronology from ancient records, have found that from the issuing of Artaxerxes' decree for rebuilding Jerusalem to the time when Jesus triumphantly entered Jerusalem on the foal of a donkey—when the throngs publicly proclaimed Him as the Messiah for the first time (see Zech. 9:9 and Luke 19:29-38)—there was an exact passage of 173,880 (483 x 360) days.[12]

As Daniel then proclaimed, *"after the sixty-two weeks the Messiah will be cut off and have nothing, and the people of the prince who is to come will destroy the city and the sanctuary. And its end will come with a flood; even to the end there will be war; desolations are determined."* Five days after His own people proclaimed Him the Messiah, Jesus Christ was "cut off." The Lord of all was crucified and nailed to a tree. He was made a spectacle and put to shame for our sake—raised up and hung on public display for the world to see. Nevertheless, He rose again on the third day, since death could not hold Him in its grip. In 70 A.D., approximately thirty-seven years after His resurrection, the people of "the prince who is to come" destroyed the city and the sanctuary. The Romans raised a siege against Jerusalem and leveled it to the ground; utterly destroying it and the temple. The temple has not been rebuilt in Jerusalem since.

With the sixty-nine weeks until the coming of Messiah completed, God's timetable for the salvation of His people Israel stopped one week, or seven years short of completion. The obvious reason for this stoppage is because the Jews rejected their Messiah, the Lord Jesus Christ. There is now an interlude between the end of the sixty-ninth week and the beginning of the seventieth. This is clear, because the predicted destruction of Jerusalem occurred thirty-seven years after the end of week sixty-nine, far outside the seven-year limit of the last, seventieth week.[13] Also, Jesus says the abomination of desolation in the middle of the final week will occur at a time just prior to His second coming (Dan. 9:27, Matt. 24:15). The ensuing interlude prior to the start of week seventy has brought salvation to the world, while birthing in it Christ's future Bride—the Church.

The last part of Daniel's prophecy dealing with the seventieth week, the time of Antichrist's reign, has yet to occur.

The Return of the Jews to Palestine

The Jews' return to Palestine, marked by the birth of Israel in 1948, is one more indicator that the start of the final climactic week is near. During the fighting of the 1967, six-day Arab-Israeli war, Israel captured all of Jerusalem and with it the revered Temple Mount. Twenty years after the Jewish state's formation, another obstacle to rebuilding the Jewish temple was removed.

Still, a major barrier remains, for the Temple Mount is sacred not only to Jews, but to Muslims as well. To Jews, it is the site of Solomon's ancient temple and of the last Jewish temple, destroyed by the Romans in 70 A.D. The Western (or Wailing) Wall, a remnant of a retaining wall that stood at the time of the last temple, is Judaism's holiest shrine. To Muslims, it is the site of the Dome of the Rock and the Al Aqsa Mosque, two of Islam's holiest shrines. After seizing the mount in 1967 and clearing the Western Wall area, Israel henceforth ceded administration of the mount itself to a Muslim council of elders.[14]

The problem that exists is, according to Jewish law, the only permissible site for rebuilding a third temple is on the site of Solomon's ancient one. And for years it was almost accepted fact that the archaeological ruins of Solomon's temple lay directly beneath the Dome of the Rock mosque. To rebuild the temple would first require destroying the Dome of the Rock. Doing this, undoubtedly, would cause an all-out holy war between Islam and Israel.

According to scholars, however, recently discovered archaeological evidence indicates the site of the old temple is not under the Dome of the Rock as originally thought, but 100 meters directly north of it.[15] If this is true, the Jewish temple could be rebuilt without harming the Dome of the Rock. To Palestinians, however, any Jewish construction on the Muslim-administered Temple Mount is unacceptable. Such opposition, in turn has not stopped extreme Jewish religious groups like the Temple Mount Faithful from desiring to seize the mount and obliterate the Islamic holy places in order to rebuild the temple.[16] Whether or not the last physical obstacle to rebuilding the Jewish temple has been removed remains to be seen.

In any case, orthodox rabbis in Israel today are training a Jewish priesthood who will be prepared to perform the temple sacrifices prescribed in the Torah once a third temple is built.[17] This gives strong evidence that devout Jews in Israel today have every intention of rebuilding their historic house of worship and ritual offering.

It is not surprising that prophetic teachers today are saying that part of the covenant the Antichrist will make with Israel after he comes into power — *"And he will make a firm covenant with the many for one week"* (Dan. 9:27)—will be to help them rebuild their temple. Some also teach that even though he will come out of Western civilization, the Antichrist will be a Jew whom Israel will accept as their Messiah. This link between the construction of a future temple and Israel's expectation of the

Messiah is strong, since orthodox Jews generally argue that a third Temple will have to await the coming of the Messiah. Jesus predicted this future Jewish impostor when, speaking to the Jews of the Messiah, He said: *"I have come in My Father's name, and you do not receive Me; if another shall come in his own name, you will receive him"* (John 5:43).

By establishing a covenant with Israel that will rebuild their temple and reinstall the Old Testament sacrifices, the Antichrist will be revered by Jews all over the world. He will honor his covenant with them until the middle of the seventieth week when, at a time shortly after Israel formally recognizes him as their long-awaited Messiah, he will astound the horrified Jews by stopping their sacrifices and by setting up the abomination of desolation in the holy place.

> *. . . but in the middle of the week he will put a stop to sacrifice and grain offering; and on the wing of abominations will come one who makes desolate . . .* (Dan. 9:27b)

Immediately after this, he will shock the earth by instituting the mark of the beast. The whole western world, subjugated by the monetary system of the ruling corporate beast and mesmerized by the lie of its New Age spirituality, will be unable to resist the violation this despot will impose through his mark.

> *And he causes all, the small and the great, the rich and the poor, and the free men and the slaves to be given a mark on their right hand, or on their forehead, and he provides that no one should be able to buy or to sell, except the one who has the mark, either the name of the beast or the number of his name.*
>
> *Here is wisdom. Let him who has understanding calculate the number of the beast, for the number is that of a man; and his number is six hundred and sixty-six.* (Rev. 13:16-18)

On the surface, the beast will be unlike his name, for he will be a perfect physical specimen. Different from the true Christ, whom Scripture says had *"no stately form or majesty that we should look upon Him, nor appearance that we should be attracted to Him"* (Is. 53:2), this man will be profoundly handsome and splendid to behold. As a leader of leaders, he will be successful without measure in the worldly sense.

In the spiritual sense, by emitting a radiant aura of "love," he will draw men and women alike, compelling them to worship and submit to him. This shouldn't be surprising, for the Bible says *"even Satan disguises himself as an angel of light"* (2 Cor. 11:14). Only those who know the truth of Jesus Christ will be able to resist worshipping him and his image, and be able to spurn receiving his mark—666—on their right hand or forehead. Many will suffer martyrdom for rejecting it.

Hunt raises an interesting question when he asks why anyone would want to receive the number 666, since the Bible identifies it with Satan and ultimate evil. In answering this, Hunt writes:

> That could be the very reason why those in the New Age would be most proud to wear this number. The use of 666 by the Antichrist would be a defiant declaration that Bible "myths" are rejected; and anyone afraid to take this mark would be considered guilty of harboring superstitious beliefs that would no longer be tolerated in the New Order. Taking this number would be a commitment to a universal new religion under the New Age Messiah (p. 214).

The Meaning of the Mark (666)

So what does the number 666 mean? And what is the significance of placing it on the forehead and the hand? For starters, we know six is the number of unregenerate man. Seven, on the contrary, represents completion. God created the heavens and the earth in seven days. Seven represents wholeness and perfection; six signifies a falling short. After their fall in the garden, Adam and Eve were no longer whole. They were spiritually dead, separated from the spiritual life of God until the promised redeemer came. Placing the mark on the hand symbolizes a man's works. Likewise, placing it on the forehead symbolizes his mind or intellect.

Humans are threefold beings, made up of a body, a soul—which most scholars agree is made up of the mind, will, and emotions—and a spirit. Science and knowledge have proven that man, via his own efforts, can do wonders to perfect the body and the mind (the soul). Even so, nothing in man's power can perfect the spirit. He can affect the mind and the body—two of the three—but not the spirit. (New Agers, in their search for spiritual truth, are in reality delving into their consciousness—their minds.) Without Christ the spirit is dead. Ironically, John in the book of Revelation wrote: *"Let him who has understanding calculate the number of the beast, for the number is that of a man; and his number is six hundred and sixty-six"* (Rev. 13:18) What do we get when we divide two by three? We get .666 . . .—sixes infinitely! The number 666 is also two-thirds of the number 1000, a number God associates with completeness.[18]

Six hundred and sixty-six is the number of unregenerate man, the person with mind and body, yet devoid of spirit. It is the number of the person who never will experience the saving grace of Jesus Christ, who alone can restore spiritual life in full. Only Christ said: *"I am the way, and the truth, and the life"* (John 14:6). Men and women who will choose to accept the mark will forever reject the saving spiritual life found exclusively in Jesus Christ.

Let everyone know then the consequences of receiving the beast's mark. If ever in the future someone wants to implant in your right hand or forehead a computer chip coded 666, or a mark with the same number, saying you will be unable to buy or sell unless you receive it, you should remember what the Bible warns:

> *If anyone worships the beast and his image, and receives a mark on his forehead or upon his hand, he also will drink of the wine of the wrath of God, which is mixed in full strength in the cup of His anger; and he will be tormented with fire and brimstone in the presence of the holy angels and in the presence of the Lamb.*
>
> *And the smoke of their torment goes up forever and ever; and they have no rest day and night, those who worship the beast and his image, and whoever receives the mark of his name.* (Rev. 14:9b-11)

For the person who takes the mark, there never can be salvation; only a future of everlasting perdition.

The One Who Restrains

Despite the many visible signs pointing to his imminent unveiling there still is one event, which will go unseen by the physical eye, that must take place before Antichrist can be revealed.

What is this supernatural event? What is keeping the Antichrist and his evil world system from coming to power? This is a question prophetic scholars have debated for decades. It was the Apostle Paul who instructed the Thessalonians that the man of lawlessness, the Antichrist, would not be revealed until the one who now restrains him is taken out of the way:

> *And you know what restrains him now, so that in his time he may be revealed.*
>
> *For the mystery of lawlessness is already at work; only he who now restrains will do so until he is taken out of the way.* (2 Thess. 2:6-7)

Although Paul indicated the Thessalonians knew, the apostle did not explicitly identify the restrainer. Paul probably didn't mention this restrainer by name because the Lord wanted it kept hidden from the Church as a whole until the last days. As a result, several attempts have been made in years past to identify this important personage. Many of these guesses now form the cornerstones of major doctrinal theories.

Is it the Holy Spirit?

The major assumption of the pretribulation-rapture teaching—which says the Church will be removed from the world before the start of tribulation—is that the restrainer is the Holy Spirit. If this is true, and the Holy Spirit must be removed before the Antichrist can be revealed, then it follows that all true Christians—those who have been born again and filled with the Holy Spirit—will be removed with Him. For God has sealed His Church with His Spirit as a pledge (2 Cor. 1:21-22, Eph. 1:13-14), and would not leave her in the world without Him. This theory places the rapture of the church before the Antichrist's unveiling.

In spite of its popularity, this interpretation causes some extreme theological problems. First, Paul's words imply that this "he" will be literally removed from the world prior to the tribulation. But if the Holy Spirit is removed, how can anyone be saved during that time? Jesus Himself said that unless a person is "born of the Spirit" he cannot enter the kingdom of God. With the Spirit gone, no one could be saved during the tribulation. Reading Revelation, however, shows this is not the case. Multitudes will be saved during the tribulation (Rev. 7:14-17), multitudes in whom the Holy Spirit must dwell. For this reason the Holy Spirit cannot be removed prior to it.

Second, how can the omnipotent Holy Spirit be "taken out the way?" He cannot be. For He is everywhere and always will be. David in his 139th Psalm proclaims:

> *Where can I go from Thy Spirit?*
> *Or where can I flee from Thy presence?*
> *If I ascend to the heavens, Thou art there;*
> *If I make my bed in Sheol, behold, Thou art there.* (Ps.
139:7, 8)

The omnipotence of the Holy Spirit in the earth is why Jesus tells us, "... *lo, I am with you always, even to the end of the age*" (Matt. 28:20b).

Several pretribulationalists have tried to resolve these doctrinal dilemmas by teaching that the Holy Spirit will abandon His role only as the restrainer. Hal Lindsey takes this view: in his book *The Rapture* he writes, "The Holy Spirit will still work as He did in the Old Testament. He will not be gone from the world [during the tribulation], but His unique. . . . Church economy ministries of indwelling, baptizing, sealing, gifting, and filling every believer will be removed with the Church" (p. 138). We should ask Lindsey where he finds the scriptural evidence to back his assertion. We should also ask why not every "pretribber" agrees with him, for many still teach the Holy Spirit will be removed from the world entirely. Dr. Roy Hicks, a pretribulationalist, writes *"Berry's Interlinear Greek-English New Testament* gives the literal meaning of 'taken out' as 'out of the midst he be gone.' How could He just step aside when His presence fills the earth? No, when He is 'taken out,' He will be taken out completely, and we will be gathered to the Lord with Him."[19] As I have already shown, Hick's views directly contradict Jesus' teachings on the role the Holy Spirit plays on earth in leading people to Christ—during the past, the present, and the future tribulation.

A less-taught view on the restrainer's identity is that *he* is the church who will restrain evil through its presence in the world until the time of the rapture. This is another teaching from the pretribulation school. But if the he who restrains is the church, then why didn't Satan reveal the Antichrist before the church? After all, the church has only been around since Christ's First Advent. In this view, Satan easily could have revealed the Antichrist before Christ was born. Besides, the Bride of Christ, the soon-to-be-glorious church is not a "he." The scriptures clearly teach it is a "she." Contrarily, the masculine singular gender (*o katechon* in the Greek) is used for the restrainer in verse seven.

Two other views on the restrainer's identity, neither of which hold much merit, are that he is Satan, or that he is the Antichrist, who restrains himself. Since the majority of biblical scholars discount these, we will not discuss them here. Still, there is one last point to make before we discover the restrainer's true identity. There is not one verse in the entire Bible that specifically describes the Holy Spirit as one who restrains. Look for yourself.

The Great Guardian of the People

The personality who is the Antichrist's restrainer is by no means unknown. His name is Michael, the powerful archangel who, as the head of God's mighty host of warrior angels, does battle against Satan and the forces of evil.[20]

Both the Christian and Jewish traditions always have regarded Michael (whose name means "Who is like God?") as a militant guardian of the people of God and as the main adversary of the angelic prince of darkness: Satan. In early and medieval Christianity, Michael came to be regarded as the helper of the Christian armies against the heathen. In Jewish rabbinic literature he is viewed variously as God's vice regent, the heavenly high priest, the keeper of the keys of heaven, and the protector of Israel.[21] Jehovah's Witnesses and Seventh Day Adventists both erroneously identify him as Jesus Christ before the Lord's incarnation. In Christian art, Michael is often depicted with a sword fighting a dragon. He is also mentioned in The Koran along with Gabriel.[22]

Michael the Prince

Michael is first mentioned in the Old Testament Book of Daniel by the angel Gabriel. Gabriel, answering Daniel's desire to know the meaning of a vision he had just received, is telling Daniel how an evil spirit withstood him from coming to him until Michael came to help:

> Then he said to me, "Do not be afraid, Daniel, for . . . I have come in response to your words.
>
> But the prince of the kingdom of Persia was withstanding me for twenty-one days; then behold, Michael, one of the chief princes, came to help me, for I had been left there with the kings of Persia. (Dan. 10:12-13)

After explaining the vision to Daniel (v. 15) and preparing to depart, Gabriel, wanting to ensure that Daniel had grasped all that he told him, asks him if he understood. After questioning him, he continued to explain to Daniel the role Michael played in battling against the princes of Persia and Greece.[23] Almost all Bible commentators agree these princes are actually Satanic angels:

> Then he said, "Do you understand why I came to you? But I shall now return to fight against the prince of Persia; so I am going forth, and behold, the prince of Greece is about to come.
>
> However, I will tell you what is inscribed in the writing of truth. Yet there is no one who stands firmly with me against these forces except Michael your prince. (Dan. 10:20, 21)

The words *stand firmly* in verse 21 come from the Hebrew word *chazaq*, which literally means, "to fasten upon, to bind, to restrain," or "to conquer." Thus, the Bible teaches beyond a doubt that Michael fills a role of restraining evil on the earth. In fact, Gabriel went so far as to tell Daniel there is no one else who stands firmly with him against these evil forces except Michael, his prince.

This is not the last place Michael is named in prophecy. For Gabriel mentions him again in Daniel, chapter 12:

> *Now at that time Michael, the great prince who stands guard over the sons of your people, will* arise. *And there will be a time of distress such as never occurred since there was a nation until that time; and at that time your people, everyone who is found written in the book, will be rescued. (Dan. 12:1)*

Gabriel is telling Daniel that at some future time, Michael, the powerful one who restrains, will "arise," after which will occur "a time of distress such as never occurred since there was a nation until that time." Gabriel's words describing the tribulation are almost identical to the ones Jesus spoke portraying the tribulation in Matthew 24. Therefore, Scripture depicts Michael's arising as the event that will usher in the tribulation.

The word *arise* in this crucial verse comes from the Hebrew root word *amad*, meaning literally, "to stand." Used in various contexts, it can mean "abide, appoint, arise, cease, continue, stand up," or "leave."[24] The correct translation of any word must bring contextual meaning not only to the sentence in which it is used, but to an entire text—in this case the book of Daniel. The word *arise* translated as "ceasing, leaving," or "standing up" before God are the only translations of the word *amad* that fit the context of verse 12, and also the Book of Daniel. To view it as meaning that he will arise on the scene, or arise (stand up) to the occasion, or arise (stand up) as a leader or prince doesn't make sense, for every other time in the Bible that Michael arises or stands up to confront evil, evil is overcome (Dan. 10:13, 20, 21, Jude 9 , Rev. 12:7-9). This time, however, it is evil that prevails as the tribulation erupts over the entire earth.

Also remember that Michael is already on the scene. He is already the restraining prince (Dan. 10:13, 21; 12:1). He does not need to *arise* on the scene, arise to the occasion, or arise as a prince because he already has. On the contrary, in Daniel 12, Michael's "arising" removes him from the scene. It removes him from being a restrainer of evil, since immediately after he arises, all hell breaks loose on the earth as the tribulation breaks out in full force. Since his "arising" takes place immediately before the tribulation and the unveiling of the Antichrist, the timing of this prophetic event is in exact unison with Paul's prophecy in Second Thessalonians 2, presenting the final evidence they are the same event.

Because of all this, I am thoroughly convinced *arising upward, ceasing,* or *leaving to stand before God* is the correct translation for the Hebrew word *amad.* Daniel 10:21 and 12:1 confirm beyond doubt that Michael is the restrainer of the Man of Sin who Paul, in Second Thessalonians 2, says will be taken out of the way. When Michael arises, he will arise from the earth to the throne of God in heaven, leaving the earth and departing from his role as the world's restrainer of evil.

And, if Satan and his evil angels arise to the throne of God for one last time with Michael and his warring hosts as shown in Job 1:6— *"when the sons of God came to present themselves [to stand] before the Lord, . . . Satan also came among them. . . . "*—then the stage will be set in heaven for the great battle of angels portrayed in the Book of Revelation. This is an event that most Bible commentators consider to be still future:

> *And there was war in heaven, Michael and his angels waging war with the dragon. And the dragon and his angels waged war, and they were not strong enough, and there was no longer a place found for them in heaven.*

> *And the great dragon was thrown down, the serpent of old who is called the devil and Satan, who deceives the whole world; he was thrown down to the earth, and his angels were thrown down with him. (Rev. 12:7-9)*

In these verses Michael, previously the restrainer of evil on the earth (Dan. 10:13, 10:20, 21, 12:1, and Jude 9), is now in heaven warring against Satan, casting him down to the earth and banishing him forever from the Lord's presence. (In order to get to heaven, Michael obviously must first arise from the earth.) Upon his defeat, Satan, vengeful and without the restraining force of Michael to contend with, will be loosed upon the earth and will proceed to unveil his Antichrist. The chronology of Revelation goes on to show this. For afterward in Revelation 13, we read: *"And he [the dragon] stood on the sand of the seashore. And I saw a beast coming up out of the sea. . . . "* (Rev. 13:1).

Michael Taken Out of the Way

What a powerful force for good will be removed from earth when Michael, the great prince and guardian of God's people, is taken out of the way. Need we wonder why Jesus wants his Bride to equip herself for the coming hardships and battles she will undoubtedly encounter? Yes, the church must be fully prepared if she is to overcome and be victorious in the face of such unrestrained evil.

In saying Michael will be taken out the way, I am not saying all angels will be removed from the earth during the tribulation. It is possible only Michael and the angels of Revelation 12 will be removed, leaving Gabriel and his messenger angels behind, along with the other ministering angels of God, to battle against the forces of darkness.[25] Or, Michael in his own right could be so powerful, he alone would have to be removed to allow Satan's loosening[26]—and the Antichrist's subsequent unveiling—upon the earth.

Whatever the case, we should note that, of all the angels named in the Bible, Michael is the only one given the title of archangel;

> *But Michael the archangel, when he disputed with the devil and argued about the body of Moses, did not dare pronounce against him a railing judgment, but said, "The Lord rebuke you.* (Jude 9)

The only other verse in the Bible where an archangel is mentioned is in First Thessalonians chapter 4, describing the Lord's second coming and the rapture: *"For the Lord himself will descend from heaven with a shout, with the voice of the archangel, and with the trumpet of God;"* (1 Thess. 4:16).

Michael, the great guardian archangel and the powerful restrainer of evil on the earth up till that future time when God takes him out of the way, will afterwards return from heaven with the Lord Jesus, bringing further glory to the Bridegroom who will be exalted by all He gathers to meet him.

Notes

1. Dave Hunt, *Peace, Prosperity and the Coming Holocaust* (Eugene, Oregon: Harvest House Publishers, 1983).

2. Marilyn Ferguson, *The Aquarian Conspiracy: Personal and Social Transformation in the 1980s* (Los Angeles, 1980), 23, quoted in Hunt, 65.

3. Otto Friedrich, "New Age Harmonies," *Time* December 7,1987, p. 62.

4. *The Next Whole Earth Catalogue,* quoted in Hunt, 82.

5. *SCP Journal,* Winter 1981-82, pp. 29,31, quoted in Hunt, 82.

6. New Ager Beverly Galyean, quoted in Hunt, 83.

7. New Age leader David Spangler, *Reflections of the Christ* (Findhorn, Scotland, 1978), 40-44, quoted in Hunt, 209.

8. Annetta Miller and Pamela Abramson, "Corporate Mind Control," *Time,* 4 May 1987, 38.

9. Levi H. Dowling, *The Aquarian Gospel of Jesus the Christ: The Philosophic and Practical Basis of the Religion of the Aquarian Age of the World* (Santa Monica, CA, 1907), 48, quoted in Hunt, 213.

10. Israel reckoned time in weeks of years as well as weeks of days (see Leviticus 25:1-7 and 2 Chronicles 36:15-23).

11. The significance of the first seven weeks is that it took forty-nine years to restore Jerusalem after Artaxerxes issued his decree.

12. Josh McDowell, *Evidence That Demands A Verdict*, 170-75.

13. Lindsey, *The Rapture*, 2-3.

14. Charles Lane, et al., "A Time Bomb at the City's Heart," *Newsweek*, 22 October 1990, 38.

15. Lindsey, *The Rapture*, 127.

16. Lane, 38.

17. Angus Deming with Milan J. Kubic, "Who Owns the Temple Mount?" *Newsweek*, 5 November 1984, 62.

18. John didn't recognize the decimal point in front of 666 because the modern decimal system wasn't invented until the eighth century A.D. See "Number System," *Encyc. Brit., Macropaedia*, 15th edition.

19. Dr. Roy Hicks, *Another Look at the Rapture* (Tulsa, OK: Harrison House, Inc., 1982), 51.

20. Shorty before this book was published I discovered Marvin Rosenthal shares this view in *The Pre-Wrath Rapture of the Church* (Nashville: Thomas Nelson Publishers, 1990).

21. See "Archangels," *Encyc. Brit., Micropaedia*, 15th edition.

22. Frederick C. Grant, "Michael," *Encyc. Amer.*, 1979.

23. The Thessalonians had insight into the restrainer's identity because Thessalonica lied on what was once the border of ancient Greece and Persia. Many battles were fought nearby and it must have been a center of intense spiritual warfare.

24. "Dictionary of the Hebrew Bible," from Abingdon's *Strong's Exhaustive Concordance Of The Bible* (Nashville: Abingdon Publishers, 41st Edition), 89.

25. It is commonly taught that God's creation of the angelic hosts consisted of three main groups: (1) the angels of worship, of which Satan was the chief angel, (2) the messenger angels, of which Gabriel is the chief angel, and (3) the warrior angels, of which Michael is the chief angel.

26. In the book *Angels on Assignment* by Charles and Frances Hunter (Kingwood, TX: Hunter Books, 1979), a story about a man named Roland Buck who reported having angelic encounters, the Hunters write concerning Buck's supposed rendezvous with Michael: " 'Up until the appointed time, our [Michael and his warrior angels] task is not to destroy Satan, but to scatter the forces of darkness, to hold them in abeyance, to overcome them and to keep them from God's people.' . . . Because of Michael's tremendous spiritual might, he [alone] was able to push back all of those forces of darkness," 167, 169.

5
THE PRETRIB RAPTURE: THE BRIDE'S GREAT ESCAPE?

Several of the cataclysmic signs heralding the impending return of Jesus Christ are the same signs that point to an approaching global apocalypse. Since these signs are predicting both our Lord's glorious coming and approaching disasters, then Christians need to ask, "Will the Church, Christ's Bride, escape the final great conflict our planet will experience immediately prior to His return?" Such a question should be asked, because a tremendously popular teaching exists today that states the church will not have to go through the tribulation, the evil time Jesus forebodes when he warned:

> . . . then there will be great tribulation, such as has not occurred since the beginning of the world until now, nor ever shall.
>
> And unless those days had been cut short, no life would have been saved; but for the sake of the elect those days shall be cut short. (Matt. 24:21, 22)

This view, called the "Pretribulation Rapture," states that Jesus will return unnoticed—"in the twinkling of an eye"—to "rapture" His church out of the world before the tribulation and the reign of Antichrist: the future evil world ruler who will attempt to destroy God's people and bring the entire earth under Satan's dominion. Hal Lindsey has popularized this view in the last twenty years through books such as, *The Late Great Planet Earth*. The teaching is especially popular in "born-again" circles, and need we ask why. What Christian in his right mind truly desires to go through the tribulation, the most terrible time of testing the world ever will experience? What believer honestly wants to suffer the pain and persecution it undoubtedly will bring? Who of us wants to suffer?

Nonetheless, the real question asks not what do Christians desire, but what does the Bible teach? Does the Bible predict the Church, Christ's Bride, will be taken out of the world before the onslaught of the tribulation? Pretribulation rapture teachers use verses such as the following to "prove" Jesus will rapture His church from the earth prior to this time of judgment and distress. Addressing the church at Thessalonica on how God will deliver His people from this coming wrath, the Apostle Paul writes:

> *[I have heard] how you . . . wait for His Son from heaven, whom He raised from the dead, that is Jesus, who delivers us from the wrath to come. . . .*

> *For God has not destined us for wrath, but for obtaining salvation through our Lord Jesus Christ. . . .* (1 Thess. 1:9, 10, 5:9)

Similarly, in the Gospel of Luke, Jesus addressed His disciples:

> *But keep on the alert at all times, praying in order that you may have strength to escape all these things that are about to take place, and to stand before the Son of Man.* (Luke 21:36)

In the book of Revelation, the risen Jesus in the same way addressed the church of Philadelphia, proclaiming:

> *Because you have kept the word of My perseverance, I also will keep you from the hour of testing, that hour which is about to come upon the whole world to test those who dwell upon the earth. (Rev. 3:10)*

These scriptures teach that God will deliver believers in His Son from the divine wrath and testing that He will bring upon an unbelieving earth in the last days. Pretribulation teachers, however, use these verses, together with Paul's teaching on the Lord's Second Coming to teach God will accomplish this deliverance via a rapture that will take place when Christ returns prior to the tribulation. Three important passages pretribulationalists say describe a pretribulation rapture are found in the New Testament epistles. In First Corinthians, Paul writes:

> *Behold, I tell you a mystery; we shall not all sleep, but we shall all be changed, in a moment, in the twinkling of an eye at the last trumpet; for the trumpet will sound and the dead will be raised imperishable, and we shall be changed.*

> *For this perishable must put on the imperishable, and this mortal must put on immortality.*

> *But when this perishable will have put on the imperishable, and this mortal will have put on immortality, then will come about the saying that is written, "Death Is Swallowed Up in victory.*

O Death, Where Is Your Victory? O Death Where Is Your Sting?" (1 Cor. 15:51-55)

Again in First Thessalonians, Paul admonishes:

For the Lord Himself will descend from heaven with a shout, with the voice of the archangel, and with the trumpet of God; and the dead in Christ shall rise first.

Then we who are alive and remain shall be caught up together with them in the clouds to meet the Lord in the air, and thus we shall always be with the Lord.

Therefore comfort one another with these words. (1 Thess. 4:16-18)

Finally in Second Thessalonians, Paul writes:

Now we request you, brethren, with regard to the coming of our Lord Jesus Christ, and our gathering together to Him . . . (2 Thess. 2:1)

Without a doubt, Paul's words refer to the Lord's second coming. They also talk about a gathering together, a being-caught-up-in-the-air—a rapture—all which will happen in the twinkling of an eye. The question that needs to be answered is, will these events take place at the start of the tribulation? In order to answer this question we need to understand these verses in the context of what Jesus taught about his second coming. And not once in the four Gospels did Jesus Christ say His second coming would occur at a pretribulation rapture. In fact, according to His chronology in Matthew of the events preceding the end of the world, Jesus put the rapture, or gathering of His elect, after the tribulation at the time of His Second Advent.

But immediately after the tribulation of those days, the sun will be darkened, and the moon will not give its light, and the stars will fall from the sky, and the powers of the heavens will be shaken, and then the sign of the Son of Man will appear in the sky, and then all the tribes of the earth will mourn, and they will see the Son of Man coming on the clouds of the sky with power and great glory.

And He will send forth His angels with a great trumpet and they will gather together His elect from the four winds, from one end of the sky to the other. (Matt. 24:29-31)

In prior verses of His discourse (Matt. 24:3-28), Jesus says absolutely nothing about a pretribulation rapture.

Pretribulation rapture teachers have provided many reasons to explain why Jesus did not mention a pretribulation rapture in Matthew 24, the most important of all Christ's sermons on the end times.

One commonly used argument is that Jesus' dialogue was a description of the Roman general Titus' leveling of Jerusalem in 70 A.D. and, except for verses 27 through 31, had nothing to do with the last days. This view is incorrect. True, Jesus talked about the destruction of Jerusalem in Luke's version of His end-times discourse (Luke 21:12-24). Matthew, however, excluded it from his version. In Luke, we know Jesus was talking about Titus' destruction of Jerusalem because he places it before the *"time of birth pangs."* After describing the birth pangs in Luke 21:8-11, Jesus stated that *"before all these things* (i.e. before the birth pangs) . . ."* certain things must take place. He then predicted the persecution of the church and the destruction of the holy city in the first century. After Titus destroyed it, the Jews were *"led captive into all the nations"* and Jerusalem was *"trampled under foot by the Gentiles"* until the times of the Gentiles were fulfilled (Luke 21:24). Only after 1948 did they start to return to the reborn nation of Israel.

Unlike Luke, however, Jesus in Matthew 24 talks solely in global, futuristic terms: *"For nation will rise against nation . . . and in various places there will be famines and earthquakes. . . . And this gospel of the kingdom will be preached in the whole world . . ."* (Matt. 24:7, 14). In fact, Jesus refers directly to the future tribulation period when he mentions the abomination of desolation, an event that will occur at the tribulation's midpoint: *"Therefore when you see the Abomination of Desolation which was spoken of through Daniel the prophet, standing in the holy place . . . then let those who are in Judea flee to the mountains"* (Matt. 24:15, 16). Thus, we can conclude that in Matthew 24 Jesus is talking about the end times.

Another argument pretribulationalists use is that Jesus, because He spoke to Jewish disciples, was referring exclusively to the Jews in His Matthew discourse, describing what they, and not the church, would go through prior to His return. Pretribulationalists say Jesus was not referring to the church at all, which is why He didn't mention her being removed at a pretribulation rapture. This viewpoint fully reflects the dispensational theology that pretribulationalism is based upon. This theology draws a sharp distinction between the church and Israel in the New Testament. The problem with teaching that Jesus spoke only of the Jews is that there is no scriptural evidence to support it. One could use the same wrong argument to contend that little of Jesus' teaching in the gospels applies to the gentile church, since almost all of His teachings (with a few exceptions) were addressed to Jews—either to His disciples or to the scribes and Pharisees. In Matthew 24, Jesus is speaking to Jewish believers, members of the church, not unbelieving ones. Hence, His words apply to all believers, whether Jew or Gentile. And, His words say that those who believe in Him will go through the tribulation.

A Second and A Third Coming?

Lastly, pretribulationalists say Matthew 24:29-31 does not refer to the rapture at all, but refers only to Jesus' Second Advent. This is because "pretribbers" have introduced a two-phased aspect to Christ's return. In their theology, Christ will return secretly before the tribulation to rapture the Church. This, they claim, is different from His Second Advent, which will occur at the end of the tribulation when He comes to set up His millennial kingdom on earth. In this model of eschatology, however, one can never reliably know which aspect of Christ's second coming a particular prophetic scripture is talking about. This is one of the great oddities of a two-phased coming of the Messiah. No matter what they say, pretribulationists teach there are two second comings. Rather, they teach there is a second and a third coming—the Lord's second coming at the rapture, and His third coming at the end of the tribulation. Nevertheless, Jesus always talked about His second coming as if it were a single event.

Still, let us assume the rapture and the Second Advent could be two separate events. Then we need to ask the following: why are all of the aspects of the rapture found in Matthew 24:29-31, a passage that most pretribulationists agree portrays the Second Advent? Let's compare Matthew 24:29-31 to 1 Corinthians 15:51-55, to 1 Thessalonians 4:16-18, and to 2 Thessalonians 2:1, three of the passages pretribulationists claim describe a pretribulation rapture. Jesus in His Matthew discourse and Paul in his epistles describe all things commonly.

First, they both describe the coming of the Lord: *"they will see the Son of Man coming on the clouds of the sky"* (Matt. 24:30), *"For the Lord Himself will descend from heaven with a shout"* (1 Thess. 4:16), and *"with regard to the coming of our Lord Jesus Christ"* (2 Thess. 2:1). Second, both speak of the gathering of His elect: *"they will gather together His elect from the four winds"* (Matt. 24:31), and *"with regard to the coming of our Lord Jesus Christ, and our gathering together to Him"* (2 Thess. 2:1). Third, both mention the presence of angels: *"He will send forth His angels"* (Matt. 24:31), and *"with the voice of the archangel"* (1 Thess. 4:16).

Fourth, both speak of trumpets: *"with a great trumpet"* (Matt. 24:31), *"at the last trumpet"* (1 Cor. 15:52), *"and with the trumpet of God"* (1 Thess. 4:16). Fifth, both mention clouds: *"the Son of Man coming on the clouds of the sky"* (Matt. 24:30), and *"we . . . shall be caught up together with them in the clouds to meet the Lord in the air"* (1 Thess. 14:15). These have too many commonalties not to be the same event.

We should also take note of the key word last in 1 Corinthians 15:52: *"in a moment, in the twinkling of an eye, at the last trumpet; for the trumpet will sound, and the dead will be raised. . . . "* If Paul calls the trumpet of 1 Corinthians 15:52 the last trumpet, then how can pretribulationalists claim it will be blown before the tribulation? The seven trumpets in the Book of Revelation (Rev 8:2) and the trumpet in Matthew 24:31 are all clearly blown during or after the tribulation. Hence, they must be blown before (with Revelation's seventh and Matthew's trumpet actually being) Paul's last trumpet in 1st Corinthians. This places the rapture after the tribulation.

For all of these reasons, the pretribulation rapture viewpoint simply does not line up with God's word. The simple, literal and chronological interpretation of Matthew 24 states nothing else: Christ's second coming, when He returns to gather together (rapture) His elect, will take place after the great tribulation at the end of the age.

The Birth of Pretribulationalism

Where then does the belief in a pretribulation rapture come from? And, how long has this popular, but questionable teaching been around? Amazingly, the teaching of a pretribulation rapture only began around 160 years ago. It is true. A London clergyman named Edward Irving first taught the view in 1830. Another Englishman, named John N. Darby, who began teaching the view shortly after Irving, however, is usually recognized as the father of pretribulationalism. During the remainder of the nineteenth century, Darby took the doctrine of Christ's coming before the tribulation and developed it into a broader theological framework called dispensational premillennialism, or dispensationalism. Darby's pretribulational theology was popularized even further in the early part of this century by C.I. Scofield, the author of *The Scofield Reference Bible*.

The prevailing story is that Irving and Darby got their notion of a pretribulation rapture from a young Scottish girl who, while speaking in tongues in 1830, announced the "revelation" that the true church would be raptured out of the world prior to the tribulation and the unveiling of the Antichrist. Whether or not this is true is debatable. One thing is clear though: The early church fathers never taught about a pretribulation rapture and there is no record that the view existed prior to 1830. For an in-depth look at the pretribulation rapture's origin (and Irving and Darby's role in it), see the Appendix.

The Question of Imminency

Darby and all other dispensational teachers have relied heavily on Jesus' sayings in the New Testament that speak of the imminency of His return to support their claim of a pretribulation rapture. The following scriptures demonstrate this.

> *But of that day and hour no one knows, not even the angels of heaven, nor the Son, but the Father alone....*
>
> *Therefore be on the alert, for you do not know which day your Lord is coming.* (Matt. 24:36, 42)

The dispensational view that an imminent return of Christ goes hand in hand with a pretribulational rapture is so stout, it led Dr. John F. Walvoord, the president of Dallas Theological Seminary, to write: "For the most part, scriptural evidence for imminency is equivalent to proof of the pretribulational viewpoint."[1] This reasoning is flawed. There are two things we know about Christ's second coming. First, it will happen in the future. Second, it could happen at anytime. Jesus says that no one, except the Father, knows the day or the hour. Jesus Himself doesn't know. This means it could just as likely occur after the tribulation as before the tribulation. That His return is impending does not by itself prove a pretribulation rapture or disprove a posttribulational one.

Pretribulationists err in claiming the Bible does not teach certain events must take place before Christ comes back to rapture His church. Chuck Smith, Pastor of Calvary Chapel, Costa Mesa, California, is so bold as to state, "I firmly believe that the coming of Christ is imminent, that not one single prophecy must be fulfilled before He catches up the church."[2] It is hard to understand how he can teach this based on Matthew, chapter 24. For as I've shown, in response to His disciples' questions—*Tell us, when will these things be? And what will be the sign of Your coming, and of the end of the age?*"—Jesus proceeded to name a whole list of events that must take place before He would come back: wars and rumors of wars, earthquakes and famines, a great tribulation and the gospel of the kingdom being preached throughout the world, the sun being darkened, and the moon not giving its light (Matt. 24:4-29). Only after these signs did He mention the rapture (Matt. 24:31).

In fact, the pretribulational viewpoint itself is not a purely imminent doctrine. Dispensationalists cannot adequately explain how the
Antichrist could have been revealed (by the removal of the Holy Spirit
at the rapture) prior to the establishment of a legitimate government in
Israel. For Daniel claims the Antichrist *"will make a firm covenant with
the many (e.g. the Israeli government) for one week"* (Dan. 9:27a). Only
after 1948 and the rebirth of the nation of Israel has pretribulationalism
become an "imminent" theology.

This then raises the question: "Why does Jesus on the one hand tell
us His coming could happen at any moment, and on the other tell us
that certain events must take place first?" I'm not sure an adequate
answer can be given to this question. The fact is, it is a duality that is
taught throughout the New Testament, and it is found in the writings
of the church throughout the centuries. And it is a healthy duality.
Christ tells us of signs to look for so that His coming will not take us
unaware. He also tells us to be ready, *"for you know not the day nor the
hour."* The fact that one is true—the imminence of His appearing, does
not make the other—that certain events must first occur—false. This
seeming paradox presents a stumbling block for dispensationalists who
have tried to remove it by inventing a dualism of their own: a two-phase
coming of Christ. Thus, the real issue is not a question of imminency
or of duality, but of doctrinal integrity, and that is where
pretribulationalism misses the mark.

The Dispensations of God

Darby argued that God's past, present, and future dealings with
mankind have been divided into various dispensations, or time periods.
He also claimed that for each dispensation, different rules exist for how
God deals with mankind. His notion was not entirely incorrect. It is
obvious God dealt differently with the people of Israel from the time of
Abraham to the time of Moses (the dispensation of Israel under
promise) than He dealt with them after He gave the Ten Commandments (the dispensation of Israel under law). Likewise, God's dealings
with the church through grace since the death and resurrection of His
Son (the dispensation of grace) have been quite different from His prior
dealings with Israel when they were under the law.

Where dispensationalists err greatly is that they exaggerate these
ideas by claiming the "dispensation of law," the very thing from which
Christ delivered us, must still be completed. According to
dispensationalists, the present "dispensation of grace" is nothing more
than a great "historical parenthesis," sandwiched between the still-to-

be-completed "dispensation of law." They claim the dispensation of law was suspended when Christ came and will resume again when the tribulation begins. Thus, they say the age of God's grace is only temporary. It will end with the start of the tribulation, the period when God pours out His wrath on an unbelieving world. At that time, God will refocus His attention on Israel. And He will revert mankind back to the Law of Moses.

It is important to understand this dispensational framework because dispensationalists use it to explain why the Church will not go through the tribulation. They say that since Christ's Bride is under God's grace, then she cannot be on the earth during the tribulation when God pours out His wrath and reinstitutes the Mosaic law of commandments. They attempt to support this from the fact the Book of Revelation does not mention the Church after chapter 3, or during the portion of John's Apocalypse that describes the great tribulation and the outpouring of God's plagues. They say that since the Church is not found thereafter, it proves she will be raptured from the earth prior to the tribulation.

Another important aspect of dispensationalism is that it draws a sharp distinction between the Church and the nation of Israel. Christ's Bride, the Church, is under grace. Israel is under the law. God turned away from Israel when they rejected Christ at His first advent. Christ subsequently founded the Church, made up of both Jews and Gentiles. Yet, dispensationalists say God hasn't abandoned His dealings with Israel; He has only postponed them. After God removes the Church at the rapture, He will turn His attention back to Israel and will fulfill His promises to them. During the seven years of the tribulation, the whole nation of Israel will be saved. Since the dispensation of law will be in effect they say, all who come to believe in Christ during the tribulation, whether Jew or Gentile, will be under the law. As a result, dispensationalists make a tremendous distinction not only between the Church and Israel, but between the Church and tribulation period believers in general. Iain H. Murray makes this clear when he quotes the founder of modern dispensationalism, John Darby:

> He held that "the Church" is a mystic body and will be complete at the "rapture." The Jews and other Gentiles converted thereafter will never be Christ's bride: "I [Darby] deny saints before Christ's first coming [at His incarnation], or after his second [at the rapture], are part of the Church." With breath-taking dogmatism Darby swept away what had previously been axiomatic in Christian theology. . . . [3]

We see this distinction again in a quote from Daniel Fuller found in Charles Ryrie's book *Dispensationalism Today*;[4]

"... the basic premise of Dispensationalism is two purposes of God expressed in the formation of two peoples who maintain their distinction throughout eternity."

The Dividing Wall Torn Down

The problem with these two central premises of dispensationalism—reinstating the Mosaic law during the tribulation, and distinguishing the church from Israel—is they are scripturally groundless. Dr. Anthony Hoekema in the book *The Meaning of The Millennium* states, "the basic Dispensational principle of an absolute distinction between Israel and the church, involving two distinct purposes of God and two distinct peoples of God, has no biblical warrant."[5] The New Testament teaches over and over that Christ has torn down the wall dividing Jew from Gentile, the law of commandments, never again for it to be rebuilt. Therefore, there is now no distinction between Jews and Gentiles who are in Christ Jesus. This is one of the Apostle Paul's most basic and fundamental teachings, for in his epistle to the Ephesians, he writes:

> But know in Christ Jesus you who formerly were far off have been brought near by the blood of Christ.
>
> For He Himself is our peace, who made both groups into one, and broke down the barrier of the dividing wall, by abolishing in His flesh the enmity, which is the Law of commandments contained in ordinances, that in Himself He might make the two into one new man, thus establishing peace, and might reconcile them both in one body to God through the cross, by it having put to death the enmity. (Eph. 2:13-16)

He writes again to the Romans and to the Galatians:

> For there is no distinction between Jew and Greek; for the same Lord is Lord of all, abounding in riches for all who call upon Him. (Rom. 10:12)
>
> There is neither Jew nor Greek, there is neither slave nor free man, there is neither male nor female; for you are all one in Christ Jesus. (Gal. 3:28)

Hence, it is puzzling why dispensationalists teach that such a distinction exists when the New Testament teaches over and over that it doesn't. As Paul taught the Ephesians, Christ destroyed the dividing wall and enmity that once distinguished Jew from Gentile, the Law of commandments contained in ordinances, when He abolished it in His flesh. The Greek word for *abolish* in Ephesians 2:15 is *katargeo*, which means to "render entirely useless." Why would God reinstate a system during the tribulation that He had previously rendered entirely useless? The old covenant will never be brought back, nor can it be, for the author of Hebrews writes:

> *For if that first covenant had been faultless, there would have been no occasion sought for a second.*
>
> *For finding fault with them, He says,*
>
> *Behold, Days are coming, says the Lord,*
>
> *When I will effect a new covenant*
>
> *With the house of Israel and with the house of Judah; . . .*
>
> *When He said, "A new covenant," He has made the first obsolete. But whatever is becoming obsolete and growing old is ready to disappear.* (Heb. 8:7, 8, 13)

Despite the clearness of God's word on the issue, dispensationalists dogmatically proclaim that God still distinguishes Israel from the Church and always will. To this I must say a distinction does exist. But as the scriptures say, this distinction exists only as long as Israel remains unsaved. As the Jewish people come to know their Messiah, the Lord Jesus Christ, the dividing wall will be removed. For it is written:

> *But to this day whenever Moses is read, a veil lies over their heart; but whenever a man turns to the Lord, the veil is taken away.* (2 Cor. 3:15, 16)

An analogy that illustrates the relationship between Israel and the Church is that of a caterpillar to a butterfly. Israel before Christ was the caterpillar, hindered in her movement and relationship with God, nevertheless still justified by faith in Him. But God had a better plan. He sent the Messiah, His Son, who completely transformed how Israel was to relate to Him. As a caterpillar weaves a cocoon, which then births a butterfly, Israel's transformation through Christ can be looked at in the same way. The end result—the butterfly, the Church—is different from the caterpillar, Israel, yet it is the same. It is not the caterpillar, yet it is. Quite a paradox, but somehow the two are still one. And God has done an even greater work than this by supernaturally making us Gentiles who believe a part of the butterfly as well. The butterfly is the completion of God's work, the transformation of His original creation. Judaism today is the empty cocoon, a discarded shell that present-day Israel refuses to abandon. Even so, as Israel makes her transformation to Christ, she too becomes the butterfly, she becomes a part of the Church.

Paul also illustrates how believing Israel and the Church are one and the same. For in Romans he portrays how the Jewish and Gentile "branches" are both part of the same olive tree, the believing Gentiles having now been grafted in by faith in place of those Jews who for not believing were broken off (Rom. 11:17-24). Consequently, only in Christ are God's promises to Israel fulfilled. Paul makes this clear when he writes:

> For I say that Christ has become a servant to the circumcision on behalf of the truth of God to confirm the promises to the fathers. (Rom. 15:8)

He confirms this again to the Corinthians and the Galatians:

> For as many as may be the promises of God, in Him [Christ] they are yes; . . . (2 Cor. 1:20)

> And if you belong to Christ, then you are Abraham's offspring, heirs according to promise. (Gal. 3:29)

Paul writes to the Galatians of how, prior to his conversion, he persecuted the Church of God (Gal 1:13). Albeit when Paul persecuted the Church, the Church comprised Jews exclusively. That they were Jews did not alter the fact that they were the Church. It will be no different when the nation of Israel is saved in the end times. Once in Christ, they will be members of His body and a part of His Church, His glorious Bride.

Who Are the Tribulation-Period Believers?

Another peculiarity of the dispensational framework is the identity of the tribulation-age believers. If they are not a part of Christ's body, or the Church as pretribbers say (even though they are believers in Jesus), then who or what are they? Some kind of mysterious, pseudo, second-class Christians? Or, could they not be Christians at all, as some pretribulationalists teach? Such claims have no scriptural basis. For the Bible strictly teaches that a believer in Jesus Christ is nothing less than a true, bona fide Christian and a member of His Church.

Granted, the Book of Revelation does not say specifically the Church will go through the tribulation. Nevertheless, Revelation and the Book of Daniel do teach that the saints will be present during the tribulation (Rev. 7:9-17; 13:7, 10; 14:12; 16:6; 17:6 and Dan. 7:21, 22), as well as those who have faith in Jesus Christ (Rev. 12:17, 14:12). Jesus says that those saved during the tribulation are His elect (Matt. 24:22, 31). Regarding these saints, the Apostle John says:

> *Let us rejoice and be glad and give glory to Him, for the marriage of the Lamb has come and His bride has made herself ready.*
>
> *And it was given to her to clothe herself in fine linen, bright and clean; for the fine linen is the righteous acts of the saints.*
> (Rev. 19:7-8)

Here John's prophecy occurs before the end of the tribulation. Thus, by deductive reasoning we must assume the "Christian" saints, who are Christ's Bride, will be present during the tribulation. How can one draw any other conclusion? We must also note that even though the word *church* is not mentioned after the third chapter of the Book of Revelation, neither is it mentioned in any of the following books of the New Testament: the gospels of Mark, Luke, and John, the 2nd Epistle of Peter, the 1st and 2nd Epistles of John, and the Epistle of Jude. Are we then supposed to conclude the teachings in these books do not apply to the Church? As you can see, this is nonsense.

Another reason why dispensationalists say Christians in the Church are distinct from tribulation believers is they claim tribulation believers, being under the law, will not operate in the power of the Holy Spirit.[6] They say this because, as mentioned in chapter 4, they believe the Holy Spirit is the restrainer who will be removed from the earth when the Church is raptured before the tribulation. As we have discovered, Michael the Archangel is the restrainer who will be removed, not the Holy Spirit. Jesus, on the other hand speaking of His Spirit, says to every disciple, "... *lo, I am with you always, even to the end of the age*" (Matt. 28:20b).

Throughout history, the church traditionally has used the term "the end of the age" when referring to the end of our present evil age. This will occur only when Jesus comes again in His Kingdom and institutes a new age of righteousness in the universe. The King James Version interprets Jesus' words as *the end of the world.*

Dispensationalists, on the other hand believe Jesus, in verse 20, is referring to the end of the Church Age.[7] That is, He will be with us in the Spirit up until the rapture of the Church, which culminates the

Church Age. Nonetheless, even if it is a practical term, the term Church Age is never used in the Bible. Age, or "present age," is almost always used in the context of "present evil." Paul demonstrates this when he writes:

> *Grace to you and peace from God the Father, and the Lord Jesus Christ, who gave Himself for our sins, that he might deliver us out of this present evil age* . . . (Gal. 1:3, 4)

Henceforth, Jesus' promise of His Spirit being with us always *"even to the end of the age,"* must include the tribulation, the most intensely evil time the world will ever know.

Paul's Witness and the Day of the Lord

The fact that the Bible teaches Christians will go through the tribulation is most clearly seen in Paul's second letter to the Thessalonians.

> *Now we request you, brethren, with regard to the coming of our Lord Jesus Christ, and our gathering together to Him,*
>
> *that you may not be quickly shaken from your composure or be disturbed* . . . *to the effect that the day of the Lord has come.*
>
> *Let no one in any way deceive you, for it will not come unless the apostasy comes first, and the man of lawlessness is revealed, the son of destruction, who* . . . *takes his seat in the temple of God, displaying himself as being God. (2 Thess. 2:1-4)*

To anyone who takes the simplistic historical view that the "day of the Lord" refers to the day when Jesus returns, there is no way to misinterpret these verses. The Lord's second coming and the rapture (when He gathers us to Him) will occur after the Antichrist's unveiling and the tribulation.

Because of this, dispensational scholars have their own interpretation of what Paul meant by "the day of Lord." Even though they acknowledge that Paul refers to the rapture in verse one, they do not believe the day of the Lord refers exclusively to a literal final day on which Christ will return. As Walvoord puts it, dispensationalists believe the day of the Lord is "an extensive time of divine judgment on the world."[8] Although they generally agree that this prolonged period includes the tribulation (and the millennium), dispensationalists disagree over when it will begin. C. I. Scofield in his popular *Reference Bible* says it will commence with the rapture of the church, will include the tribulation and the millennium, and will end at the ushering in of the

new heavens and the new earth on the day of God (2 Pet. 3:10-13).[9]
Lindsey adds a slightly different twist, saying it will begin "shortly after
the Antichrist is revealed" (p. 119), which will occur after the rapture of
the church.

In 2 Thessalonians 1-4, dispensationalists believe the people of
Thessalonica were afraid they had missed the rapture and were already
living in the tribulation and the "day of the Lord." Dispensationalists
claim Paul dispelled the Thessalonians' fears of the day of the Lord
having arrived ("has come," v. 2) by reassuring them that their gathering
together to Christ at the rapture (v. 1) had not yet occurred. Consequently, the day of the Lord and the tribulation (which were to occur
after the rapture) could not have come either. Paul continued by saying
the day of the Lord will not come until after the apostasy and the
revealing of the man of sin.

There are several problems with this interpretation. First, it assumes
both Paul and the Thessalonians believed in a pretribulation rapture.
Quite the contrary, the early Church had no knowledge or belief in a
pretribulation rapture. The early Church fathers writings on the second
coming demonstrate this. They all believed Christ would come after the
unveiling and destruction of the Antichrist.

Second, pretribulationists assume the Thessalonians held the dispensational view that the day of the Lord is synonymous with the
tribulation. The early Church father Tertullian demonstrates, nonetheless, that the early church believed that the day of the Lord referred not
to the tribulation, but to Christ's second coming. Tertullian directs his
prayers towards "the end of the world, to the passing away thereof at the
great day of the Lord—of His wrath and vengeance—the last day, which
is hidden (from all), and known to none but the Father."[10]

Third, why would Paul so vividly portray the unveiling of the
Antichrist, describing him sitting down in the temple of God, display-
ing himself as being God, if Christians wouldn't be around to witness
it? In describing Antichrist's unveiling, Paul is giving the Thessalonians
and the Church a sign to look for, just as Jesus did in Matthew:

> *Therefore when you see the Abomination of Desolation
> which was spoken of through Daniel the prophet, standing in the
> holy place (let the reader understand)* . . . (Matt. 24:15)

Finally, the dispensationalist interpretation of the day of the Lord
does not hold water chronologically. Scofield says it will be inaugurated
by the rapture of the church. But, according to pretribulation theology,
the rapture of the church, which occurs when the restrainer is taken out

of the way, must happen before the Antichrist can be revealed. Scofield thus puts the beginning of the day of the Lord (at the rapture) *before* the Antichrist's unveiling. Paul, however, said exactly the opposite. He specifically stated that the day of the Lord will not come until the apostasy comes *first* and the man of lawlessness is revealed. Probably realizing this, Hal Lindsey states the day will begin "shortly after the Antichrist is revealed," which will happen sometime after the removal of the Holy Spirit's restraining ministry at the rapture. This solves a part of their chronology problem, but by putting a time period between the rapture and the start of the day of the Lord, Lindsey further separates the relationship of the day of the Lord to Christ's second coming. The immediate context of 2 Thessalonians 2:1-3 implies Paul does not even bother distinguishing between them, as he refers to the coming of our Lord Jesus Christ, and then writes that the day of the Lord—the day of His coming—will not come until the man of lawlessness is revealed. Scripture further teaches the two go hand in hand. Peter and Paul both likened the day of the Lord to the coming of a thief in the night (1 Thess. 5:2, 2 Pet. 3:10), while Jesus referred to His second coming in the same manner (Matt. 24:43, 44).

In Joel chapter 2, Joel describes the heavenly signs that will occur before the Lord's coming:

> *The sun will be turned into darkness,*
> *And the moon into blood,*
> *Before the great and awesome day of the Lord comes.* (Joel 2:31)

These heavenly signs, which Joel says will occur before the day of the Lord, are shown by Matthew to occur *after* the tribulation just prior to the Second Advent of Christ (Matt. 24:29). In order to fit the dispensational framework, however, these signs would have to occur *before* the tribulation, since dispensationalists say the day of the Lord begins at the tribulation.

Still, the chronological problems are not all that is wrong with the dispensational definition of the day of the Lord. Its single worst problem is that it tries to fit the long and diverse time periods that pretribulationists say include the tribulation, the millennium, and the destruction of the world into scriptures like the following from Saint Peter's second epistle:[11]

> *But the day of the Lord will come like a thief, in which the*
> *heavens will pass away with a roar and the elements will be*

destroyed with intense heat, and the earth and its works will be burned up.

Since all these things are to be destroyed in this way, what sort of people ought you to be in holy conduct and godliness, looking for and hastening the coming of the day of God, on account of which the heavens will be destroyed by burning, and the elements will melt with intense heat!

But according to His promise we are looking for new heavens and a new earth, in which righteousness dwells. (2 Pet. 3:10-13)

Peter says the day of the Lord will come like a thief, in which the heavens will pass away with a roar and the earth and all its works will be burned up. How in the world can these verses, which are warnings of such a quick, immediate, and irreversible judgment, be understood to include a seven-year tribulation wherein many will be saved and, especially, a glorious 1000-year earthly reign of Jesus Christ? Nevertheless, dispensationalists do exactly that.

The Day of the Lord is the Last Day

As shown by 2nd Peter, the day of the Lord is the Last Day, the Judgment Day. It is the day when Christ will come to receive His Bride, to judge the world, to destroy the present heavens and earth, and to make a new heavens and a new earth in which righteousness dwells. Although it will be utterly unique, the scriptures imply it will be a single day—not a period of days or years as dispensationalists say. It is synonymous to the day of God, the day of Jesus Christ, the day of judgment, and to the "last day" spoken of by Jesus:

For this is the will of My Father, that everyone who beholds the Son and believes in Him, may have eternal life, and I Myself will raise him up on the last day. (John 6:40)

If you take Jesus' words literally, the "last day" means just that. Jesus isn't talking about a time frame that includes the rapture, the tribulation, the second coming, the millennium, and the end of the world. He isn't talking about the last day of the church age. He is talking about the final day on which the dead will be raised and man will give account to his Maker—the day of the Lord. In fact, within the pretribulational framework, the last day (with its resurrection) cannot fit within the time frame of the day of the Lord. For the last day would have to begin at the rapture with the resurrection of believers, while the day of the Lord, as Lindsey says, must begin after the rapture "shortly after the Antichrist is revealed" (p. 119).

The truth of the last day proves by itself that a pretribulation rapture is unscriptural. Jesus said everyone who believes in Him will be raised on the last day. But by teaching the rapture of the Church and the resurrection of believers (1 Thess. 4:16 and 1 Cor. 15:52) will occur before the tribulation, Dispensationalists place the resurrection of the dead in Christ not on the last day, but on a day at least seven years (the length of the tribulation) prior to it. They directly contradict what Jesus taught. This isn't the only time of such contradiction, as the rest of this chapter will clearly show.

The Story of the Two in the Field

Jesus never taught about a pretribulation rapture. Before I began writing this book I would not have believed this, for every time I read the parable of "the two in the field" (Matt. 24:36-44), even though I was a "posttribber," it seemed to speak literally of a pretribulation rapture. Indeed, these are verses that most Christians believe refer to a pretribulation rapture. The parable goes as follows:

> *For the coming of the Son of Man will be just like the days of Noah. . . . there shall be two men in the field; one will be taken, one will be left.*

> *Two women will be grinding at the mill, one will be taken, and one will be left.*

> *Therefore be on the alert, for you do not know which day your Lord is coming.* (Matt. 24:37, 40-42)

In 1985, I discovered exactly what Jesus meant in this parable. In so doing I found out many leading proponents of the pretribulation viewpoint do not even believe this parable refers to the rapture. Two such scholars are Walvoord, who states this view in *The Rapture Question* (pp. 188-190), and Dr. Charles Taylor, who has authored several books on a pretribulation rapture. Both of them believe Jesus was teaching not on the rapture, but on the judgment of the wicked. The ones taken are not Christians as commonly believed, but are unbelievers, as is clear if you read the passage in context of the days of Noah:

> *For as in those days which were before the flood they were eating and drinking, they were marrying and giving in mar-*

riage, until the day that Noah entered the ark, and they did not understand until the flood came and took them all away; so shall the coming of the Son of Man be.

Then there shall be two men in the field; one will be taken, one will be left.

Two women will be grinding at the mill, one will be taken, and one will be left. (Matt. 24:38-41)

The key word here is *taken* (and its past tense *took*). As in the days of Noah when the flood came and took them all away, so also at the coming of the Son of Man will the wicked first be taken out of the world to a terrible place of judgment. The parallel passage from Luke demonstrates this even more clearly. Luke's version says:

There will be two women grinding at the same place; one will be taken, and the other will be left.

["Two men will be in the field; one will be taken and the other will be left."]

And answering they said to Him, "Where,* Lord?" And He said to them, "Where the body is, there also will the vultures be gathered." (Luke 16:35-37)

Jesus' words in verse 37 used to baffle me. Now that I understand them, they make very much sense. Jesus answered the disciples' questions about where they would be taken by exclaiming, *"Where the body is, there also will the vultures be gathered."* He did not respond by saying the elect would be taken out. He responded by describing the wicked being taken to a place of final judgment—to the land of the dead, a place where the vultures gather.

The Wicked—Not The Righteous—Are Removed First

That the wicked, not the righteous, will be taken out of the world first at the end of the age is consistently taught throughout the New Testament. This is best demonstrated in Jesus' parable about the wheat and the tares (Matt. 13:24-30, 36-43). In this parable the field is the world (v. 37). The *"one who sows the good seed is the Son of Man"* (v. 37), while *"the enemy"* who sows the bad seed *"is the devil"* (v. 39). The wheat

---

* i.e. "Where will they be taken?"

are the righteous, *"the sons of the kingdom"* (v. 38), and the tares are the wicked, *"the sons of the evil one."* The *"harvest is the end of the age"* and the *"reapers are angels"* (v. 39). Regarding the crop, Jesus states:

> *Allow both to grow together until the harvest; and in the time of the harvest I will say to the reapers, "First gather up the tares and bind them in bundles to burn them up; but gather the wheat into my barn."* (Matt. 13:30)

Jesus, the final authority, plainly states that the tares, the doers of iniquity, will be gathered first. They will be bound and burned. Then the reapers will gather the wheat into His barn.

> *Therefore just as the tares are gathered up and burned with fire, so shall it be at the end of the age.*
>
> *The Son of Man will send forth His angels, and they will gather out of His kingdom all stumbling blocks, and those who commit lawlessness, and will cast them into the furnace of fire, in that place there shall be weeping and gnashing of teeth.*
>
> *Then the righteous will shine forth as the sun in the kingdom of their Father. He who has ears, let him hear.* (Matt. 13:40-43)

The Lord emphasizes this sequence once again later in His sermon when he recites the kingdom parable about the dragnet. Describing how the angels will separate the bad fish from the good fish, Jesus says:

> *So it will be at the end of the age; the angels shall come forth, and take out the wicked from among the righteous, and will cast them into the furnace of fire, there shall be weeping and gnashing of teeth.* (Matt. 13:49-50)

That the wicked will be removed before the gathering of the saints is also seen in 1 Thessalonians 4:17, a verse pretribulationists claim describes a pretribulation rapture:

> *Then we who are alive and remain shall be caught up together with them in the clouds to meet the Lord in the air, and thus we shall always be with the Lord.* (1 Thess. 4:17)

A key word in verse 17 is *remain*. The living Christians who *remain*, after the angels have taken the wicked away to judgment (Matt. 13:36-43, 24:38-41, Luke 16:34-37), will be caught up in the clouds together with the resurrected saints to meet the Lord in the air at His coming. And so we shall always be with the Lord.

Heaven Must Receive Him (Until His Enemies Are Made His Footstool)

As much as His Bride longs to receive Him, the New Testament teaches Jesus must remain in heaven until the time comes for God to restore all things. In the Book of Acts, the author writes:

> *He must remain in heaven until the time comes for God to restore everything, as He promised long ago through His holy prophets.* (Acts 3:21, NIV)

In 1 Corinthians Paul wrote that Christ's return would take place only after the defeat of all His enemies, including death.

> *. . . then comes the end, when He delivers up the kingdom to the God and Father, when He has abolished all rule and all authority and power.*
>
> *For He must reign until He has put all His enemies under His feet.*
>
> *The last enemy that will be abolished is death.* (1 Cor. 15:24-26)

In verse 25 Paul was referring to Psalm 110, David's famous vision of the Messiah where he wrote, *"The Lord says to my Lord: Sit at My right hand, Until I make Thine enemies a footstool for Thy feet"* (Ps. 110:1). Taking these three passages in context clearly shows Jesus' second coming, when He leaves His Father's right hand and descends from heaven with a shout, will occur only after all His enemies, the last being death, have been put under His feet. And when will the last enemy— death—be abolished? The Apostle John reveals this in the Revelation where he writes how in the end God shall:

> *. . . wipe away every tear from their eyes; and there shall no longer be any death; there shall no longer be any mourning, or crying, or pain; the first things have passed away.* (Rev. 21:4)

Death will only be abolished after the completion of all things, including the tribulation, at the end of the age when Christ will have put it under His feet along with all rule, authority, and power. Jesus must reign in heaven, seated at the Father's right hand, until the time comes for God to restore everything.

When is the Wedding of the Lamb Complete?

The rapture of the Church at our Lord's second coming, that glorious moment when we the Bride will be caught up to meet Him in the air, is commensurate to the joining of a bride and bridegroom on their wedding night. In the Jewish wedding tradition of Christ's day, the wedding was consummated on the night when the bride and the bridegroom came together in the bridal chamber. And this happened only after celebrating the wedding feast (see Gen. 29:21-23). The Book of Revelation shows the wedding feast of the Lamb and His Bride will take place at the end of the tribulation.

> *Let us rejoice and be glad and give the glory to Him, for the marriage of the Lamb has come and His bride has made herself ready.*
>
> *. . . And he [the angel] said to me, "Write, Blessed are those who are invited to the marriage supper of the Lamb." . . . "These are true words of God."* (Rev. 19:7, 9)

Consequently, it is imperative that the rapture—the joining of Bride to Bridegroom—take place after the wedding feast described here, and after the end of the tribulation. Nonetheless, pretribulation rapture teachers, by teaching the rapture will occur beforehand, put the consummate joining of the Bridegroom and the Bride before the wedding feast.

Could it be that the Bride, because of her grand desire to be one with her Bridegroom, wants things to happen sooner than what her Father has planned?

Notes

1. John F. Walvoord, *The Rapture Question* (Grand Rapids, MI: Academie Books, 1979), 2nd ed., 73.

2. Chuck Smith, "The Second Coming: Any Day Now," *Charisma and Christian Life*, February 1989, 47.

3. John Darby, *The Puritan Hope* (London: The Banner of Truth Trust, 1971), 200, quoted in Dave MacPherson, *The Unbelievable Pre-Trib Origin* (Omega Publications, P.O. Box 4130, Medford, OR 97501), 33-34. Used by permission.

4. Daniel Fuller, *Dispensationalism Today* (Chicago, IL: Moody Press, 1965), 44-45.

5. Anthony Hoekema, taken from *The Meaning of the Millennium* edited by Robert G. Clouse, p.55. © 1977 InterVarsity Christian Fellowship of the USA. Used by permission of InterVarsity Press, P.O. Box 1400, Downers Grove, IL 60515.

6. Lindsey, *The Rapture,* 138 (see note 2, ch. 3, p. 64)

7. Lindsey, 137.

8. Lindsey, 118.

9. *New Scofield Reference Bible* (New York: Oxford University Press, Inc., 1967), 929.

10. George Eldon Ladd, *The Blessed Hope* (Grand Rapids: Wm. B. Eerdmans Publishing Co., 1984), 27-28. Used by permission of Wm. B. Eerdmans Publishing Co.

11. Scofield, 1341.

6

DELIVERED FROM WRATH (BUT NOT FROM PERSECUTION)

Of the Small Number of the Lovers of the Cross

> Jesus has many lovers of His kingdom . . . but . . . few bearers of His Cross. Many desire His consolation, but few desire His tribulation. . . . All men would joy with Christ, but few will suffer anything for Christ. . . .
>
> But those who love Jesus purely for Himself, and not for their own profit . . . bless Him as heartily in temptation and tribulation . . . as they do in . . . consolation. And if He never sent them consolation, they would still always bless and praise Him. . . . I think none such can be found, unless it be far away in far countries.[1]

As a humble Roman Catholic monk named Thomas á Kempis wrote nearly 560 years ago during his nearly lifelong stay at the German monastery of Mount Agnes, there truly are few lovers of Jesus' cross. There are many who will love Him so long as He blesses them. There are many who will claim protection in His name from the sufferings, persecutions, and martyrdoms of this world. Nonetheless, how many would still believe in Him if it meant living in poverty? How many would still follow Him if they knew someday they might have to suffer or even die for Him? How many would love Him if they saw loved ones killed and tortured for His name's sake?

Judging from the witness of history, from the treatment of Christians in the third world and communist countries, and most of all from the Holy Scripture, it is beyond comprehension that many in America today teach that the Church will not suffer persecution. Nevertheless, this is what pretribulation rapture preachers are teaching: "The Bride will not have to endure tribulation." "Few or none will be martyred for the name of Christ." They claim the sufferings and calamities of the tribulation will be so severe (and indeed they will be) that God would never allow His Church, His beloved Bride, to live through such immense persecution and distress. It would be against His nature. Christians are just too special to Him.

The problem with this outlook is that the Bible and the historical witness of the Church do not support it. Jesus Himself specifically warned His disciples about the persecution that awaited them:

> *Then they will deliver you to tribulation, and will kill you, and you will be hated by all nations on account of My name.* (Matt. 24:9)

In John's gospel He says again:

> *If you were of the world, the world would love its own; but because you are not of the world, but I chose you out of the world, therefore the world hates you.*
>
> *Remember the word that I said to you, `A slave is not greater than his master.' If they persecuted Me, they will also persecute you.* (John 15:19, 20a)

The Early Christians

Jesus' prophecy of impending persecution came true to the very word. Every apostle, except John, died a martyr's death. The great persecution of the early Church began in Jerusalem with the stoning of Stephen (Acts 7:54-60). It continued when the Apostle James, the son of Zebedee and brother of John, was beheaded at Herod's bidding (Acts 12:1, 2), for which that evil king paid a grievous price, being eaten by worms (Act 12:23). The fate of James and the rest of the apostles is graphically depicted in the sixteenth-century Christian classic, *Foxe's Book of Martyrs*.[2] Based mainly on tradition, its tales of the apostles' martyrdoms and of the sufferings endured by the Christians of the Roman Empire paint an illustrious picture of the kinds of dangers and persecutions Christ's first brave disciples faced in a cruel, ancient world.

Justin Martyr (100-165 A.D.) was an early Church father who lived under the cruel hand of Roman oppression. Beyond intimidation, he displayed the fearless attitude of one whose faith is grounded in Jesus Christ. He wrote:

> Now it is evident that no one can terrify or subdue us who have believed in Jesus over all the world. For it is plain that, though beheaded, and crucified, and thrown to wild beasts, and chains, and fire, and all other kinds of torture, we do not

give up our confession; but the more such things happen, the more do others and in larger numbers become faithful, and worshippers of God through the name of Jesus (Dialogue with Trypho, 110).[3]

The late Dr. George Eldon Ladd, author of *The Blessed Hope*, writes of Martyr, "Justin, who himself became a martyr, feels that the sufferings to be inflicted by the 'man of apostasy,' the Antichrist, will be little worse than what Christians were already gladly and fearlessly suffering for Christ."[4]

The Martyrs of the Twentieth Century

Until now, we in America have been so blessed by God's protection from persecution, we have forgotten—or don't realize—other Christians the world over are not so fortunate. In some Muslim countries, the penalty for converting to Christianity is death. In most other Islamic countries, in many of the remaining communist nations, in Israel, in Hindu Nepal, and in Buddhist Tibet, it is illegal to preach the Gospel or to proselytize. Scores of Christians in this century alone have paid a grievous price, many with their lives, for following Christ's command of carrying the gospel to these lands and to the farthest reaches of the globe. The book *By Their Blood—Christian Martyrs of the 20th Century* by James and Marti Hefley[5] (a continuation of *Foxe's Book of Martyrs*), documents the many stories of men and women—Protestant and Catholic, black and white, people of every race and nationality—who in this century have sacrificed their lives for spreading the gospel of Jesus Christ in Africa, China, Latin America, and countless other countries.

In light of all this, can you see why it is so difficult to reconcile these undaunted sufferings and fearless persecutions, past and present, with today's positive pretribulation rapture message? Can you see why it is difficult to seriously accept a message that states that "true believers" in Jesus Christ will not have to suffer persecution, die for their faith, or go through the Great Tribulation?

If true Christians will not have to endure these hardships, then why does history show they already have? I have heard some pretribulationists say those early Christians must not have been true, Spirit-filled believers (otherwise God would have protected them). Well if those early Christians were not true believers—those who laid their lives down even unto death for their faith in Jesus Christ—then who in heaven's name is? If Peter, Paul, and the rest of the apostles, awesome men of God and warriors for the faith of Christ Jesus, did not have God's Spirit, then which of us can dare claim we do? If all of these were not exempt from the cost that Jesus stated comes from following Him—even a person's very life—then which of us can claim we are?

What makes American Christians believe they are so special to God that He would allow other Christians in the past and the present to go through suffering, persecution and death for His name's sake and not us? What makes us think we are more favored in His eyes? Where does the Bible say American Christians will not have to suffer persecution? How can we believe this?

We should take to heart the following words of Corrie ten Boom, author of the best selling book *The Hiding Place*,[6] who herself suffered tremendous persecution at the hands of the Nazis during World War II. Speaking of the Chinese Christians and of their sufferings under communist rule she said, "The Christians were told that they didn't have to go through tribulation and we all know how it is now in China." She adds that, "All other Christians in free lands had better be prepared for what is coming to them also." In her article "The Coming Tribulation," in the November-December 1974 issue of *Logos Journal*, she wrote, "Those teaching there will be no tribulation and that Christians will be able to escape all this, are really the false teachers Jesus was warning us to expect in the latter days."[7]

Jehovah Is a Shield about Us

In spite of the possibility of death and martyrdom, the Bible and Church tradition also portray God as the one who will protect His people from their enemies. God loves His children and is very jealous for them. Whenever we are in trouble, we know He is there watching over us. Two stories of deliverance found in the book of Daniel beautifully demonstrate this. The first is of Shadrach, Meshach, and Abednego, three Hebrew youths whom the Babylonian King Nebuchadnezzar tossed into a fiery furnace. The second is the story of Daniel in the lion's den. These are two of the Bible's most comforting stories about the divine protection God bestows upon his people.

Daniel tells how Shadrach, Meshach, and Abednego were brought before the king for refusing to worship an enormous golden image Nebuchadnezzar had erected and commanded those within his kingdom to worship. Furious because the three disobeyed his command to worship the image, even after he gave them a second chance, King Nebuchadnezzar ordered that the youths be tied and cast into a furnace of blazing fire. Nevertheless, the three Jewish youths told the king:

> *If it be so, our God whom we serve is able to deliver us from the furnace of blazing fire; and He will deliver us out of your hand, O king.*
>
> *But even if He does not, let it be known to you, O king, that we are not going to serve your gods or worship the golden image that you have set up.*
>
> *Then Nebuchadnezzar was filled with wrath, and his facial expression was altered toward Shadrach, Meshach, and Abednego. He answered by giving orders to heat the furnace seven times more than it was usually heated.* (Dan. 3:17-19)

The symbolism behind Nebuchadnezzar's heating the furnace "seven times" hotter than normal could well be in reference to the seven-year length of the tribulation. Albeit, God marvelously delivered Shadrach, Meshach, and Abednego from the fiery flame, just as He will deliver His Bride from the coming tribulation. He did not abandon them but was present with them through the entire ordeal.

> *Then Nebuchadnezzar the king was astounded and . . . said to his high officials, "Was it not three men we cast bound into the midst of the fire?" They answered and said to the king, "Certainly, O king."*
>
> *He answered and said, "Look! I see four men loosed and walking about in the midst of the fire without harm, and the appearance of the fourth is like a son of the gods [i.e., a Son of God]!" . . .*
>
> *And . . . the king's high officials . . . saw . . . that the fire had no effect on the bodies of these men nor was the hair of their head singed, nor were their trousers damaged, nor had the smell of fire even come upon them.* (Dan. 3:24-25, 27)

What a marvelous story this is of perseverance and trust in God even in the face of death! Shadrach, Meshach, and Abednego have set an example for every Christian today on how to persevere and triumph even in the midst of tribulation.

An equally impressive tale of courage and bravery is the story of Daniel being thrown into a den of lions (Daniel 6). Daniel trusted in God in the jaws of death, and God delivered him. It is difficult to imagine the kind of faith it took for the mighty prophet to endure this trial. Daniel had the kind of trust that only comes through constant communion with the Father and with his son, Jesus Christ.

It was this same kind of trust that delivered the apostle John, Jesus' beloved disciple, from a tortuous death when the Roman emperor Domitian had him plunged into a cauldron of boiling oil. Legend has it that when John was thrown in, the oil erupted violently out of the cauldron and slew those who had attempted the vile deed. John walked away unharmed, the oil not even leaving a small burn on him.[8]

Further legend explains the ancient Church tradition of attributing to John the emblem of a chalice with a viper on it. This is in memory of the challenge made to John at Ephesus by the high priest of Diana to drink a poisoned cup. Tradition has it that as John made the sign of the cross over the chalice, a serpent manifested itself from the midst of the drink and left the vessel. The Apostle proceeded to drink from the cup without being harmed. The high priest of Diana, hoping to match John's feat, proceeded likewise to drink from the cup only to fall over dead. He was poisoned by the lethal brew because the serpent had suddenly entered back into it.[9]

The Great Paradox

God delivered John, just as he delivered Daniel and Shadrach, Meshach, and Abednego. This creates a great paradox of our faith. Why does God at certain times deliver His people from the perils of death, while at other times He allows them to be tortured and killed by their enemies? Why did He deliver Daniel but not all of the other prophets? Why did He deliver John but not James, Peter, and Paul (although He certainly protected them earlier in their lives)? Why does the Bible say God will protect Christians from their enemies, but in other places say many will die for their faith? These are difficult questions to answer.

Could it be that God, in order to achieve the higher purpose of His will, often will allow his holy ones to suffer and even die for His name's sake? And what is His will? God's ultimate will is for His Bride to grow, to become strong, and to be made pure. His perfect will is for the world to be saved. God wants countless more people to enter His kingdom and to discover the saving knowledge of His Son Jesus Christ. History clearly shows that during times when the Church is suffering persecution, God's greatest power is manifested through her. It is during these times that scores upon scores, after witnessing the faithful endurance of a righteous church, have committed their lives to Christ. John Foxe, referring to the sufferings of the early Christians, writes, "And yet, notwithstanding all these continual persecutions and horrible punishments, the Church daily increased, deeply rooted in the doctrine of the apostles and of men apostolical, and watered plenteously with the blood of saints."[10]

The churches in China and Africa are two spots during this current century that have experienced the remarkable spread of the Gospel of life. They are rooted in the ground soaked by the blood of their martyrs. Those faithful missionaries and early converts gave the ultimate sacrifice. They defied death in this life to bring the message of eternal life to their fellow countrymen.

Purified Through Suffering

God also uses the trials and tribulations of this age to strengthen and to purify His church. Those who say otherwise have looked at neither the witness of history nor the Bible. In China today, where Christians have suffered terribly under communist rule, is a case in point of a church that has flourished under the relentless hand of persecution.

James 1:2 says *"to consider it all joy when we encounter various trials."* Christians today use this scripture when they are experiencing the trials and problems of life. When James wrote this, it was to Jewish believers in Christ after Jerusalem had been razed in 70 A.D. Many of them were killed and the remainder, along with the rest of the Jews, were scattered across the ancient world. What greater tribulation can a people experience than this? And still James instructed them to consider it all joy!

> *James, a bond-servant of God and of the Lord Jesus Christ, to the twelve tribes who are dispersed abroad, greetings.*
>
> *Consider it all joy, my brethren, when you encounter various trials, knowing that the testing of your faith produces endurance.*
>
> *And let endurance have its perfect result, that you may be perfect, lacking in nothing.* (James 1:1-4)

The last chapter of Daniel speaks also of being purified through tribulation. Speaking of the Great Tribulation to come in the last days, the angel tells Daniel:

> *Many will be purged, purified and refined; but the wicked will act wickedly, and none of the wicked will understand, but those who have insight will understand.* (Dan. 12:10)

The concept of the Church being purified by tribulation was so common in the early Church because they were accustomed to suffering and enduring under dire persecution. This is vividly portrayed by the early Christian writing called *The Shepherd of Hermas* (cir. 150 A.D.),[11] the tale about a shepherd named Hermas and his encounter with a fearful beast. Almost all Biblical scholars agree this beast symbolizes the Great Tribulation. Hermas makes the point that the tribulation will serve to perfect the Church, even as gold tempered in the fire is perfected.

A Selfless Attitude

Yes, it is a great paradox that says the God who so dearly loves us and divinely protects us also will allow some of His children to die so that His ultimate desire will be accomplished through them. Without remorse, we should all gain solace in knowing that every martyr who has died and every fiery trial that has been endured for our Lord has planted a seed that will produce a future harvest for the Kingdom of God—a harvest that will yield future souls and a more resolute spirit in the Church awaiting the return of her Bridegroom.

Dying for Christ may sound foreign, but it is something all of us should be able to face. After all, Jesus did require it of us, saying that anyone who comes to Him without hating even his own life cannot be His disciple (Luke 14:26). Surely we are all not going to die for our faith during the tribulation. As we will see in chapters 7 and 8, the great majority of believers who go through the Great Tribulation will live to see its end. But we need to be prepared for it.

No soldier goes into a war expecting to die. He goes into it hoping to return after the war to his home and loved ones. Regardless, every soldier knows that some who enter the battle will not return. They know that in any war there will be casualties. A true soldier also knows you cannot prepare for war unless you expect to be in one. Why should the tribulation be different? It will be a war. The forces of Antichrist will seek to destroy the Church, just as the Roman emperors sought to destroy the early Christians. And if the time of death comes, nothing can change it. Some of us may be like Stephen and James, who were killed fairly early in their Christian journeys and during the midst of powerful ministries. Some of us might be like Peter and Paul, who were martyred after completing the race the Lord gave them to run. And many of us might be like John, who escaped death at the hands of his enemies. I hope we can all be like John. Still, we need to have the attitude of John, who like his brother James was willing to drink the cup the Lord drank at Calvary:

> But Jesus answered and said, "You do not know what you are asking for. Are you able to drink the cup that I am about to drink?" They said to Him, "We are able." He said to them, "My cup you shall drink. . . ." (Matt. 20:22, 23a)

The key to being ready for the Great Tribulation lies in our attitudes. If we could possess the same selfless attitude described in á Kempis' *The Imitation of Christ*—"but those who love Jesus purely for Himself, and not for their own profit or convenience, bless Him as heartily in temptation and tribulation . . . as they do in . . . consolation"[12]—we would do well indeed. Only by dying to ourselves and becoming conformed to the person and image of Jesus Christ, allowing Him to live His life through us each and every day, will we obtain this attitude and be able to face death and tribulation with victory.

Delivered From Wrath

In spite of the dreadful prospect of suffering persecution and death for their faith, Christians never need fear suffering God's vengeful wrath. The persecution that believers will receive and the wrathful judgment God will pour out upon the earth during the tribulation are two, entirely different things. The seven-year tribulation, particularly the Great Tribulation during its last three-and-a-half years, will be a time of terrible judgment for our planet's inhabitants. God will unleash tremendous plagues, wars, and famines without restraint. It will be a time of distress such that Jesus said, *"For those days will be a time of tribulation such as has not occurred since the beginning of the creation . . . until now, and never shall"* (Matt. 24:21). Despite the fact Christians will go through this fiery trial, we need to be fully assured that if we keep His word, we will be divinely protected by Jesus from the wrath the Father will pour out on an unbelieving world. We know this because Jesus gave us His word.

The idea of the Church's being on the earth when God's divine wrath falls is another stumbling block for pretribulation rapture teachers. They reason that since the Church cannot suffer divine wrath, she cannot be in the world during the tribulation. Lindsey makes this point in *The Rapture* by writing, "If it can be demonstrated that Divine wrath falls on the earth prior to the second coming, then their theory [of a posttribulation rapture] contradicts itself."[13]

The problem with this view is that divine wrath already has fallen on the earth. The great flood in Noah's day was most certainly an outpouring of God's anger. So were God's destruction of Sodom and Gomorrah by fire and brimstone, as were the seven plagues He poured out on the land of Egypt during Israel's exodus. God has poured out His wrath in centuries past, and His precedent every time has been not to take His people out of the world, but rather to keep them in the world while providing them protection and deliverance.

Consider the children of Israel, who were in the land of Egypt when God worked His wonders through Moses and Aaron. The Israelites were in Egypt during every plague that God poured out on the Egyptians: during the plague of the water becoming blood (Exod. 7:20), during the plague of the frogs (Exod. 8:6), of the gnats (Exod. 8:17), of the insects (Exod. 8:24), of the boils (Exod. 9:10), of the hail (Exod. 9:23), of the locusts (Exod. 10:14, 15), and during the smiting of all the firstborn of Egypt (Exod. 12:29, 30). These plagues are in many ways similar to the judgments God will pour out during the tribulation—except that the tribulation judgments will be worldwide. Still, God protected His people from all of them. That is why we shouldn't be afraid when we read in the book of Revelation about God's wrath being poured out upon the earth. He will never fail to deliver and protect His people through the midst of it all.

We must, however, belong to Christ and be living our lives for Him if we are going to be spared from God's heavy hand. For Paul wrote:

> *There will be tribulation and distress for every soul of man who does evil, of the Jew first and also of the Greek, but glory and honor and peace to every soul of man who does good, to the Jew first and also to the Greek.* (Rom. 2:9, 10)

If we fall away and turn our backs on His wondrous grace, we will be as those who do not know Him. But, if we are the totally committed, glorious Bride He is coming for, we have nothing to fear.

For these reasons, every Christian must realize the future seal, trumpet, and bowl judgments, as well as the mark of the beast, which are spoken about in Revelation are reserved only for the unrepentant. God's judgment will fall only on those who refuse to repent from their wicked ways and turn to Him. It will fall on those who willingly reject His love and forgiveness. Nowhere does it show that it falls on anyone else. This is clearly shown throughout the Book of Revelation.

> *And the rest of mankind, who were not killed by these plagues, did not repent of the works of their hands, so as not to worship demons, and the idols of gold and silver and of brass and of stone and of wood, which can neither see nor hear nor walk; and they did not repent of their murders nor of their sorceries nor of their immorality nor of their thefts.* (Rev. 9:20, 21)

> *And the first angel went and poured out his bowl into the*
> *earth; and it become a loathsome and malignant sore upon the*
> *men who had the mark of the beast and who worshipped his*
> *image. . . .*
>
> *And the fifth angel poured out his bowl upon the throne of*
> *the beast; and his kingdom became darkened; and they gnawed*
> *their tongues because of pain, and they blasphemed the God of*
> *heaven because of their pains and their sores; and they did not*
> *repent of their deeds.* (Rev. 16:2, 10-11)

These certainly are not Christians who are spoken of here. Christians need to know beyond a doubt that Jesus will keep them from the hour of testing that is to come upon the whole earth, just as He spoke to the church of Philadelphia in John's time.

> *Because you have kept the word of My perseverance, I also*
> *will keep you from the hour of testing, that hour which is about*
> *to come upon the whole world, to test those who dwell upon the*
> *earth.* (Rev. 3:10)

Noah and his family, who alone believed God, escaped the great flood that blotted out all living flesh. Lot and his family escaped from Sodom, moments before God rained down burning sulfur upon that wicked city. And the children of Israel rested safely—protected by the blood of the Passover lamb smeared on their door posts—as the angel of death passed over them and smote every firstborn Egyptian:

> *And the blood shall be a sign for you on the houses where you*
> *live; and when I see the blood I will pass over you, and no plague*
> *will befall you to destroy you when I strike the land of Egypt.*
> (Exod. 12:13)

So too are we who believe safe from God's coming wrath by the blood of the true eternal Passover Lamb, the Lord Jesus Christ. As with Noah, Lot, and the sons of Israel, God may not take us out of the world, but He will protect us from its evils. For remember, Jesus asked the Father on our behalf:

> *I do not ask Thee to take them out of the world, but to keep*
> *them from evil.* (John 17:15)

Notes

1. Thomas á Kempis, *The Imitation of Christ*, ed. Harold C. Gardiner, S.J. (Garden City, NY: Doubleday & Company, Inc., 1955), 92-93.

2. John Foxe, *Foxe's Book of Martyrs* (Springdale, PA: Whitaker House, 1981).

3. George Eldon Ladd, *The Blessed Hope* (Grand Rapids, MI: Wm. B. Eerdmans Publishing Co., 1956), 24. Used by permission of Wm. B. Eerdmans Publishing Co.

4. Ladd, 24-25.

5. James and Marti Hefley, *By Their Blood-Christian Martyrs of the 20th Century* (Milford, MI: Mott Media, 1981).

6. *The Hiding Place* (Old Tappan: Spire Books, 1971).

7. Quoted in Gary Greenwald's Bible study tape entitled "The Great Rapture Cover-up (Part I)," no. 313, The Eagle's Nest.

8. David Hugh Farmer, *The Oxford Dictionary of Saints* (New York, NY: Oxford University Press, 1982), 214.

9. Farmer, 214.

10. Foxe, 18.

11. Ladd, 23-24.

12. á Kempis, 92-93.

13. Lindsey, *The Rapture*, 91.

7
DANIEL'S SEVENTIETH WEEK: THE TRIBULATION

Russia's defeat at Gog/Magog and the rise of a global corporate empire will be the two major visible events signaling the impending beginning of Daniel's final seventieth week. The removal of Michael the restrainer, on the other hand, will be imperceptible to the human eye. His departure will be the single unseen event ushering in the tribulation, the time of greatest trial and fiery testing the world will ever know.

The tribulation has had volumes written about it. Still, most Christians know little about it other than as a time when God will pour out His wrath on an unbelieving world. In fact, few people know of it as Daniel's seventieth week, the seven-year biblical time frame that will encompass the salvation of the Jewish people and the reign of the Antichrist, the beast whose mark—666—will be given out during its last three-and-one-half years (Rev. 13:5). By saying that Christians won't be on the earth to experience it, dispensationalists have emphasized the tribulation as a time of judgment and world holocaust—the world's penalty for having rejected faith in Jesus Christ.

The Church, however, will be on the earth during the tribulation. Thus, in spite of its extreme distress, the tribulation undoubtedly will be a time of revival and salvation on the earth. It will be a time for refining and purifying the Church, a time of victory for the saints of the Most High, a time for ushering in the kingdom of Christ's glorious Bride. As a clash between Satan's worldly realm and God's heavenly kingdom, the tribulation will be the ultimate power encounter, shaking the earth and all who dwell in it to the very core.

Revelation: The Sequence

Before we can take an in-depth look at the single Bible book that says the most about the tribulation, the Book of Revelation, we must answer a major question with regard to Revelation's order of events. Simply put, do the future events predicted by John occur sequentially in the exact order he wrote them, or do they lack an absolute chronology and overlap in time? Knowing this is crucial to interpreting the events of the tribulation.

One of the keys that determine the order of events in Revelation lies in understanding how the judgments of the seven seals (Rev. 6, 8), the seven trumpets (Rev. 8, 9, 11), and the seven bowls (Rev. 15, 16)—the three series of judgments that dramatize God's wrath poured out upon the world—relate to one another. Almost all Bible scholars who espouse a pretribulation rapture, including Hal Lindsey[1] and C.I. Scofield,[2] contend that these judgments will occur consecutively: the seven seals first, with the last seal unleashing the seven trumpets, and with the seventh and last trumpet unleashing the final seven bowls. Those who support a posttribulation coming of Christ, including Robert Gundry[3] and Jim McKeever,[4] usually have these judgments overlapping or occurring in a parallel manner. No doubt, a scenario that has the seals, trumpets, and bowls occurring sequentially intensifies the effects of each and aligns itself more with the pretribulational teaching, which emphasizes the tribulation as a time of God's punishment. Nonetheless, the Book of Revelation contains abundant evidence to support at least a partial overlap of these three series of judgements; an overlap that supports the posttribulational viewpoint.

Let's begin with the seven seals. Remember that the breaking of the seven seals and their subsequent judgements, including the loosing of the Four Horsemen of the Apocalypse, began shortly after Christ's sacrifice at the cross. In Revelation, chapter 5, Jesus' ability to break the seven seals is tied to His being the Lamb of God who died for the sins of the world. For the angel spoke:

> *Worthy art Thou to take the book, and to break its seals; for Thou wast slain, and didst purchase for God with Thy blood men from every tribe and tongue and people and nation.* (Rev. 5:9)

Compare also Ezekiel 14:21, a prophecy of Jerusalem's destruction in 70 A.D., with Revelation 6:8. Both mention the four judgements—sword, famine, wild beasts, and plague—that the Four Horsemen unleashed upon the earth. In chapter 1, we saw how the earth, since Christ's resurrection, has suffered the wrath of these four dreaded horsemen who conquer, wage war, spread famine, and kill mankind. Billy Graham also implies this in *Approaching Hoofbeats*, his book on the Four Horsemen of the Apocalypse. The galloping hoofs of the four horsemen are now pounding the earth, and they will continue up to, and throughout the tribulation. Consequently, the four seals of the horsemen will overlap and encompass the trumpet and bowl judgements that occur during the tribulation.

Secondly, there are strong parallels between two key seal and trumpet judgement passages and prophecies portraying Christ's second coming. First, examine the sixth-seal judgement of Revelation 6:

> *And I looked when He broke the sixth seal, and there was a great earthquake; and the sun became black as sackcloth made of hair, and the whole moon became like blood;*
>
> *and the stars of the sky fell to the earth, as a fig tree casts its unripe figs when shaken by a great wind.*
>
> *And the sky was split apart like a scroll when it is rolled up; and every mountain and island were moved out of their places.*
>
> *And the kings of the earth and the great men and the commanders and the rich and the strong and every slave and free man, hid themselves in the caves and among the rocks of the mountains;*
>
> *and they said to the mountains and to the rocks, "Fall on us and hide us from the presence of Him who sits on the throne, and from the wrath of the Lamb; for the great day of their wrath has come; and who is able to stand?"* (Rev. 6:12-17)

Compare these verses with the following prophecies on the events immediately preceding Christ's return and the end of the world:

> *And there will be signs in sun and moon and stars, and upon the earth dismay among nations, . . .*
>
> *men fainting from fear and the expectation of the things which are coming upon the world; for the powers of the heavens will be shaken.*
>
> *And then they will see The Son of Man coming in a cloud with power and great glory.* (Luke 21:25a-27)
>
> *The sun will be turned into darkness, And the moon into blood, Before the great and awesome day of the Lord comes.* (Joel 2:31)
>
> *The heavens are the works of Thy hands;*
> *They will perish, but Thou remainest;*
> *And they will all become old as a garment,*
> *And as a mantle Thou wilt roll them up; . . .* (Heb. 1:10b-12a)

Can you see the similarities of the sixth-seal judgement to these passages? These scriptures definitely pertain to Christ's second coming. The sun becomes dark and the moon turns red. Stars fall from the sky. Men shake from fear and hide for dread of what is coming upon the earth. The skies and the heavens are rolled up like a scroll. The only conclusion we can draw is the sixth seal judgement unleashes the cosmic disturbance that will immediately precede the day of Christ.[5] This means the majority of trumpet and bowl judgements, events that no doubt occur during the tribulation and before the Lord's return, must precede the sixth seal. Therefore, the three series of judgements cannot occur sequentially.

This same reasoning applies to the seventh trumpet, whose blowing heralds the establishment of God's kingdom.

> *And the seventh angel sounded; and there arose loud voices in heaven, saying, "The kingdom of the world has become the kingdom of our Lord, and of His Christ; and He will reign forever and ever. . . ."*
>
> *And the nations were enraged, and Thy wrath came, and the time came for the dead to be judged, and the time to give their reward to Thy bond-servants the prophets and to the saints and to those who fear Thy name, the small and the great, and to destroy those who destroy the earth.* (Rev. 11:15, 18)

The voices triggered by the seventh trumpet state the fact that the Father's kingdom has come: *"The kingdom of the world has become the kingdom of our Lord, and of His Christ. . . ."* Verse 18 also describes events that signify the consummation: *"and Thy wrath came, and the time came for the dead to be judged, . . ."* Further evidence on the finality of the seventh trumpet is found in Revelation, chapter 10, where another angel cries out:

> *But in the days of the voice of the seventh angel, when he is about to sound, then the mystery of God is finished, as He preached to His servants the prophets.* (Rev. 10:7)

Finally, remember how Paul in 1 Corinthians 15 described the angel's sounding of the last (seventh) trumpet as the proclamation of Christ's coming and the resurrection of the dead, a phenomenon Paul also described as a mystery;

> *Behold, I tell you a mystery; . . . in a moment, in the twinkling of an eye, at the last trumpet; for the trumpet will*

sound, and the dead will be raised imperishable, and we shall be changed. (1 Cor. 15:51a, 52)

Since the seventh trumpet will herald the Second Advent of Christ and the establishment of His kingdom among men, it cannot precede the bowl judgements, which will occur during the tribulation. Hence, the trumpet and bowl judgements must overlap.

One last important point is the similarity between the sixth trumpet (Rev. 9:13-21) and the sixth bowl judgements (Rev. 16:12-16). After reading them, one can easily conclude that both of them deal with the gathering of the Eastern armies at the great river Euphrates prior to the battle of Armageddon at the end of the tribulation. Lindsey, in *Planet Earth* assigns a force of 200 million to this great Oriental army,[6] the number spoken of by the angel of the sixth trumpet.

> *And the number of the armies of the horsemen was two hundred million; I heard the number of them.* (Rev. 9:16)

Since the sixth trumpet and the sixth bowl occur concurrently, the sixth trumpet must follow the first five bowl judgements. This, along with the parallelisms of the sixth seal and seventh trumpet to other Bible prophecies on Christ's second coming, provides sufficient proof that the seal, trumpet, and bowl judgements in Revelation do not occur completely in succession and that John's apocalypse is not perfectly sequential. This is a strong key to interpreting the book of Revelation and the events of the Great Tribulation.

Events Signaling the Beginning of Daniel's Seventieth Week

With the culmination of events—Russia's catastrophic defeat at Gog/Magog, the demise of the U.S. government, the rise of a unified transnational corporate empire grounded on the principles of the New Age, and the removal of Michael, the powerful restrainer—the stage is now set for the Antichrist's unveiling. Once revealed, this man known as the beast, the little horn, and the man of lawlessness or sin will rise to head the global corporate beast and quickly will consolidate power by uprooting three of its original ten TNC members.

> *While I was contemplating the horns, behold, another horn, a little one, came up among them, and three of the first horns were pulled out by the roots before it; and behold, this horn possessed eyes like the eyes of a man, and a mouth uttering great boasts.* (Dan. 7:8)

The seven remaining transnational corporations will form the foundation of the beast's kingdom.

To a world longing for peace after experiencing the violence of war, this man will appear on the world scene as the ultimate spokesman for peace, boldly enticing all humanity. Eyeing the one region of the world that has eluded peace, the Middle East, he will first seek to establish a covenant with Israel and their surrounding Arab neighbors. *"And he will make a firm covenant with the many for one week, . . ."* (Dan. 9:27). For her part in the treaty, Israel will be allowed to rebuild her temple on the temple mount without fear of Arab reprisal. After its completion, Israel will reinstitute the temple sacrifices. With the signing of this "firm" covenant, Daniel's seventieth week, the seven-year tribulation, will begin.

The First Half of the Tribulation: Continuing Birth Pangs

Rather than being a time of pseudo-peace brought about by the Antichrist's Middle Eastern covenant, the earth during the first three-and-one-half years of the tribulation will experience a marked increase in both the frequency and intensity of the birth pangs cited in chapter 1. The Four Horsemen of the Apocalypse will continue to gallop over the earth, bringing deception, war, famine, and death wherever they roam. Wars and rumors of war will continue to escalate. Earthquakes, volcanic eruptions, tidal waves, hurricanes, tornadoes, and other natural disasters will increase in ferocity. Famines will continue to spread across the globe. Pestilences, in the form of chemical and nuclear spills, will continue to lethally contaminate land and sea. For Christians, religious deception will no longer be a disturbing observation of a growing trend, but a hard-core reality of an adverse establishment.

Antichrist's transnational corporate beast will entrench itself politically and economically across the far reaches of Western civilization, gaining absolute power in all of Europe, Russia, America, Canada, Australia, and most of Latin America and Africa. Because of its undeviating opposition to biblical Christianity, the New Age spirituality that constitutes the beast's heart and soul will embark on a deliberate campaign of persecution against Western Christians. Christians will be removed from all positions of power. All reference to the Judeo-Christian God will be removed from school textbooks. Despite the rampant spread of AIDS, there will be no tolerance for any absolute moral teaching with regard to extramarital sexual activity, homosexuality, birth control, or abortion. Any religion that teaches Christ as the only way to God will be outlawed. And in third world countries, Christians will continue to be persecuted to the death. This brings us close to the middle of the seventieth week, and to the fifth seal (Rev. 6:9-11).

In the vision of the fifth seal, the apostle sees the souls of all who through the centuries have been martyred for their faith in God and for their testimony of Jesus Christ. Crying out in a loud voice, they plead for the Lord to avenge their blood on those who have spilled it on the earth. Comforting them with the white robe of holiness, the Lord tells them to rest for a little while longer until the number of their fellow brethren, who are to be killed even as they were, is completed. The Great Tribulation is about to begin. But first, another supernatural phenomenon must take place: God's sealing of his chosen people—Israel.

The Sealing of Israel

During the first three-and-one-half years after the signing of the Antichrist's middle eastern covenant and the rebuilding of the temple, Jews from every nation will gather en masse to the land of Israel. The majority of the world's Jews will be gathered to Palestine. Near the midpoint of the seventieth week and the outbreak of His wrath, God, out of love for His chosen people, will do something remarkable. John writes:

> *And I saw another angel ascending from the rising of the sun, having the seal of the living God; and he cried out with a loud voice to the four angels to whom it was granted to harm the earth and the sea,*
>
> *Saying, "Do not harm the earth or the sea or the trees, until we have sealed the bond-servants or our God on their foreheads."*
>
> *And I heard the number of those who were sealed, one hundred and forty-four thousand sealed from every tribe of the sons of Israel. (Rev. 7:2-4)*

Regarding the identity of these 144,000 bond-servants, who we must note are different from the 144,000 mentioned in Revelation 14 (to be discussed in chapter 13), Shearer writes: "Thus, there can be no doubt as to their identity: the 144,000 of Revelation 7 being Israel, . . ."[7]

Identifying the 144,000 of Revelation 7 with Israel is the greatest contribution of Shearer's book. Previous dispensational scholars, Lindsey among them, have claimed the 144,000 are an exact number of Jews who will evangelize the world during the tribulation,[8] a literal view that has a weak scriptural basis. If these 144,000 are to be interpreted literally, then shouldn't the Antichrist, instead of being a man, appear to us as a seven-headed, scarlet beast with ten horns? Of course not. We must remember that the Book of Revelation and the rest of the prophetic scriptures are filled with symbolism, and that it is vital to grasp the symbolism underlying each prophetic passage. One hundred and forty-four thousand, like the numbers 12 and 1,000 that make it up (12,000 from each of the 12 tribes of Israel), represents completeness. It represents how the full, complete number of Israel will be sealed on their foreheads with the seal of the living God before the Great Tribulation.

And why must they be sealed? So they will be protected during the Great Tribulation, from both the wrath of God poured out on unbelievers and from the persecution of the Antichrist. For in Revelation, chapter 9, at the sounding of God's fifth trumpet, locusts (who are demons) are released from the bottomless pit and go forth to torment all unbelievers on the earth *"who do not have the seal of God on their foreheads"* (Rev. 9:1-4).

So then, shouldn't Christians for their own protection have their foreheads sealed also? No, for as Shearer explains:

> the Church . . . has already been sealed. Those in the Church—when they received Christ as their Savior—were "sealed by the Holy Spirit of Promise" . . . and there is no further need to reseal them. . . .[9]

Regarding this, the Apostle Paul wrote:

> *In Him, you also, after listening to the message of truth, the gospel of your salvation—having also believed, you were sealed in Him with the Holy Spirit of promise,*
>
> *Who is given as a pledge of our inheritance* . . . (Eph. 1:13, 14a)

In addition to being sealed by the Holy Spirit, the Church is protected by the blood of the Passover Lamb. Thus, those within the body of Christ have no need to be resealed.

As for Israel, the question now becomes, "and should the Jews be sealed despite their unbelief in Christ?" The answer is *yes,* for it is by their unbelief that we Gentiles have come to know God. Even as Paul writes:

But by their transgression salvation has come to the Gentiles,
to make them jealous. . . .

For if their rejection be the reconciliation of the world, what
will their acceptance be but life from the dead? (Rom. 11:11b,
15)

Just because a person is a Jew, however, doesn't mean he will be
delivered from the tribulation. For Paul also wrote:

There will be tribulation and distress, for every soul of man
who does evil, of the Jew first and also of the Greek [the
Gentile], . . .

For there is no partiality with God. (Rom. 2:9, 11)

Therefore, the righteous of Israel will be sealed by God on their
foreheads prior to the midpoint of the seventieth week. Concerning this
chosen remnant, the prophet Daniel wrote:

And there will be a time of great distress such as never
occurred since there was a nation until that time; and at that
time your people, everyone who is found written in the book, will
be rescued. (Dan. 12:1b)

With Israel sealed, all hell is about to break loose on the earth. The
Great Tribulation is ready to begin.

The Abomination of Desolation

Speaking about the start of the Great Tribulation, Jesus Christ said:

Therefore, when you see the Abomination of Desolation
which was spoken of through Daniel the prophet, standing in the
holy place (let the reader understand),

Then let those who are in Judea flee to the mountains; . . . for
then there will be a great tribulation, such as has not occurred
since the beginning of the world until now, nor ever shall. (Matt.
24:15-16, 21)

Jesus linked the start of the Great Tribulation—the last and most
severe three-and-one-half years of Daniel's seventieth week—to the
Abomination of Desolation. This event will unfold after the Antichrist
has invaded Israel. The most likely scenario that will bring this about is
that radical Islamic militants will vehemently protest the peace treaty
their moderate Arab governments will make with Israel and the Anti-

christ at the start of the week. This opposition will erupt into violent revolutions throughout the Islamic world. After falling under the control of Islamic fundamentalists, these nations will begin a new war with Israel. Since the Arab's will have broken the peace accord, the Antichrist will enter the war on the side of Israel by invading the Middle East. Daniel described the conflict when he wrote:

> *And at the end time the king of the South will collide with him [the Antichrist], and the king of the North will storm against him with chariots, with horsemen, and with many ships; and he will enter countries, overflow them, and pass through.* (Dan. 11:40)

Lindsey equates the attack by the king of the North with Russia's attack at Gog/Magog, thereby placing the events of Ezekiel 38 and 39 at the midpoint of the tribulation.[10] We have already seen, however, why Gog/Magog must take place at least seven years prior to the Abomination of Desolation. In addition, earlier in chapter 11 Daniel defines the "king of the South" and the "king of the North" as rulers of two of the four kingdoms (Macedonia, Syria, Egypt, and Asia Minor) that were to be remnants of Alexander the Great's Greek Empire.[11] The most prominent dispensational scholar, C.I. Scofield, equates the king of the South with the traditional ruler of Egypt, whereas he identifies the king of the North as the ruler of Syria.[12] Thus, it is Egypt and Syria, not Russia, who will attack the Antichrist immediately prior to his invasion of Israel. Nevertheless, the iron-willed Antichrist will prevail. For Daniel writes:

> *He will also enter the Beautiful Land [Palestine], and many countries will fall; but these will be rescued out of his hand: Edom, Moab and the foremost of the sons of Ammon.*
>
> *Then he will stretch out his hand against other countries, and the land of Egypt will not escape.* (Dan. 11:41-42)

Upon entering the Beautiful Land after defeating Israel's Arab enemies, the Beast, with the False Prophet heralding the way, will be proclaimed as the Jewish Messiah. Upon entering Jerusalem, however, he will horrify the Jews by taking up his seat in the temple of God, proclaiming himself as God (2 Thess. 2:4). The Abomination of Desolation will have happened as Jesus and Daniel the prophet spoke. The fate of Israel and the world will be at hand.

The Woman in the Wilderness

Note that three countries—described as Edom, Moab, and the sons of Ammon—will escape the Antichrist's grasp. This will not happen by chance, the Book of Revelation predicts God will prepare a sanctuary in the desert for Israel where she will flee for protection from the Antichrist and from the horrors of the tribulation. As the seal of God on their foreheads will protect Israel from God's wrath, this haven in the wilderness will protect her physically from Satan and the Beast.

> *And a great sign appeared in heaven: a woman clothed with the sun, and the moon under her feet, and on her head a crown of twelve stars. . . .*
>
> *And the woman fled into the wilderness where she had a place prepared by God, so that there she might be nourished for one thousand two hundred and sixty days.* (Rev. 12:1, 2, 5, 6)

The woman's dress in this passage closely parallels Joseph's dream in Genesis, chapter 37, where he envisions the sun, the moon, and eleven stars bowing down before him. After Joseph related this dream to his father, Jacob (whom God earlier had renamed Israel) angrily interpreted the sun, the moon and the eleven stars to mean himself, his wife and Joseph's eleven brothers. Based on this, there is no doubt about the identity of the woman in Revelation 12. She is Israel and the crown of twelve stars on her head represents the twelve tribes of Israel.

Shearer writes about the three countries that will escape the Antichrist's grasp after he invades Palestine (Edom, Moab, and Ammon):

> This [area] is the "wilderness" spoken of in Revelation Chapter 12 where the woman (Israel) is to flee immediately after the Abomination of Desolation. . . . It is that portion of land east of the river Jordan which sweeps in a large arc (with the Dead Sea as the fulcrum) from about 40 miles northeast of the Dead Sea southward to about 50 miles due south, southeast of the same sea—a barren, mountainous, and desolate wilderness devoid of any significant vegetation. . . . Here God will care for His people much in the same fashion that He cared for them when Moses led the people out of Egypt.[13]

Further evidence that Israel will occupy the land of Edom, Moab, and the sons of Ammon in the last days is found in prophecies by Isaiah (Isa. 11:14) and Zephaniah (Zeph. 2:9).

As to why Israel will need the physical protection of this barren mountainous sanctuary, and the Church will not, Shearer continues:

> . . . since Israel, by the time of the Abomination of Desolation, has not yet fully recognized her Messiah as Christ, their spirits do not yet . . . contain the protecting presence of the Holy Spirit; thus, extraordinary care must be taken in the case of Israel that is not necessary with regard to the Church. Israel must be offered physical protection . . . for if they were to die as a result of the turmoil of the [Great tribulation] . . . they would share the same fate common to all unbelievers who die outside of Christ [separation from God]. . . . the same is not true of those who die in Christ (i.e., the Church). . . . (p. 110)

Israel therefore, upon witnessing the Abomination of Desolation, will abandon the promised land and the holy city of Jerusalem, fleeing from the Antichrist to a wilderness area that is now a part of modern-day Jordan. This "desolation" of Israel and Jerusalem should not be confused with Titus' destruction of Jerusalem and the dispersion of the Jews described in Luke 21:20-24. In Luke, the Jews were *"led captive into all the nations . . . until the times of the Gentiles be fulfilled."* Here, however, the woman (Israel) flees into the desert to a place prepared for her by God where she is protected for 1,260 days. Notice how at this time, Satan, who has just been cast out of heaven by Michael and his angels (Rev. 12:7-9), and knowing that Michael is no longer around to protect her, immediately tries to attack Israel. God, however, thwarts the devil's attack by supernaturally protecting Israel in her wilderness haven:

> *And when the dragon saw that he was thrown down to the earth, he persecuted the woman. . . .*
>
> *And the two wings of the great eagle were given to the woman, in order that she might fly into the wilderness . . . from the presence of the serpent.*
>
> *And the serpent poured water like a river out of his mouth after the woman, so that he might cause her to be swept away with the flood.*
>
> *And the earth helped the woman, and the earth opened its mouth and drank up the river which the dragon poured out of his mouth. (Rev. 12:13, 15-16)*

Enraged with their inability to destroy the woman, Satan and the Beast will turn their attention to making war on the rest of her offspring—those *"who keep the commandments of God and hold to the testimony of Jesus"* (Rev. 12:17)—the Church.

War on the Saints of the Most High

The Apostle John describes the fearful state of the world at this future moment:

> *And the whole earth was amazed and followed after the beast; and they worshipped the dragon, because he gave his authority to the beast; and they worshipped the beast, saying, "Who is like the beast, and who is able to make war with him?"*
>
> *And there was given to him a mouth speaking arrogant words and blasphemies; and authority to act for forty-two months was given to him. . . .*
>
> *And it was given to him to make war with the saints and to overcome them; and authority over every tribe and people and tongue and nation was given to him.* (Rev. 13:3b, 4, 5, 7)

John makes it perfectly clear. After the Abomination of Desolation, there will be no more illusions about the Antichrist. He will set out to be worshipped as God and to institute his mark—666—in the whole earth. All who resist him will be marked for death, and Christians will be his prime target. For this reason Jesus' words, *"when you see the Abomination of Desolation standing in the holy place, then let those who are in Judea flee to the mountains"* (Matt. 24:15, 16), apply not only to those who are in Judea, but to all Christians. Christ is warning all Christians to flee to safety; to a place of sanctuary in the mountains or in the desert. For the beast of the earth will seek to destroy Christ's Bride. Daniel, describing the little horn's assault on God's holy ones, writes:

> *I kept looking, and that horn was waging war with the saints and overpowering them. . . .*
>
> *And he will speak out against the Most High and wear down the saints of the Highest One, and he will intend to make alterations in times and in law; and they will be given into his hand for a time, times, and half a time [3-1/2 years].* (Dan. 7:21, 25)

Attempting to do away with every semblance of Christianity, the Antichrist will even alter the world's calendar. Time no longer will be dated from Christ's birth. More terribly, the Church will be given into his hand for three-and-one-half years. The Antichrist and all who have taken his mark will persecute the saints of the Most High with a zeal surpassing the killings and persecutions Nero inflicted upon first-century Christians.

Nevertheless, through this and the afflictions suffered during the first half of the tribulation, Christians will pray all the more fervently to the Lord their God, and He will hear and go forth to battle for them, for immediately after the Antichrist's onslaught at the start of the Great Tribulation, Yahweh will answer the prayers of His people by doing an amazing thing: He will unleash angels to sound the first five trumpets of His wrath.

The First Five Trumpets

Writing of the seven trumpets of God, John says:

> *And I saw the seven angels who stand before God; and seven trumpets were given them.*
>
> *And another angel came and stood at the altar, holding a golden censer; and much incense was given to him, that he might add it to the prayers of all the saints upon the golden altar which was before the throne.*
>
> *And the smoke of the incense, with the prayers of the saints, went up before God out of the angel's hand. . . .*
>
> *And the seven angels who had the seven trumpets prepared themselves to sound them.* (Rev. 8:2-4, 6)

These verses clearly show the seven trumpets are God's answer to the prayers of His people; prayers rising up to God throughout the tribulation and especially after the Abomination of Desolation, requesting Him to intervene on their behalf against the forces of Antichrist.

After the scene at the altar, the apostle describes the first five trumpets and the judgements of God that accompany them—the first woe. The first five trumpets are partial judgements, which do not affect the entire earth. With the blowing of the first trumpet, a third of the earth, a third of the trees, and all the green grass are burned up (Rev. 8:7). The second, like a great mountain burning with fire and thrown into the sea, causes a third of the sea to become blood, a third of the creatures in the sea to die, and a third of its ships to be destroyed (Rev. 8:8,9). The third trumpet, a great star falling from heaven, burning like a torch and called "Wormwood," causes a third of the fresh waters—rivers, lakes, and springs—to become bitter, killing many who drink from them (Rev. 8:10, 11). The fourth causes a third of each of the sun, the moon, and the stars to be darkened so that a third of the day and a third of the night no longer give off light (Rev. 8:12). The fifth releases demons from the bottomless pit so they might go forth to torment for five months—like scorpions when they sting—all who do not have the seal of God on their foreheads (Rev. 9:1-11). They are not permitted, however, to harm the grass of the earth, nor any green thing, nor any tree. This shows the grass which was burned up by the first trumpet is not permanently destroyed.

Because these judgements are partial and are sent in response to His people's prayers, God most probably will deliver them solely against the Antichrist and his forces. Sanctuaries inhabited by Christians, Israel, the Far East, and the Orient (i.e., the kings of the East) will be spared from these judgements. Also, the blowing of the five trumpets will occur right at the start of the Great Tribulation, within seven or eight days of the Abomination of Desolation. The reason for this soon will become apparent.

The first five trumpets will make it clear to the Antichrist and those with his mark that they have a war on their hands against God's saints, a war which God will not idly watch. Rather, the Almighty Father and His Son will fight in the thick of the battle for their people. Seeing this will remind Christians of Christ's eternal promise:

> *Because you have kept the word of My perseverance, I also will keep you from the hour of testing, that hour which is about to come upon the whole world, to test those who dwell upon the earth.* (Rev. 3:10)

After the sounding of the fifth trumpet, John writes: *"The first woe is past; behold, two woes are still coming after these things"* (Rev. 9:12).

The Two Witnesses

Immediately after the first woe, another supernatural phenomenon will take place that will further inspire the hearts and minds of God's people. God's two witnesses will appear on the scene immediately after the blowing of the first five trumpets. Scribing the angel's words, John portrays these two overpowering figures and their mighty deeds:

> *And I will grant authority to my two witnesses, and they will prophecy for twelve hundred and sixty days, clothed in sackcloth,*

> *These are the two olive trees and the two lampstands that stand before the Lord of the whole earth.*
>
> *And if anyone desires to harm them, fire proceeds out of their mouth and devours their enemies; and if anyone would desire to harm them, in this manner he must be killed.*
>
> *These have the power to shut up the sky, in order that rain may not fall during the days of their prophesying; and they have power over the waters to turn them into blood, and to smite the earth with every plague, as often as they desire.* (Rev. 11:3-6)

Much has been written about these two witnesses. Shearer claims they are Israel and the Church. This interpretation causes problems for several reasons. First, Israel since her rejection of Christ no longer is a part of the olive tree (Rom. 11:17-24). Second, the lampstand traditionally has symbolized the Church (Rev. 1-3), not Israel. Finally, the two witnesses are killed after their testimony and are raised from the dead three-and-one-half days later. Shearer's interpretation means the entire Church, as well as Israel, will have to be killed near the end of the tribulation and then raised from the dead after three-and-one-half days. There is no scriptural basis for teaching this.

Many evangelicals believe they will be either Moses and Elijah or Enoch and Elijah sent by God. Of these two possible pairings, the latter is more realistic. Moses has died (Jude 9), whereas Enoch and Elijah were taken up alive into heaven (Gen. 5:24 and Kings 2:11).[14] Whoever they are, the two witnesses will be two indomitable Christian warriors operating in the full power of the Holy Spirit who appear during the second half of the tribulation. This is known because prior to granting authority to the two witnesses, the angel announces to John that the nations will tread the holy city of Jerusalem under foot for forty-two months (Rev. 11:2), something that will take place during Israel's safe exile in the wilderness during the Great Tribulation.

They will prophesy for twelve hundred and sixty days—nearly the *entire length* of the Great Tribulation—and will operate as a medium of God's wrath against the forces of Antichrist and God's enemies; having power to destroy with fire from their mouths, to shut up the sky, to turn the waters into blood, and to smite the earth with every plague. Thus, unlike the first woe, the two witnesses' judgements will be worldwide and not solely restricted to the realm of the Antichrist. Yet, they will be selective in delivering these judgements. For they have power *"to smite the earth with every plague, as often as they desire"* (verse 6). Because of this, Christians will be safe from their wrath.

They will perform their awesome works until their testimonies are complete, after which the beast who comes up from the abyss (the Antichrist) will make war on them and kill them. He will leave their corpses lying on the streets of the "great city" for three-and-one-half days for viewing by the nations (Rev. 11:7-9). The great city here is not Jerusalem (Heb. 13:12). Rather, it is Mystery Babylon, *"the great city, which reigns over the kings of the earth"* (Rev. 17:18). After the three-and-one-half days, God will breath life into their dead bodies and will take them up into heaven. As put by John:

> And after the three and a half days the breath of life from God came into them, and they stood on their feet; and great fear fell upon those who were beholding them.

> And they heard a loud voice from heaven saying to them, "Come up here." And they went up into heaven in the cloud, and their enemies beheld them.

> And in that hour there was a great earthquake, and a tenth of the city fell; and seven thousand people were killed in the earthquake, and the rest were terrified and gave glory to the God of heaven.

> The second woe is past; behold, the third woe is coming quickly. (Rev. 11:11-14)

The two witnesses prophecy to, and torment *"the peoples and tribes and tongues and nations . . . those who dwell on the earth"* (Rev. 11:9, 10). For this reason, the bulk of their testimony will be directed toward the inhabitants of countries and continents outside of the Antichrist's direct domain; toward the peoples of China, Japan, Africa, India, and the remaining third world nations. Notice also that after God raises the two witnesses from the dead and a subsequent earthquake strikes the city, those who survive it are terrified and give glory to God. Therefore, the two witnesses' wrath and testimony are intended to win people to faith in the true God of the Bible. This is apparently what it will take to win over many a devout Muslim, Buddhist, Hindu, and Sikh to faith in Jesus Christ, God's only Son.

Once the two witnesses are removed, John says the second woe is past. Hence, God's wrath delivered through the two witnesses is the second woe, a woe that will last for 1,263 days[15] of the 1,278 day-long[16] Great Tribulation. Since the first woe must precede the second, the blowing of the first five trumpets—the first woe—must take place right at the start of the Great Tribulation, within seven or eight days of the

Abomination of Desolation. Since the third must succeed the second, this is also why the seven bowls (and the sixth trumpet) that make up the third woe must be poured out during the final seven days of the tribulation.

God's second woe, His two mighty witnesses, will undoubtedly be a source of great inspiration for Christ's Bride throughout the Great Tribulation.

The Witness of the Saints

Although the scriptures say the Antichrist will overcome the saints and that Christians will be given into his hand for forty-two months, the outcome of the tribulation makes it clear he never will totally conquer God's people. Adolf Hitler overpowered the entire continent of Europe, which was given into his hand for nearly sixty months. Millions died during his reign of terror. Nonetheless, in every occupied land, partisan guerrilla movements sprouted up to combat the evils of Nazi Germany. In France, in Russia, in Poland, in Italy, in Yugoslavia, and in every other European country, the underground resistance battled the Nazis until total victory was ultimately achieved.

This will symbolize Christ's Bride throughout the Great Tribulation. This underground church, her faith immediately strengthened through God's intervention, via the first woe, and continually uplifted by the mighty acts of His two witnesses, will wage an all-out guerrilla war in the Spirit against the Antichrist and the men of his mark. From bases in countries not under the beast's direct domain (the Islamic countries, the nations of Asia, and parts of Latin America) the saints will send in Christian "battalions" to reinforce the Church in occupied territories, to preach the Gospel, to heal the wounded, and to minister to new believers.

Likewise, the Antichrist will not be able to retain a stranglehold over the information technology he will use in attempting to bring Western civilization under his submission. Instead, he will be tricked by his own devices. Larry Martz in the article "Revolution by Information," writes: "George Orwell long ago warned that technology would be an instrument of tyranny—a warning symbolized by Big Brother's two-way telescreen in *1984*. Orwell was right, and tyrants are indeed using the latest electronic gadgetry to eavesdrop, pry, and monitor their subjects' behavior. He was also wrong: somehow technology keeps giving people new ways to get around the oppression it makes possible."[17] The computer information networks that the Antichrist hopes will control every subject in his dominion, "the System of the Beast," will constantly be attacked by Christian computer "hackers" and other saboteurs throughout his realm. Christians and other dissidents will cut network lines, disrupt communications, and infest his central computer facilities with disruptive computer "viruses." Reminiscent of the Chinese student's pro-democracy movement at Beijing's Tiananmen Square, which was a "revolution by fax machine, [and] computer and word of mouth, by photocopier and wall poster, by direct-dialed phone calls, shortwave radio and letters in the mail,"[18] Christians will likewise spread the Gospel of Jesus Christ through all these media, reaching millions in the Antichrist's realm with the message of salvation. Through it all, God's awesome love shall inspire them onward, as Saint Paul's exhortation echoes in their hearts: *"Who shall separate us from the love of Christ? Shall tribulation, or distress, or persecution, or famine, or nakedness, or peril, or sword?"* (Rom. 8:35).

Wherever they go, miraculous works will follow in their footsteps. Strengthened through prayer, empowered by His word, and united by a continual celebration of the Eucharist—their Lord's body and blood—this awesome Christian army will step out in the might of His Spirit, performing great signs and wonders throughout the earth. Since they will be unable to buy or sell without the mark, God's people will survive the Antichrist's economic tyranny through tremendous acts of charity—much like the early Christians. Feeding the hungry by multiplying food *(Matt. 14:16-21)*, clothing the poor, healing the sick, giving sight to the blind, raising the dead; and not harmed by any serpent, or affected by any deadly poison, withstanding hardships beyond description—and through it all exhibiting an agape love that pierces the hearts of all who cross their paths—Christians will win over to Christ the frightened multitudes who have not fallen prey to the Antichrist's mark, baptizing thousands into the faith! And to those who have been called to such a witness—martyrdom. For it is written of them all: *"And they overcame him [Satan] because of the blood of the Lamb and because of the word of their testimony, and they did not love their life even to death."* (Rev. 12:11)

With the Lord's unselfish love lived out through her, Christ's Bride will reap from the earth a rich harvest of souls, causing the angels of heaven to rejoice. This is the Father's ultimate purpose behind the tribulation. Visualizing this harvest of mankind while on the island of Patmos, John writes:

> *And I looked, and behold, a white cloud, and sitting on the cloud was one like a son of man, having a golden crown on His head, and a sharp sickle in His hand.*

> *And another angel came out of the temple, crying out with a loud voice to Him who sat on the cloud, "Put in your sickle and reap, because the hour to reap has come, because the harvest of the earth is ripe."*

> *And He who sat on the cloud swung His sickle over the earth; and the earth was reaped.* (Rev. 14:14-16)

This is the harvest John is talking about when:

> *After these things I looked, and behold, a great multitude, which no one could count, from every nation and all tribes and peoples and tongues, standing before the throne and before the Lamb, clothed in white robes, and palm branches were in their hands; . . .*

> *These are the ones who come out of the great tribulation, and they have washed their robes and made them white in the blood of the Lamb.* (Rev. 7:9, 14b)

These are also the ones of whom Zechariah the Prophet wrote:

> *And I will bring the third part through the fire,*
> *Refine them as silver is refined,*
> *And test them as gold is tested.*
> *They will call on My name,*
> *And I will answer them;*
> *I will say, "They are My people,"*
> *And they will say, "The Lord is my God."* (Zech. 13:9)

Enraged at God because He has wrestled from them what they coveted for themselves, Satan and the Antichrist with great fury will begin to wear down the saints of the Highest One (Dan. 7:25). By this time the world will be teetering on the brink of destruction. Consequently, on behalf of His Bride and the abundant harvest that He has just reaped, God will interrupt the drama with great wrath. The third woe is about to come.

The Seven Bowls[19]

In portraying the seven bowls of the third and last woe, the Apostle John writes:

> *And I saw another sign in heaven, great and marvelous, seven angels who had seven plagues, which are the last, because in them the wrath of God is finished.*

> *And I saw, as it were, a sea of glass mixed with fire, and those who had come off victorious from the beast and from his image and from the number of his name, standing on the sea of glass. . . .*
>
> *And one of the four living creatures gave to the seven angels seven golden bowls full of the wrath of God, who lives forever and ever. . . .*
>
> *And I heard a loud voice from the temple, saying to the seven angels, "Go and pour out the seven bowls of the wrath of God into the earth."* (Rev. 15:1, 2a, 7; 16:1)

In between describing the seven last and most severe plagues of God's wrath, the seven bowls, John tells how he saw standing before God *"those who had come off victorious from the beast and from his image and from the number of his name."* These are God's victorious saints, including the great harvest of the tribulation. When the harvest is complete, seeing no further reason to risk His elect, God will intervene on behalf of His people by pouring out the seven bowls, and by sounding the sixth trumpet of His wrath. These judgements constitute the *third woe*. And the redeemed, standing on the sea of glass, symbolize Christ's Bride who will be guarded from this *third woe*.

The *third woe* differs from the first and second in that its purpose is not to bring men to repentance. Since it comes after the great harvest and the testimony of the two witnesses at the end of the Great Tribulation,[20] its judgements will be poured out upon those who are so hardened, they will by this time be beyond repentance. For John says, *"they did not repent, so as to give Him glory"* (Rev. 16:9b). This disdainful attitude will be exhibited not only toward God's seven bowls, but toward His sixth trumpet as well (Rev. 9:20, 21). Hence, these plagues are strictly meant to punish mankind. And since they are covered by the blood of the Lamb, Christians will be divinely protected from them.

When the first angel pours out his bowl into the earth, it becomes a loathsome and malignant sore upon the men who have the beast's mark and who worship his image (Rev. 16:2). The second bowl, when poured out, causes the sea to turn to blood, killing every living thing in it (Rev. 16:3). The third angel pours out his bowl on the earth, causing the rivers and springs of fresh water to become blood also (Rev. 16:4-6). The fourth is poured out upon the sun, causing it to scorch men with fire and fierce heat (Rev. 16:8, 9). The fifth angel pours out his bowl upon the throne of the beast, causing his kingdom to become darkened (Rev. 16:10). After the fifth bowl, John exclaims how men *"gnawed their* tongues because of pain, and . . . blasphemed the God of heaven because of their pains and their sores; and . . . [they] did not repent of their deeds."

Those who might argue that the church would suffer from the wrath God inflicts through the first five bowls, should note that: (1) the first bowl is poured out specifically on men with the mark of the beast; the fifth bowl is poured out on the throne of the beast; and the fourth is poured on evil, unrepentant men, (2) true, the second and third bowls cause all the waters of the earth to turn to blood, but it happens so close to (within a week of) the end of the tribulation and the coming of God's glory. As God delivered His saints through seven years of tribulation, so we can count on Him to deliver us through the tribulation's final seven days.

As the initial bowls of God's wrath are poured out upon the earth, the armies of the whole world, including the massive army of the kings of the east, will gather together in the holy land for the greatest war of annihilation in history. The last two bowls and the sixth trumpet of God's wrath all pertain to this great battle: the Battle of Armageddon.

Notes

1. Lindsey, *The Rapture*, 90-100.

2. *Scofield Reference Bible*, 1360, 1363.

3. Robert Gundy, *The Church and the Tribulation* (Grand Rapids, MI: Zondervan Publishing, 1973), 75.

4. Jim McKeever, *The Coming Climax of History* (Medford, OR: Omega Publications, 1982), 163-176.

5. Since the sixth seal precedes the cosmic disturbances before the day of the Lord, then the seventh seal could describe a half-hour of silence in heaven prior to the day of the Lord's actual onset (cf. Zeph. 1:7).

6. Taken from the book, *The Late Great Planet Earth* by Hal Lindsey, p. 75. Copyright © 1970, 1977 by Zondervan Publishing House. Used by permission of Zondervan Publishing House.

7. Shearer, *The Beginning of the End*, 106.

8. Lindsey, *The Rapture*, 146.

9. Shearer, 106.

10. Lindsey, *The Rapture*, 94.

11. Most Bible scholars agree the "first king" in Daniel 8:21 and the "mighty king" in Daniel 11:3 both refer to Alexander the Great.

12. *Scofield Bible*, 911, 915-916.

13. Shearer, 111.

14. This would be the first authentic case of time travel.

15. The 1,260 days plus three-and-one-half days their dead bodies lie in the streets.

16. Assuming a leap year is included, three-and-one-half 365 day years equate to 1,278 days. Although Daniel's seventieth week is based on 360 day years, the last half of the week, the Great Tribulation, does not appear to be.

17. Larry Martz, "Revolution by Information," *Time*, 19 June 1989, 28. Used by permission.

18. *Ibid*, 29.

19. The third woe includes the sixth trumpet.

20. Since the second woe, the testimony of the two witnesses, will last through approximately the 1,271st day of the Great Tribulation, the judgments of the third woe must all occur in its final seven days.

8
ARMAGEDDON: THE LORD'S BATTLE

The first question that needs to be answered with regard to Armageddon is: Where is it? In answering this, Hal Lindsey, quoting Dr. J. A. Seiss, author of the book *The Apocalypse*, writes:

> Harmageddon (Armageddon) means the Mount of Megiddo, which has also given its name to the great plain of Jezreel which belts across the middle of the Holy Land, from the Mediterranean to the Jordan. The name is from a Hebrew root which means to cut off, to slay; and a place of slaughter has Megiddo ever been.[1]

Continuing, Lindsey says:

> In Biblical history countless bloody battles were fought in this area. Napoleon is reported to have stood upon the hill of Megiddo and recalled this prophecy [Rev. 16] as he looked over the valley and said, ". . . all the armies of the world could maneuver for battle here."[2]

The prelude to the Battle of Armageddon will begin when the sixth angel pours out his bowl upon the great river Euphrates, drying up its waters so the way can be prepared for the kings of the East (Rev. 16:12). The sixth bowl unleashes something else too, as the Apostle John writes:

> *And I saw coming out of the mouth of the dragon and out of the mouth of the beast and out of the mouth of the false prophet, three unclean spirits like frogs;*
>
> *For they are the spirits of demons, performing signs, which go out to the kings of the whole world, to gather them together for the war of the great day of God, the Almighty.*
>
> *And they gathered them together to the place which in Hebrew is called Har-Magedon.* (Rev. 16:13-14, 16)

The sixth bowl's purpose will be to gather the earth's armies to Armageddon. The sixth trumpet, the trumpet of war, will unleash these armies into the fury of combat. The following passage depicts this great conflict's first wave of destruction:

> *And the sixth angel sounded, and I heard a voice . . . , one saying to the sixth angel who had the trumpet, "Release the four angels who are bound at the great river Euphrates."*
>
> *And the four angels, who had been prepared for the hour and day and month and year, were released, so that they might kill a third of mankind.*
>
> *And the number of the armies of the horsemen was two hundred million; I heard the number of them.*
>
> *And this is how I saw in the vision the horses and those who sat on them: the riders had breastplates the color of fire and of hyacinth and of brimstone; and the heads of the horses are like the heads of lions; and out of their mouths proceed fire and smoke and brimstone.*
>
> *A third of mankind was killed by these three plagues, by the fire and the smoke and the brimstone, which proceeds out of their mouths.*
>
> *For the power of the horses is in their mouths and in their tails; for their tails are like serpents and have heads; and with them they do harm.* (Rev. 9:13a, 14-19)

The sixth trumpet releases four angels who are bound at the Euphrates river. These angels, before being released, are the restraining force that keeps the armies of the East from crossing the great river. Once released, they are given power to kill a third of mankind. They perform their great destruction through the army of the Beast and the rest of the armies of the earth gathered at Armageddon. These massive armies will total a phenomenal 200 million troops. John the Revelator, while on the island of Patmos 1,900 years ago, had no notion or understanding of armored cavalry units made up of monstrous tanks and mobile, armored nuclear missile launchers, so he portrays them in the language of his day. He describes them as horses with the heads of lions, out of whose mouths proceed fire and smoke and brimstone. John tells how the power of the horses are in their mouths and in their tails. He pictures their tails as serpents with heads—a vivid portrayal of a finned missile propelling a nuclear warhead. And with them they do much harm, so much harm that a third of mankind will be destroyed through nuclear annihilation.

The Church, however, will miraculously remain unscathed by this great end-time, atomic holocaust. John makes clear this wrath will fall only upon the ungodly, those so hardened that he writes:

> *And the rest of mankind, who were not killed by these plagues, did not repent of the works of their hands, so as not to worship demons, and the idols of gold and of silver and of brass and of stone and of wood, which can neither see nor hear nor walk; and they did not repent of their murders nor of their sorceries nor of their immorality nor of their thefts.* (Rev. 9:20, 21)

Quickly after the outbreak of Armageddon, God will pour out the final, seventh bowl of His wrath on the unbelieving of this world (Rev. 16:17-21). Flashes of lightening and peals of thunder, and a great and mighty earthquake, one such has not occurred since man walked upon the earth, will shake our planet. So great an earthquake will it be, that John exclaims, *"every island fled away, and the mountains were not found"* (v. 20). It will also split the "great city" into three parts, and cause the cities of the nations to fall. After the earthquake, huge hailstones, weighing about one hundred pounds each, will rain down upon men from heaven, causing them to blaspheme God because of their severity. Also with the seventh bowl, Babylon the great will be remembered before God and will be given the cup of the wine of His fierce wrath.

Babylon the Great:
The Great Harlot of the Kings of the Earth

Babylon the Great: This central figure plays a major role in the book of Revelation and throughout the Great Tribulation. Leading up to this judgment, the Apostle John writes:

> *And one of the seven angels who had the seven bowls came and spoke with me, saying, "Come here, I shall show you the judgment of the great harlot who sits on many waters,*
>
> *With whom the kings of the earth committed acts of immorality, and those who dwell on the earth were made drunk with the wine of her immorality."*
>
> *And he carried me away in the Spirit into a wilderness; and I saw a woman sitting on a scarlet beast, full of blasphemous names, having seven heads and ten horns.*

And the woman was clothed in purple and scarlet, and adorned with gold and precious stones and pearls, having in her hand a gold cup full of abominations and of the unclean things of her immorality,

And upon her forehead a name was written, a mystery, "BABYLON THE GREAT, THE MOTHER OF HARLOTS AND OF THE ABOMINATIONS OF THE EARTH."

And I saw the woman drunk with the blood of the saints, and with the blood of the witnesses of Jesus. And when I saw her, I wondered greatly.

And the angel said to me, "Why do you wonder? I shall tell you the mystery of the woman and of the beast that carries her, which has the seven heads and the ten horns." (Rev. 17:1-7)

Volumes have been written regarding the mystery of Babylon the Great, the great harlot of the Book of Revelation. As an end-times personality, she is no doubt distinct from ancient Babylon, where the Jews of Daniel's day spent seventy years in captivity. As the woman who sits on the scarlet, seven-headed and ten-horned beast of Revelation 13—the corporate beast of the Antichrist and the Antichrist himself—we know she will be in league with him and have a special relationship to him. We also know she will be a great persecutor of the Church of Jesus Christ (v. 6). So just who is she? Before we answer this question, let's find out who she isn't.

First let us lay some groundwork. It is vital to note many current, evangelical scholars believe Babylon the Great possesses a two-fold nature. They believe there actually are two Babylons spoken of in Revelation, chapters 17 and 18: a spiritual or religious Babylon, and a commercial or political Babylon.

One extremely popular theory embraced by many evangelicals, pre and posttribulationists alike, is that religious Babylon is the Roman Catholic Church, which some within this group of Christians believe is an apostate form of Christianity. As spiritual Babylon, she supposedly will become the religion of the Antichrist. This view was popularized early by Hislop in his work *The Two Babylons*. The views of those who interpret this way, it is sad to say, are rooted much deeper in bigotry than they are in Scripture, for Revelation provides no evidence whatsoever to support the existence of two Babylons, much less that one of them, the religious Babylon, is the Roman Catholic Church.

Before refuting their weak scriptural arguments, it is difficult to believe anyone could have even gotten the notion that the Antichrist's religion will come out of the Roman Catholic Church; the same Church which eagerly professes: "I believe in God the Father Almighty, Maker of heaven and earth. And in Jesus Christ His only Son our Lord: . . ." For why would the same Church that continuously proclaims these opening lines to the Apostle's Creed support the Antichrist; the Beast who, in denying the Father and the Son, will proclaim himself as God and go about killing Christians throughout the world?

Nevertheless, a major scripture that is quoted by those who believe this way is Revelation 17:9. Speaking of the Beast on which Babylon sits, it says: *"Here is the mind which has wisdom. The seven heads are seven mountains on which the woman sits, ..."* Many claim these seven mountains represent the seven hills upon which Rome is built. Hence, they claim the Vatican, which sits on these hills, is the Great Harlot. Nevertheless, if we read the next verse we find out exactly what verse 9 means, for verse 10 continues: *"and they are seven kings; . . . ."* The seven heads described initially as seven mountains also happen to be seven kings. If we remember from the last chapter, these are the seven remaining, foundational transnational corporations on which the Antichrist will establish his throne. They have *nothing* to do with the Roman Catholic Church.

Still, there are some who try to support their view that John is writing of two Babylons by pointing out an apparent duality in Revelation. Describing it, Shearer writes:

> That TWO Babylon are spoken of here is evident from the fact that when Spiritual Babylon [the woman] is destroyed . . . , she is destroyed because of the jealousy and hatred of the Ten Kings and the Beast (Revelation 17:6). But when Commercial Babylon is destroyed, these same kings . . . are sorrowful and mourn her destruction (see Revelation 18).[3]

Since the kings lament over Babylon on the one hand, while on the other they destroy her with great jealousy and hatred, it seems to imply they are dealing with two separate entities.

The truth, however, is that the Babylons are not the separate entities in Revelation 17 and 18; it is the kings who are separate. The ten kings of Revelation 17 are not the same as the kings of the earth who mourn Babylon's destruction in Revelation 18. The ten kings of chapter 17 are ten illegitimate, evil, and power-hungry, individuals who are brought into power temporarily by the Beast for only one hour in order to destroy the Great Prostitute.

> *And the ten horns which you saw are ten kings, who have not yet received a kingdom, but they receive authority as kings with the beast for one hour.*

> *These have one purpose and they give their power and authority to the beast. . . .*

> *And the ten horns which you saw, and the beast, these will hate the harlot and will make her desolate and naked, and will eat her flesh and will burn her up with fire.*

> *For God has put it in their hearts to execute His purpose by having a common purpose, and by giving their kingdom to the beast, until the words of God should be fulfilled.*

> *And the woman whom you saw is the great city, which reigns over the kings of the earth.* (Rev. 17:12, 13, 16-18)

These ten kings rule only during the one-hour period of the harlot's destruction. Coming out of the Beast's kingdom, they must obviously rise out of western civilization.

The kings of Revelation 18, however, are established kings (rulers) who have reigned for much longer periods of time; long enough to have committed adulterous acts and to have lived with the harlot in luxury before her ruin (Rev. 18:3). These kings include the kings of the east, the rulers of the Orient. Concerning them, John writes:

> *And the kings of the earth, who committed acts of immorality and lived sensuously with her, will weep and lament over her when they see the smoke of her burning,*

> *Standing at a distance because of the fear of her torment, saying, "Woe, woe, the great city, Babylon, the strong city! For in one hour your judgment has come."* (Rev. 18:9, 10)

There can be no doubt the kings in Revelation 17 and 18 are two different groups. There can be no doubt also that the Babylons spoken of in Revelation 17 and 18 are one and the same since, in both chapters, their destruction comes about in one hour.

In the face of this, there is absolutely no scriptural basis to support there are two distinct Babylons in the Book of Revelation and that one of them is the Roman Catholic Church. Such thinking is simply backwash from an inquisition that took place centuries ago. Surely the

Catholic Church should be deplored for her acts during this period, but if one would deplore her, one had better deplore John Calvin, who had the Spanish heretic Miguel Servetus burned at the stake,[4] and deplore Martin Luther, who while advocating the burning of witches declared: "An example should be made of them to terrify others." Likewise, Luther's attitude toward Anabaptists was: "Nor should any mercy be shown to Anabaptists, who deny the validity of infant baptism."[5] Or, how about Ulrich Zwingli, who as the leader of the Swiss canton of Zurich during the Reformation imposed political and economic sanctions on Switzerland's Roman Catholic districts. In response to their upheaval, Zwingli ultimately led Zurich's army into battle against them, where he fell by the sword.[6] Such was the religious zeal of men during that day.

We in America often ridicule people of other nations for bearing centuries-old hatreds. Yet in America, Protestants and Catholics still carry grudges and prejudices that were born centuries ago.

John sees one Babylon in Revelation 17 and 18, and she is not the Roman Catholic Church. This is not to say that Babylon will not have a religious side to her. But as we read in chapter 4, this nature will emanate from the New Age spiritual counterfeit that is now spreading deceptively throughout the world. So then, if Babylon is not the Roman Catholic Church, who is she?

End-Times Babylon: The Greatest Nation

Revelation 18 gives the rest of the clues needed to determine the identity of this mysterious personality. This explicit passage helps us to recognize some of the Great Harlot's most vital characteristics. First, it is obvious that instead of being just a single great city, she is much, much more. She is a grand and mighty nation; a land which sits in the midst of many waters, surrounded by abundant waters (Rev. 17:1). She is a proud and arrogant country, one who highly exalts herself (Rev. 18:7). As the Great Harlot, she is a sorceress and extremely immoral, corrupting the nations of the world with her sorceries and adulteries (Rev. 18:3, 4, and 23). She is the richest nation on the face of the earth, importing massive cargoes of every product imaginable—even cargoes of slaves and the souls of men—making the merchants of the world rich through her insatiable appetite for luxury (Rev. 18:11-19). From her many mills, she produces her own grain (Rev. 18:22). In her are found the finest musicians, artists, and craftsmen known to man (Rev. 18:22). She is a lamp to the world, the source of its enlightenment (Rev. 18:23). And in her were found the voice of the Bridegroom, Jesus Christ, and of His Bride, the Church (Rev. 18:23).

In addition to these, Shearer does an excellent job in pointing out many of her other outstanding traits from Old Testament prophecies of prophetic Babylon. From Jeremiah, she is said to be one who *"dwells by many waters, abundant in treasures"* (Jer. 51:13). There is a *"mixed multitude in the midst of her"* (Jer. 50:37). She is exceedingly powerful militarily, *"the hammer of the whole earth"* (Jer. 50:23). She was once a God-fearing nation, *"a golden cup in the hand of the Lord"* (Jer. 51:7). But now she is a land of materialistic possessions (vv. 12-16) that have become her idols: *"For it is a land of idols, and they are mad over fearsome [timid] idols"* (Jer. 50:38). And finally, she is a nation that has reached for the stars, to outer space; for *"Though Babylon should ascend to the heavens, and though she should fortify her lofty stronghold, from Me destroyers will come to her,"* declares the Lord (Jer. 51:53).

So who is prophetic Babylon, this Great Harlot of the kings of the earth? She is the United States of America. David Wilkerson, author of *The Cross and the Switchblade*, writes: "modern day Babylon is present-day America. . . . No other nation on earth fits the description in Revelation 18 but America, the world's biggest fornicator with the merchants of all the nations."[7] Shearer, in his book, also clearly states: the United States is the Babylon of the end times.[8]

What country could more appropriately ride aboard the great global corporate beast—the kingdom of the Antichrist—than the United States of America? None! The terrifying, prowling, four-headed winged Leopard from Daniel, upon her government's decline and the rise of the Antichrist's TNC empire, instead of disappearing from the global scene, will be transformed into the Great Harlot spoken of in Revelation. She will ride aboard the Beast, in luxurious union with it, as the great city-nation who reigns over the kings of the earth. Because of this, those kings and merchants of the earth who commit adultery with her (in Revelation 18) will include the eastern trading powers of Japan, Korea, Hong Kong, Taiwan, and Singapore—those nations who today are profiting the most from her insatiable appetite for luxury. And, as the Antichrist's Great Harlot, in the future she will become the great persecutor of Christ's Bride on the earth.

Because of her great sins against God—her blatantly perverse sexual immorality and pornography; her extravagant materialism as the rest of the world starves; her insatiable addiction to drugs; her undisguised racism; her persecution and denial of the God of the Bible; her playing the role of God in the areas of medicine, genetic- and bio-engineering, creating new life forms on the one hand,[9] while destroying more than 60 million unborn children on the other; and, as the heartland of New Age spirituality, her proud boast that she is God—this great and marvelously wise country in the end will be judged by God. In pronouncing her judgment, the Lord spoke through the Apostle John:

> *Fallen, fallen is Babylon the great! . . . For all the nations have drunk of the wine of the passion of her immorality. . . .*
>
> *After these things I heard . . . a loud voice . . . in heaven, saying, "Hallelujah! Salvation and glory and power belong to our God;"*
>
> *Because . . . He has judged the great harlot who was corrupting the earth with her immorality, and He has avenged the blood of His bond-servants on her."*
>
> *And a second time they said, "Hallelujah! Her smoke rises up for ever and ever.* (Rev. 18:2, 3; Rev. 19:1-3)

As the battle of Armageddon rages, her previous lover, the Antichrist, with his ten evil kings, will betray the Great Harlot. By God's prompting, they will turn their entire nuclear arsenal against her, bringing about her total downfall in just one hour.

But before her destruction, the Lord will command His saints:

> *Come out of her, my people, that you may not participate in her sins and that you may not receive of her plagues;*
>
> *For her sins have piled up as high as heaven, and God has remembered her iniquities.* (Rev. 18:4b, 5)

Jesus will rescue His Bride from the Harlot's midst so that she does not partake in her punishment. And the blood of all Christ's saints will be avenged on Babylon, the Great Harlot, as she suffers complete and utter ruin. Woe to the Great Harlot! Woe to the Great Prostitute who has corrupted all the nations of the earth! Woe! For the Lord God Almighty who judges her is strong.

And as Babylon is being judged during the great battle, something else will happen: the Jews will leave their haven in the wilderness to recapture the city of Jerusalem.

The Siege of Jerusalem

While the Battle of Armageddon rages, the Israeli military will observe the mass confusion and disarray amongst the warring armies of the earth. They will notice also the forces of the Antichrist distracted by both the battle and by their vengeance upon Babylon. Hence, the Jews—yet to be converted to Jesus Christ—will seize this opportunity to retake Jerusalem. This is prophesied in the twelfth chapter of Zechariah, a chapter that Bible commentators agree is an account of the Battle of Armageddon. Here, Zechariah predicted:

> *In that day I will make the clans of Judah like a firepot among pieces of wood and a flaming torch among sheaves, so they will consume on the right hand and on the left all the surrounding peoples, while the inhabitants of Jerusalem again dwell on their own sites in Jerusalem.*
>
> *The Lord also will save the tents of Judah first in order that the glory of the house of David and glory of the inhabitants of Jerusalem may not be magnified above Judah.* (Zech. 12:6, 7)

The King James Version translates the last part of verse six as: *"Jerusalem shall be inhabited again in her own place, even in Jerusalem."* This implies a reoccupation of the city. Jerusalem, occupied by the forces of the Antichrist during the previous forty-two months of the Great Tribulation, will now be recaptured by the Jews. The men of Judah—the Israeli army—will bring this about by driving a wedge through the surrounding peoples, consuming them on the right hand and on the left, and clearing a path for the inhabitants of Jerusalem to pass through. That the men of Judah live in tents rather than in permanent dwellings implies they are on a military campaign; a campaign that will begin with the trek from their base in the Jordanian wilderness. With the road to Jerusalem cleared, the Jews will repossess the holy city.

While Jerusalem is being reinhabited, the armies of the earth who are fighting each other in the valley of Armageddon suddenly will gather against Jerusalem to besiege it. But since the time of Israel's calling is at hand, the Lord God will go forth to fight for His chosen people. Zechariah writes:

> *Behold, I am going to make Jerusalem a cup that causes reeling to all the peoples around; and when the siege is against Jerusalem, it will also be against Judah.*
>
> *And it will come about in that day that I will make Jerusalem a heavy stone for all the peoples; all who lift it will be severely injured. And all the nations of the earth will be gathered against it. . . .*

> *In that day the Lord will defend the inhabitants of Jerusalem, and the one who is feeble among them in that day will be like David, and the house of David [Israel] will be like God, like the angel of the Lord before them.*
>
> *And it will come about in that day that I will set about to destroy all the nations that come against Jerusalem.* (Zech. 12:2–3, 8–9)

In that day the Lord will strike every horse with bewilderment and its rider with madness. Every horse of the men who have gone to war against Jerusalem and Judah will be struck blind (Zech. 12:4). God will also strike every soldier with a plague. Their flesh will rot while they stand on their feet. Their eyes will rot in their sockets and their tongues will rot in their mouths (Zech. 14:12). And a great panic will fall on them. Remembering how just hours before they were enemies, they will lift up their swords against each other, destroying one another (Zech. 14:13). Judah, the Israeli army, will also fight against them at Jerusalem (Zech. 14:14).

Just when Israel is realizing the Lord's victory, God by His sovereign call will do something remarkable. Much as he did to the Apostle Paul on the road to Damascus, the Lord Jesus Christ through His Spirit will reveal Himself to His people, Israel. The prophet Zechariah writes:

> *And I will pour out on the house of David and on the inhabitants of Jerusalem, the Spirit of grace and of supplication, so that they will look on Me whom they have pierced; and they will mourn for Him, as one mourns for an only son, and they will weep bitterly over Him, like the bitter weeping over a first-born.* (Zech. 12:10)

The Jews after so many years will finally come to know their Messiah. Notice the words, *"an only son"* and *"a first-born,"* that Zechariah uses. Jesus Christ is the only begotten Son of God, the first-born of all creation. Realizing the great unbelief that blinded them for 2,000 years, the people of Israel at this heart-rending moment will behold Him whom they have pierced—not only physically when they nailed Him to a tree, but also spiritually when their eyes pierced through and failed to see or acknowledge Him, although throughout the centuries He was there to be seen. With a genuine and grievous lamentation, the Jewish people will lament for the Messiah who so greatly loved them, the same Messiah they will now so greatly love.

In that day there will be great mourning in Jerusalem. . . .

And the land will mourn, every family by itself; the family of the house of David by itself, and their wives by themselves; the family of the house of Nathan by itself, and their wives by themselves; . . . (Zech. 12:11-12)

Israel, by coming to know her Messiah, will be saved. She will once more be a branch on God's olive tree (Rom. 11)—that tree which now is His church. While her salvation is taking place, however, the tribulation clock will be winding down toward its last tick: a tick that could spell doomsday for the world.

The Lord's Battle

Regarding the last days of the Great Tribulation, Jesus said, *"And unless those days had been cut short, no life would have been saved; but for the sake of the elect those days shall be cut short"* (Matt. 24:22). With the judgment of the Great Harlot complete, with the Antichrist and his followers raging in hatred toward God and seeking to destroy His Church, with Jerusalem besieged, with mankind embattled at Armageddon and the world on the brink of nuclear annihilation, God will go forth to rescue His Bride. This will be the scenario on earth when a great and mighty multitude cry out in heaven:

Hallelujah! For the Lord our God, the Almighty, reigns.

Let us rejoice and be glad and give the glory to Him, for the marriage of the Lamb has come and His bride has made herself ready.

And it was given to her to clothe herself in fine linen, bright and clean; for the fine linen is the righteous acts of the saints. (Rev. 19:6b-8)

The Bride of Christ, refined as gold through the fire, unified without any division or denomination or sect, has made herself ready. The period of the Antichrist's dominion over her has run its course. The Lord Jesus, unwilling for the world that He created to be destroyed, but rather desiring it to be ruled by His glorious Bride, will step forward to fight the battle. Looking into the heavens, John in our passage describes our mighty Lord as He marches into battle:

And I saw heaven opened; and behold, a white horse, and He who sat upon it is called Faithful and True; and in righteousness He judges and wages war. . . .

> *And I saw the beast and the kings of the earth and their armies, assembled to make war against Him who sat upon the horse, and against His army.*
>
> *And the beast was seized, and with him the false prophet who performed the signs in his presence, by which he deceived those who had received the mark of the beast and those who worshipped his image; these two were thrown alive into the lake of fire which burns with brimstone.*
>
> *And the rest were killed with the sword which came from the mouth of Him who sat upon the horse, and all the birds were filled with their flesh.* (Rev. 19:11, 19-21)

Christ, the King of Kings and Lord of Lords, the eternal Word of God and the leader of the mighty heavenly army, will destroy the Antichrist and the men with his mark, along with the False Prophet and the rest of the world's armies who, as enemies of God, seek to destroy the earth. He will do so through the power of the Holy Spirit that radiates from His church—the Spirit He is now pouring out over all the world; the Spirit that is bringing His people Israel to the revelation of Him; the very same Spirit that proceeds from His mouth like a sword to slay His enemies, flowing like fire from the throne of God as it destroys the kingdom of the Beast. Daniel, describing this awesome sight, writes:

> *I kept looking*
> *Until thrones were set up,*
> *And the Ancient of Days took His seat; . . .*
> *A river of fire was flowing*
> *And coming out before Him. . . .*
> *I kept looking until the beast was slain, and its body was destroyed and given to the burning fire. (Dan. 7:9a,10a,11b)*

Yes, the time to judge the horrible Beast has come and he has been given over to the burning fire. The time has now come for the saints to reign on the earth. Just as Daniel the prophet wrote:

> *and judgment was passed in favor of the saints of the Highest One, and the time arrived when the saints took possession of the kingdom. (Dan. 7:22b)*

> *But the court will sit for judgment, and his [the Beast's] dominion will be taken away, annihilated and destroyed forever.*

> *Then the sovereignty, the dominion, and the greatness of all the kingdoms under the whole heaven will be given to the people of the saints of the Highest One; His kingdom will be an everlasting kingdom, and all the dominions will serve and obey Him.* (Dan. 7:26, 27)

Christ and His Bride have triumphed victoriously over the Beast of the earth. The hour has come for Her to reign for an appointed period of time.

Notes

1. Dr. J. A. Seiss, *The Apocalypse* (Zondervan Publishing House: Grand Rapids, Michigan, 1962), taken from the book, *The Late Great Planet Earth* by Hal Lindsey, p. 152. Copyright © 1970, 1977 by Zondervan Publishing House. Used by permission of Zondervan Publishing House.

2. Lindsey, *Planet Earth*, 152-153.

3. Shearer, *The Beginning of the End*, 124. Used by permisssion.

4. John T. McNeill, "John Calvin," *Encyc. Amer.*, 1979.

5. Merle Severy, "The World of Martin Luther," *National Geographic*, vol. 164, no. 4 (Oct. 1983), 450.

6. Wilhelm Pauck, "Ulrich Zwingli," *Encyc. Amer.*, 1979.

7. David Wilkerson, *Set the Trumpet to Thy Mouth* (Lindale, Texas: Word Challenge, Inc., 1985), 3.

8. Shearer, *The Beginning of the End*, 141-144.

9. The following excerpts make light of this (From *The Third Wave* by Alvin Toffler. Copyright © 1980 by Alvin Toffler. Used by permission of Bantam Books, a division of Bantam Doubleday Dell Publishing Group, Inc.):

"The distinguished science commentator, Lord Ritchie-Calder, explains that 'Just as we have manipulated plastics and metals, we are now manufacturing living materials.' "

"Major companies are already in hot pursuit of commercial applications of the new biology. . . . They have already demanded and won the right to patent new life forms" (p. 146).

"Today genetic engineers in laboratories around the world are capable of creating entirely novel life forms. They have end-run evolution itself" (p. 293).

9
THE BRIDE'S REIGN FOR A SEASON AND A TIME: PART I

After the last chapter describing the end of the Great Tribulation, many readers are probably wondering: Did Jesus return or not? I say this, because throughout history, Christ's second advent almost always has been placed at the end of the Great Tribulation. The early church fathers Irenaeus and Justin Martyr—believing Christ would return with great power to slay the Antichrist, to raise the dead, and to judge the world—both placed His return at the end of the tribulation. Hence, asking if Jesus will return at the end of the tribulation is an extremely important question.

Before answering, it would help to present the major views on Christ's second coming concerning the end of the tribulation and Christ's return. Today, there are four major millennial systems on the end times: (1) dispensational premillennialism, which advocates the pretribulation rapture of the Church, (2) historical premillennialism, which advocates a posttribulation rapture, (3) postmillennialism, which says Jesus will return after a millennial reign of the Church, and (4) amillennialism, which states that there will be no millennium.[1]

Without a doubt, premillennialism, whether it be pre or posttribulational, is the most popular view within evangelical circles. This system of interpretation places Christ's second advent at the end of the Great Tribulation, at which time He will judge the earth's inhabitants and inaugurate a 1,000-year millennial reign on earth.

Dispensationalists say Jesus will return with his glorified saints—those raptured before the tribulation—to initiate the Millennial Kingdom. Historical premillennialists say that when Jesus returns, He will rapture the Church, meeting her in the air from where they will return to destroy the Antichrist and rule on the earth for a thousand years. After that, the earth will be destroyed and the new heavens and the new earth of the ages to come will be created. Despite the fact there is no detailed or established exposition of premillennialism found in the writings of the early fathers,[2] this view was supposedly predominant during the first three centuries of the Christian era. Among its adherents were Papias, Irenaeus, Justin Martyr, Tertullian, Hippolytus, and Lactantius.[3]

Postmillennialists say the Church will overcome the world and bring a millennial period of peace and perfect harmony to the earth. After this millennial age of spiritual prosperity, Christ will come to receive the kingdom from His Church. Postmillennialism relies heavily on allegories. The view was prominent in the late nineteenth and early twentieth centuries, when optimism over the Church's missionary success was high. World War I severely damaged this view, and as Lindsey says, "World War II all but wiped it out."[4]

In the traditional amillennial scheme—amillennial meaning "no millennium"—Jesus comes at the end of the world to raise the dead, to judge mankind, to create a new heavens and a new earth, and to initiate eternity. Amillennialists usually deny a literal seven-year period of tribulation, the fulfillment of Daniel's prophecy on the seventieth week and, as their name implies, a thousand-year earthly millennial reign of Jesus Christ.

Nonetheless, amillennialism was the dominant theology of the end times for more than a thousand years, ever since the renowned Church father, Augustine, articulated the position. His teachings were so fully accepted, that at the council of Ephesus in 431 A.D., belief in the millennium was condemned as superstitious.[5] Augustinian amillennialism proceeded unchallenged through the Church's medieval period and the Reformation, and is still today a foundational doctrine of the Roman Catholic church.

Augustinian amillennialism was prominent during the Middle Ages because, rather than placing its emphasis on a supposed millennial reign of Christ, it placed the entire emphasis of Christ's second coming on the last day and the final judgment. Christ's return would bring about the bodily resurrection of the dead and usher in the eternal state of God's Kingdom, that final state for which every Christian yearns. The last judgment is a major theme of Augustine's classic work, *The City of God.*

Augustine interprets the first resurrection of Revelation, chapter 20, as a spiritual resurrection—a resurrection of the soul brought about by the redemptive work of Christ. Those who reign via the first resurrection are the Church. He interprets the 1,000 years in this same passage as "the whole duration of this world" from the time of Christ, where "the number of perfection [1000]" is employed "to mark the fullness of time."[6]

Regarding those who believe in a literal millennium, Augustine writes:

> And this opinion would not be objectionable, if . . . the joys of the saints . . . be spiritual, and consequent on the presence of God; for I myself, too, once held this opinion. But, as they assert . . . those who . . . rise again shall enjoy the leisure of immoderate carnal banquets, furnished with an amount of meat and drink . . . not only to shock the feeling of the temperate, but even to surpass the measure of credulity itself, such assertions can be believed only by the carnal. They who do believe them are called by the spiritual Chiliasts, which we may literally reproduce by the name Millenarians.[7]

In addition to Augustine, the great reformers Martin Luther and John Calvin rejected belief in the millennium. Paul Althaus, author of the book *The Theology of Martin Luther,* writes: "Luther agrees with the catholic church in its rejection of chiliasm [millennialism]. He too does not interpret Revelation 20 in terms of the end of history but as a description of the church."[8] Instead, Luther placed his emphasis on the resurrection of the last day, which he calls "the most happy Last Day."[9]

Calvin is even more condemning of chiliasm. Heinrich Quistorp, author of *Calvin's Doctrine of the Last Things*, voices Calvin's protests:

> Any one who prescribes for the children of God only a thousand years' enjoyment of their inheritance in the future does not see what a disgraceful implication this is for Christ and His kingdom. . . . These people . . . are either entirely inexperienced in all heavenly things or with secret malice are trying to shake the grace of God and the power of Christ. Like the opponents of the resurrection . . . in 1 Corinthians 15, they make the Christian hope into a hope that is merely relative to this world and thereby dissolve the true hope which is directed to the eternal future of the Lord and His coming kingdom. The saving work of God in Christ finds its secure and abiding fulfillment only if on the day of the Lord sin is effaced, death is swallowed up in victory, and the kingdom of eternity is fully and wholly established.[10]

While he provided plenty of reasons for disavowing millennialism, Calvin, nonetheless, did not provide any new insights into the millennium passage of Revelation 20. He followed the basic teaching of

Augustine with a slight variation: He equated the first resurrection to a spiritual regeneration of the soul, and the thousand years to the spiritual reign of Christ over "individual" souls in their earthly lives.

From the prior discussion on the present major systems of eschatology, the only two that literally place Christ's return at the end of the Great Tribulation are the premillennial systems. Postmillenialism and amillennialism, as they presently stand, do not even address the Great Tribulation, much less Jesus' coming at the end of it. As an amillennialist, this is one of my reasons for writing this book. I do believe in a literal, seven-year tribulation and believe that the teaching of it should be included in any study of eschatology.

The time has now come to answer the question, Will Jesus return at the close of the Great Tribulation? The answer is vital to the eschatology in the remainder of this book—a prophetic system I describe as "Kingdom Amillennialism." The answer is no, Jesus' second coming will not occur at the end of the tribulation. After the tribulation, and before Jesus comes again, there will be an undetermined period of time wherein the Bride of Christ, His Church, will reign on the earth via the Kingdom of God. The remainder of this book is devoted to showing you why.

We will begin by taking a look at what is by far the most popular system of prophetic interpretation in the evangelical church today—the same system that advocates a pretribulation rapture: dispensational premillennialism.

Dispensational Premillennialism

Dispensationalists, or pretribulationists, say that when Jesus returns He will come riding on a white horse accompanied by His saints— those in the Church whom He raptured before the tribulation. They quote Revelation 19:11-21 to support this. At that time, Jesus will proceed to save Israel, to destroy the Antichrist, and to judge the inhabitants of the earth (Matt. 25). Jesus and His glorified saints—who will have imperishable, spiritual bodies—will then proceed to reign on the earth for a thousand years (Rev. 20:4-6) over a redeemed, but still-mortal Israel and those Gentiles who as believers during the tribulation (the sheep of Matt. 25:33) passed His judgment and are allowed to physically enter into the millennial kingdom. In this scheme, Israel will have an exalted ranking above the saved Gentile nations. Pretribulationalists draw heavily on the "kingdom prophecies" of the Old Testament to paint a picture of Israel's kingdom during the millennium. Israel, however (because of physical, mortal bodies), will still be subject to the glorified Church, who along with Christ will reign over the earth. Dispensational premillennialism, as shown in chapter 5, was developed in the mid-nineteenth century by John Darby.

One of the reasons for the popularity of dispensational premillennialism, irrespective of the positive, comforting message it communicates (that the Church will be raptured before the tribulation), is that out of all the views presented, it is the only one that offers a detailed, well-structured system of theology that attempts to piece together all of the prophetic scriptures on the end times, both New Testament and Old. Postmillennialism, which is based almost entirely on allegory, does not make any such attempt. Amillennialism, which well addresses the prophecies on Christ's second coming, the resurrection of the dead, and the last judgment, does not adequately address the Old Testament "kingdom prophecies" (Is. 2:1-4, Is. 11:6-10; Ezek. 43:1-8, Ezek. 47, 48; Zech. 14:16-21). Neither does it do justice to the first resurrection and the 1000-year reign described in Revelation 20. By "kingdom prophecies," I mean all those prophetic passages describing a future blissful kingdom on the earth prior to the consummation, including Israel's role in it.

Historic premillennialism comes the closest to this goal, but it falls short of answering a critical question; a question asked repeatedly by dispensationalists: Who will populate the Millennial Kingdom? All of the kingdom prophecies indicate that those entering the "millennial age" will be mortals. Lindsey, in *The Rapture,* shows how those entering this period will be able to bear children (Jer. 23:3-6) and to marry (Is. 4:1-3). Due to man's existence in sinful flesh, there will nonetheless still be disobedience and discipline on the earth (Zech. 14:16-19), as well as aging and death.[11]

The problem with the posttribulation rapture scheme is, since it has all living believers transformed into immortal, spiritual beings (1 Cor. 15:35-58) and all unbelievers destroyed and cast into hell (1 Thess. 1:7-10, Matt. 13:36-43, Matt. 25:31-46) at the Lord's second coming, it only allows for redeemed immortals, members of the church, to enter the millennial kingdom. Both the Old Testament prophecies that portray mortals entering the kingdom, and John's account in Revelation 20 of the rebellion of the nations at the end of the 1000 years (Rev. 20:7-10), however, make this impossible. Thus, the historic premillennial view cannot answer the question of who will populate the kingdom. Hence, it loses much of its credibility. Besides, what would be the purpose of such a thousand-year reign if only immortals could enter it? There would be none. This is why Augustine and the rest of the Church, including Luther and Calvin, rejected the view for well over a thousand years.

Dispensationalists, since they believe the transformation of the Church will occur before the tribulation, answer the question by saying when Jesus comes back, those living believers who survive the Great Tribulation, whether Jew or Gentile, will enter the millennial kingdom as mortals. They also say that since the millennium is God's fulfillment of the Messianic, Davidic kingdom, Israel will hold an exalted position over the saved gentile nations.

Nevertheless, in answering the question of who will populate the kingdom, dispensationalists cause even more confusion. Just because dispensationalism is a well-developed theology that can answer questions does not mean it is the truth. (Mormons and the Jehovah's Witnesses also have well-developed theologies that can answer questions about their doctrine.) To demonstrate its errancy, let's first look at the dispensational interpretation of Matthew 25—the last judgment parable that dispensationalists say describes the judgment of the mortal Gentiles who survive the tribulation. Jesus says these believers, whom He calls *"blessed of My Father,"* will enter into eternal life:

> *But when the Son of Man comes in His glory, and all the angels with Him, then He will sit on His glorious throne.*

> *And all the nations will be gathered before Him; and He will separate them from one another, as the shepherd separates the sheep from the goats; and He will put the sheep on His right, and the goats on the left.*

> *Then the King will say to those on His right, "Come, you who are blessed of My Father, inherit the kingdom prepared for you from the foundation of the world.*

> *For I was hungry, and you gave Me something to eat; I was thirsty, and gave Me drink; I was a stranger, and you invited Me in;"*

> *Then He will say also to those on His left, "Depart from Me, accursed ones, into the eternal fire which has been prepared for the devil and his angels; for I was hungry, and you gave Me nothing to eat; I was thirsty, and you gave Me nothing to drink; . . ."*

> *And these will go away into eternal punishment, but the righteous into eternal life.* (Matt. 25:31-35, 41, 42, 46)

From Jesus' words, we must ask, if the righteous who survive the tribulation will inherit eternal life, how can Lindsey and other dispensationalists say they are mortals who enter a millennium in physical, temporal bodies—bodies destined to both age and die? Entering into eternal life as a mortal is a contradiction of terms. Rather, Matthew 25 describes believers entering the eternal state of the Father's kingdom in immortal, resurrected bodies.

Also, how can those Jesus calls *"blessed of My Father"* be among those Zechariah describes in the following "millennial" passage?

> *And it will be that whichever of the families of the earth does not go up to Jerusalem to worship the King, the Lord of hosts, there will be no rain on them.*
>
> *And if the family of Egypt does not go up or enter, then no rain will fall on them; it will be the plague with which the Lord smites the nations who do not go up to celebrate the Feast of Booths.* (Zech. 14:17-18)

Zechariah's prophecy describes punishment for many mortals during the "millennium," while Jesus described blessing upon His return, for all who believe.

Consequently, dispensational premillennialism contradicts Matthew 25 by saying that (1) believers will enter the millennium in physical, mortal bodies, and that (2) punishment—not blessings—will be inflicted on some of these believers.

Still, these misinterpretations are small compared with what is the greatest peculiarity of dispensational theology: Since pretribulationists believe Jesus will return with His glorified Church after the tribulation, they also teach, as stated by Lindsey, that "Believers from the Church will enter the Millennial Kingdom . . . in immortal bodies as priests and co-rulers with the Lord Jesus."[12]

So according to the dispensational view, the earth during the millennium will have as its inhabitants not only the Lord Jesus, the mortal children of Israel, and the mortal surviving Gentiles, but also the glorified, resurrected, and immortal members of the Church! When I first heard this, I cannot explain how baffled I was. Loraine Boettner best describes my feelings towards this view when he writes:

> A curious situation surely does arise when Christ and the resurrected and translated saints return to earth to set up the

millennial kingdom in association with men still in the flesh.
That condition, semiheavenly and semiearthly, with Christ
reigning . . . in Jerusalem, with two radically different types
of people (the saints in glorified, resurrected bodies and
ordinary mortals still in the flesh mingling freely throughout
the world for the long and almost unending period of one
thousand years) strikes me as so unreal and impossible that I
wonder how anyone can take it seriously. Such a mixed state
of mortals and immortals, terrestrial and celestial, surely
would be a monstrosity. It would be as incongruous as for the
holy angels now to mingle in their work and pleasure and
worship with the present population of the world, bringing
heavenly splendor into a sinful environment. Exalt the
millennium as you please, it still remains far below heaven.
It could not be other than a great anticlimax for those who
have tasted of the heavenly glory to be brought back again to
have a part in this life. Such positions of authority and
rulership as might be given them in this world would be a
poor compensation for the glory that they have enjoyed in
heaven . . . The idea of a provisional kingdom in which
glorified saints and mortal men mingle finds no support
anywhere in Scripture.[13]

Boettner is correct; even when you read Revelation 20, the chapter
on the "Millennium," you will find no mention of mingling between the
mortal and the immortal. Dispensationalists who teach that the resurrected saints will rule and reign with Christ on the earth over a mortal
population of both Jews and Gentiles are basing their teaching on
something else besides scripture.

Another perplexity about the teaching of an earthly millennium is
that if Christ—the eternal Son of God—is visibly ruling on the earth
during this period, and teaching mortal men the ways of salvation and
the errors of rejecting it, how could these who have seen with their eyes
the glory of the Almighty rise up in rebellion against Him at the end of
the 1000 years (Rev. 20:7-10)? This scenario totally defies reason.[14] The
Bible says when all who are in the heavens and the earth stand before
Him, every knee shall bow and every tongue shall confess that Jesus
Christ is Lord, to the glory of God the Father (Phil. 2:11). The basic
premise of faith is that we believe in Him whom we cannot see. If God
were to stand before us this very instant, everyone would believe, even
the greatest atheist or infidel. There would be no reason for faith.

> *Now faith is the assurance of things hoped for, the convic-*
> *tion of things not seen. . . .*
>
> *And without faith it is impossible to please Him. . . .* (Heb.
> 11:1, 6a)

It isn't difficult to see why men like Augustine, Luther, and Calvin rejected the idea of an earthly millennium, considering it to be, as Quistorp puts it, "a childish fantasy which hardly deserves the credit of refuting."[15]

I must make one final point concerning the dispensational premillennial view. It concerns Lindsey's contention that Augustine's teachings on amillennialism became the philosophical basis for "Christian" anti-Semitism. As he puts it:

> . . . from the time that amillennialism began to be taught
> (about the fourth century, beginning with Augustine A.D.
> 345-430), it became a philosophical basis for anti-Semitism.
> Amillennialism teaches that the Church has been given the
> promises made to the Israelites because they crowned a
> history of unbelief by rejecting the Messiah.[16]

True, Augustine and traditional amillennialists teach that the Church, through Christ's sacrifice on the cross, is now the inheritor of all the promises made to Israel. They also teach that Israel, by rejecting the Messiah, had the kingdom taken away from her. But the modern-day writers Jim McKeever,[17] a historic premillennialist, and Loraine Boettner,[18] a postmillennialist, express the same view; since it is nothing more than what the New Testament teaches. As shown in chapter 5, Paul repeatedly taught how the Church is now a partaker in the promises made to Israel. And regarding the kingdom being taken away from Israel, let us remember Jesus' words to the Jews: *"Therefore I say to you, the kingdom of God will be taken away from you, and be given to a nation producing the fruit of it"* (Matt. 21:43). The *"nation"* Jesus is speaking of is His Bride, the Church, of whom Peter writes: *"But you are a chosen race, A royal priesthood, a holy nation, a people for God's own posses-sion, . . ."* (1 Pet. 2:9a).

Even so, Augustine in *The City of God*, shows consistency with Paul's teaching that the promises of God still apply to the Israelites; promises they will receive when they return to Christ by faith. For concerning God's promise of the land of Canaan to Abraham, ". . . for all the land which you see, I will give it to you, and to your descendants [seed] for ever . . . ," Augustine writes:

> Further, the promise here made may be understood not only of the nation of Israel, but of the whole seed of Abraham [the church] . . . because, although the Israelites are expelled from Jerusalem, they still remain in other cities . . . of Canaan, and shall remain even to the end; and when that whole land is inhabited by Christians, they also are the seed of Abraham.[19]

By referring to the condition of Israel in his time, Augustine shows his clear understanding that the Abrahamic covenant still applies to Israel. But, now they can receive its full blessings only with the Church through Jesus Christ.

It was not that Augustine had no harsh words to say about the Jews and their rejection of Christ; but to call them "the philosophical basis for "[Christian] anti-Semitism," ignores the evidence of history. Anti-Jewish attitudes can be found in the writings of many of the early church fathers—fathers who were supposed premillenarians. For instance, regarding the Eucharist, Irenaeus wrote: "The Jews do not offer such an oblation, for their 'hands are full of blood;' for they did not receive the Word of God through whom the offering is made to God." Tertullian wrote concerning those who ate the Lord's body after having sacrificed to idols: "The Jews laid hands on Christ but once; these men offer sacrifice to his body every day." Even Tertullian, before Augustine applied the notion of a restored Israel to the Church, writing:

> As for the restoration of Judea, however, which even the Jews themselves . . . hope for just as it is described [in the Old Testament], it would be tedious to state at length how the figurative interpretation is spiritually applicable to Christ and His church, and to the character and fruits thereof (Adv. Marcion, 3,25).[20]

I'm not saying the anti-Jewish sentiments of the early Church are to be condoned, but the question needs to be asked: How did they arise? Evidence clearly states they arose because the Jews were among the greatest persecutors of the Church for its first three-hundred-fifty years. The Jews indeed were the greatest persecutors of the Church through its first fifty years, as the Acts of the Apostles clearly points out. Lindsey does not point this out in any of his books; rather, he directs the blame for anti-Semitism toward Augustinian amillennialism, instead of toward its root cause: Jewish persecution of the early Church.

In reality, dispensational premillennialism, even if indirectly, contains one of the most anti-Semitic views on the end times. For in portraying Israel's 1000-year kingdom under Christ, it relegates Israel to a millennium spent in mortal, aging, sin-laden bodies, under the subjection of an immortal, glorious and sin-free Church. I cannot see how any Jew, saved or unsaved, could desire this 1000-year predicament.

And, if today amillennialism is a cause for anti-Semitism, then without a doubt, dispensationalism is a cause for both anti-Palestinian and anti-Arab sentiments. For having attributed Israel to an exalted place, many American evangelicals and fundamentalists looked with satisfaction as Israel repossessed its former, biblical territories; and not even batting an eyebrow at the inhuman plight experienced by the former natives of these lands—the Palestinian Arabs, people for whom Christ also died. I can still recall the many Christians who enthusiastically observed Israel's invasion of Lebanon in 1982, proclaiming how Israel's "reclaiming" of the land promised to them by God signified the beginning of the end.

Dispensational premillennialism is a theology that inadvertently draws distinctions between peoples. It does not clearly sound the Apostle Paul's words, which say: *"For there is no partiality with God"* (Rom. 2:11). It also strips away from the victorious tribulation saints their rightful place of rulership in the world after the Great Tribulation.

The Kingdom of the Saints

Dispensational premillennialism, with its three-tiered system of power—the glorified Church, Israel, and the surviving Gentile nations—teaches that those saints who endure and survive the tribulation will enter the millennium, not as a part of Christ's Bride, or as the victorious saints portrayed in the book of Revelation and Daniel, but at the bottom of the ladder, subject to the nation of Israel.

Nonetheless, in speaking of the tribulation saints, Daniel says: *"and the time arrived when the saints took possession of the kingdom"* (Dan. 7:22). Daniel is talking about the Church here! Christ's Bride, having persevered through the tribulation and having triumphed over the forces of the Antichrist, will inherit a kingdom—not a millennial kingdom where Christ physically reigns on the earth, but one very similar: In this kingdom, Jesus from His heavenly throne will reign through the saints of the Most High.

Just as Daniel wrote concerning the judgment of the Antichrist and the establishment of the saints' kingdom, other scriptures in Isaiah, Ezekiel, Zechariah, and the minor prophets—passages previously referred to as the "kingdom prophecies"—indicate there will an interim, blissful kingdom upon the earth after the Great Tribulation, and before the end of the world.

The Book of Revelation also indicates some type of span, for in Revelation, chapter 20, after the destruction of the Antichrist and of the False Prophet following the tribulation, Satan is bound for a "thousand years" so that he should not deceive the nations any longer. After the thousand years, Satan is then released and leads a rebellion against the saints before God intervenes and casts him into the lake of fire and brimstone where, John says, the Beast and the False Prophet are there already.

Daniel again implies there is some kind of interim period after the seventieth week, saying that from the Abomination of Desolation, there will be 1335 days (Dan. 12:12); even though the Great Tribulation can, at most, last 1,278 days (three-and-one-half years) after the Abomination of Desolation.

The key to proving that Jesus will reign from heaven through His Bride, the Church, during this period—rather than in a bodily fashion after His second advent—is twofold. First, evidence must be given to show that Jesus' second coming will not occur at the end the Great Tribulation. Second, it must be proven that Jesus' second coming is the final consummation—that it brings about, in quick succession, the last judgment, the destruction of our present world, the creation of the new heavens and the new earth, and the initiation of the Father's eternal kingdom. If these two points can be proven, then the "kingdom prophecies," the same ones premillennialists say describe the millennium, can be fit into the interim period of the Bride's rule.

The Close of Daniel's 70th Week: The Salvation of the Jews

Another errant premillennial teaching related to the second coming is on the salvation of the Jewish remnant, spoken of in Zechariah, chapter 12. Many premillennialists claim Israel's salvation in this passage will occur at the instant of Christ's coming. In other words, when the Jews, who are besieged at Jerusalem during the battle of Armageddon, see Jesus descending from heaven with His army of saints, they will believe in Him and accept Him as their savior. Among the historic premillennialists who have taught, or still teach this view, are Alexander Reese[21] and Robert Gundry.[22] Dispensationalists who believe this include Dwight Pentecost.[23] The verse from Zechariah that they rely on states:

> *And I will pour out on the house of David and on the inhabitants of Jerusalem, the Spirit of grace and of supplication, so that they will look on Me whom they have pierced; and they will mourn for Him, as one mourns for an only son. . . .* (Zech. 12:10a)

The problem with teaching that Israel will be delivered when the Jews see Jesus descending from heaven at His second advent is, such teaching contradicts the New Testament scriptures that say only those who believe in Christ when He returns will be saved. Everyone who does not believe, including the unregenerate of Israel, will be punished by His eternal wrath. As put by Paul:

> *the Lord Jesus shall be revealed from heaven with His mighty angels in flaming fire,*
>
> *dealing out retribution to those who do not know God and to those who do not obey the gospel of our Lord Jesus.*
>
> *And these will pay the penalty of eternal destruction, away from the presence of the Lord and from the glory of His power.* (2 Thess. 1:6b-9)

If the Jews do not know Christ by the time of His second coming, it will be too late. Many of Jesus' parables (like the parable of the wedding feast cited in Matt. 22:1-14) bear this out. Nonbelieving Jews will be treated no differently than any other nonbelievers, *"For there is no partiality with God."* There will be no second chances once Jesus comes back.

Nevertheless, Zechariah's passage clearly states Israel will come to know her Messiah. This is why Zechariah cannot be addressing the second coming in his prophecy. Some astounding intervention of God other than Christ's second advent, will bring about the conversion of the Jews. It will make Israel realize the price Jesus paid on the cross and will cause Israel to see Christ and know Him just as we do. For in our spirits, *". . . we see Jesus, who was made a little lower than the angels for the suffering of death, crowned with glory and honor. . . ."* (Heb. 2:9, NKJV).

The awesome intervention of God that will bring about the conversion of the Jews also will bring about the destruction of the Antichrist. We will talk about this supernatural event in the next chapter.

Notes

1. Two more dispensational views are the midtribulation rapture viewpoint and the more recent Pre-wrath viewpoint. Since many of the arguments against a pretribulation rapture apply to them, I've chosen not to cover them in this book. The arguments against premillennialism apply to them as well.

2. John F. Walvoord, *The Rapture Question* (Findlay, Ohio: Dunham Publishing Co., 1957), 50, quoted in Dave MacPherson, *The Unbelievable Pre-Trib Origin* (Omega Publications, P.O. Box 4130, Medford, OR 97501), 27.

3. Taken from *The Meaning of the Millennium* edited by Robert G. Clouse, p. 9. © 1977 InterVarsity Christian Fellowship of the USA. Used by permission of InterVarsity Press, P.O. Box 1400, Downers Grove, IL 60515.

4. Lindsey, *The Rapture*, 27, 29.

5. Clouse, 9.

6. St. Augustine, *The City of God*, Trans. by Marcus Dods, D.D. (New York: Random House, 1950), 720. Used by permission.

7. *ibid*, 719.

8. Paul Althaus, *The Theology of Martin Luther*, Trans. by Robert C. Shultz (Philadelphia: Fortress Press, 1966), 419. Reprinted from *The Theology of Martin Luther* by Paul Althaus, copyright © 1966 Fortress Press. Used by permission of Augsburg Fortress.

9. *ibid*, 420-21.

10. Heinrich Quistorp, *Calvin's Doctrine of Last Things*, Trans. Harold Knight (Richmond, VA: John Knox Press, 1955), 159.

11. Lindsey, *The Rapture*, 143-44.

12. *The Rapture*, 156.

13. Clouse, 49.

14. Boettner writes, "premillennialists fail to take into consideration the overpowering majesty of the risen and glorified Christ. They imagine that men will be in personal contact with him as he reigns from an earthly throne. Apparently they assume he will be as he was in the days of his humiliation. But when the ascended and glorified Christ appeared to Saul on the road to Damascus, Saul was stricken blind by the light and fell to the ground. . . . And, John says, "When I saw him, I fell at his feet as though dead" . . . If such glory was so overpowering that the beloved disciple John fell at his feet as though

dead, how much less shall ordinary mortals, sinners, be able to stand before him! . . . His period of humiliation is over, and his divine glory forbids the approach of those who are tainted with sin. . . ." Taken from Clouse, p. 49.

15. *Calvin's Doctrine of Last Things,* 158.

16. *The Rapture,* 30.

17. McKeever, 49.

18. Clouse, 101.

19. *The City of God,* 544.

20. George Eldon Ladd, *The Blessed Hope* (Grand Rapids, MI: Wm. B. Eerdmans Publishing Co., 1984), 27. Used by permission of Wm. B. Eerdmans Publishing Co.

21. Alexander Reese, *The Approaching Advent of Christ* (Grand Rapids, MI: Grand Rapids International Publications, 1975), 37.

22. Robert Guidry, *The Church and the Tribulation* (Grand Rapids, MI: Zondervan Publishing House, 1973), 82-83.

23. Dwight Pentecost, *Things to Come* (Grand Rapids, MI: Dunham Publishing Co., 1964), 507.

10
THE BRIDE'S REIGN FOR A SEASON AND A TIME: PART II

The End of the Great Tribulation: The Destruction of the Beast

Since its early days, the Church traditionally believed Jesus would destroy the Antichrist and his cohorts at His second coming. The Apostle John's vision in Revelation 19—describing Jesus riding on a white horse, followed by the armies of heaven and battling the beast and his forces (Rev. 19:11-21)—appears to support this. It is clear from the passage that Jesus' destruction of the beast is the event that brings the Great Tribulation to a close.

Paul shines further light on this when he writes:

> And then that lawless one will be revealed whom the Lord will slay with the breath of His mouth and bring to an end by the appearance of His coming [presence]. . . . (2 Thess. 2:8)

Nevertheless, neither John in Revelation 19, nor Paul in Second Thessalonians, is talking about Christ's second coming. This is a bold statement, for when many prophetic teachers talk about the second coming of Christ, they refer to the Revelation passage, saying how Jesus will come back riding on a white horse, leading an enormous army of saints to destroy the Antichrist. Jesus, however, never talked about His return in this fashion. Remember what the two angels said to Jesus' disciples as they watched Him ascend into heaven after His resurrection:

> Men of Galilee, why do you stand looking into the sky? This Jesus, who has been taken up from you into heaven, will come in just the same way as you have watched Him go into heaven. (Acts 1:11)

Instead of teaching that He would return riding a white horse accompanied by His raptured saints, Jesus taught that He would come back just as he ascended, accompanied by His holy angels. Paul teaches the same thing (2 Thess. 1:7). Only once in the New Testament does Paul say Jesus will return with the saints, in 1 Thessalonians 3:13. The

Greek word Paul uses for saints in this verse, *hagios*, means "holy ones." Consequently, *hagios* can also refer to angels. Even if Paul is speaking of the saints in verse 13, there are two scenarios that could account for this. First, knowing that the dead will be raised at Jesus' second coming, the departed saints of ages past must return with Jesus so their spirits can be reunited with their resurrected bodies. These saints, however, will in no way wage war on the Antichrist and his hordes. Still, we must realize that the emphasis in the New Testament is placed on Jesus' returning with His mighty angels who *"will gather out of His kingdom all stumbling blocks, and those who commit lawlessness"* (Matt. 13:41b).

There are two more reasons Revelation 19 does not refer to the second coming. First, Jesus says that at the onset of the day of the Lord—the day of His return—men will be *"fainting from fear and the expectation of the things which are coming upon the world"* (Luke 21:26). John also writes in Revelation 6, *"the kings of the earth and the great men and the commanders . . . and the strong . . . hid themselves in the caves and among the rocks of the mountains . . . from the wrath of the Lamb"* (Rev. 6:15, 16). To think that men, when they see Jesus coming back in the glory of His Father, will rise up to make war on Him with earthly weapons is nonsensical. The Bible says that when they see Him, *"all the tribes of the earth will mourn over Him"* (Matt. 24:30, Rev. 1:7). In Revelation 19, however, men's hearts are so hardened and blinded, they do not hide in fear but instead join their armies against *"Him who sat upon the horse, and against His army"* (Rev. 19:19). Second is the method of judgment. The gospel accounts of Christ's second coming never show Jesus slaying the wicked upon His return as He does in Revelation 19. The wicked are always gathered in some fashion by His angels—being either bound and cast into the fiery furnace (Matt. 13:30, 41, 42), or outer darkness (Matt. 22:13), or removed to a place of judgment (Luke 17:34-37, Matt. 25:31-41).

It must be noticed how John saw *"heaven opened; and behold, a white horse, and He who sat upon it is called Faithful and True; and in righteousness He judges and wages war. . . . And the armies which are in heaven, clothed in fine linen, white and clean, were following Him on white horses. And from His mouth comes a sharp sword, so that with it He may smite the nations"* (Rev. 19:11, 14-15). John sees Christ and His army in heaven, and from heaven He wages war. Nowhere in the vision does he see Christ and His army coming down from heaven.

For these reasons I believe the symbology in Revelation 19 is threefold. First, Christ in heaven identifies Himself with His saints on earth as they war against the Antichrist at the end of the tribulation, just as He identifies Himself with His people in Matthew 25, *"Truly . . . to the extent that you did it to . . . even the least of them, you did it to Me."* Consequently, when the Beast and his armies make war on the saints, they are also making war on Christ (see Matt. 25:45). Second, Christ's Bride, clothed *"in fine linen, bright and clean"* (Rev. 19:8), is waging war against the Antichrist in the Spirit—in the heavenly realm—just as the Beast is waging war against her in the Satanic realm. This explains why John sees Christ's army in heaven. Two Old Testament references that depict this heavenly army waging war in the spiritual realm on behalf of God's people are where Joshua met the Captain of the Lord's host wielding a drawn sword (Josh. 5:13-15) and where Elisha discerned the army of the Lord equipped with chariots of fire drawn up for battle against the armies of Aram (2 Kin. 6:17). For as Paul writes:

> *For our struggle is not against flesh and blood, but against the rulers, . . . the powers, . . . the world forces of this darkness, against the spiritual forces of wickedness in the heavenly places.* (Eph. 6:12)

The third meaning behind John's vision—a meaning that ties in Paul's words from Second Thessalonians—will be discussed at the end of this chapter. But first, what do some other Bible passages say concerning the destruction of the Antichrist and the end of the Great Tribulation?

Daniel's Vision of the Beast

The text that gives the most information on the destruction of the Man of Sin is found in Daniel. Speaking of the judgment of the fourth, ten-horned, end-times beast, and of the judgment of the little horn which it sprouted, Daniel writes:

> *While I was contemplating the horns, behold, another horn, a little one, came up among them and three of the first horns were pulled out by the roots before it; and behold, this horn possessed eyes like the eyes of a man, and a mouth uttering great boasts.*

> *I kept looking*
> *Until thrones were set up,*
> *And the Ancient of Days took His seat;*
> *His vesture was like white snow,*
> *And the hair of His head like pure wool.*
> *His throne was ablaze with flames,*
> *Its wheels were a burning fire.*

> *A river of fire was flowing*
> *And coming out from before Him;*
> *Thousands upon thousands were attending Him,*
> *And myriads upon myriads were standing before Him;*
> *The court sat,*
> *And the books were opened.*

> *Then I kept looking because of the sound of the boastful*
> *words which the horn was speaking; I kept looking until the beast*
> *was slain, and its body was destroyed and given to the burning*
> *fire.*

> *As for the rest of the beasts, their dominion was taken away,*
> *but an extension of life was granted to them for an appointed*
> *period of time.* (Dan. 7:8-12)

There are certain points to observe about Daniel's vision. The first point is the method of judgment. Daniel sees the Ancient of Days take his seat, His throne ablaze with flames and a river of fire flowing out from before Him. Bible scholars, including C.I. Scofield,[1] agree that the Ancient of Days refers to God the Father: Upon taking His seat with the court, the books are opened—a verse indicating judgment is being passed. After this the judgment is carried out; the Beast is slain, along with the little horn that spoke boastful words against the Most High, and its body is given to the burning fire. The method of judgment is fire. This parallels Revelation 19, which says the Beast and the False Prophet will be thrown into the lake of fire which burns with brimstone. Daniel's vision, however, does not say Christ's second coming will accomplish this. It simply says the Beast is destroyed with fire.

Now, it is crucial to grasp this next point. In reading Daniel's account, there is every reason to believe the passage is sequential. The next thing Daniel sees after the destruction of the Antichrist and his kingdom is the fate of the three remaining beasts he saw earlier in his vision. As we saw in chapter 2, these three beastly kingdoms are Great Britain, Russia, and the United States. Of them Daniel writes:

> *As for the rest of the beasts, their dominion was taken away,*
> *but an extension of life was granted to them for an appointed*
> *period of time.* (Dan. 7:12)

The phrase *"appointed period of time"* comes from the Hebrew root word *zeman*, which means "an appointed occasion, a season," and *iddan*, which means "a set time." Thus, Daniel 7:12 says the three end-time beasts to be supplanted by the Antichrist's kingdom will be granted an extension of life for an appointed period of time after his destruction, howbeit they will be forever stripped of their former dominion.[2] This is an extremely important point, for by sharp contrast, Matthew 25 teaches that when Christ comes again all unbelievers will be condemned, and that all that will remain of the human race will be the reigning believers in eternal, resurrected bodies.

Daniel's account, however, not only says the saints will take possession of the kingdom after the beast's destruction (vv. 22, 26, 27), but it says the remnants of the former great kingdoms of the earth (excluding the Antichrist's) will be granted an extension of life in this kingdom for a season and a time. Taken in context of Matthew and other New Testament passages, Daniel implied Christ's second coming will not occur at the end of the Great Tribulation when the Antichrist is destroyed. A season of time—when the saints will reign—must intervene.

If we continue reading Daniel's vision, we find the second coming of Christ.

> *I kept looking in the night visions,*
> *And behold, with the clouds of heaven*
> *One like a Son of Man was coming,*
> *And He came up to the Ancient of Days*
> *And was presented before Him.*
> *And to Him was given dominion,*
> *Glory and a kingdom,*
> *That all the peoples, nations, and men of every language*
> *Might serve Him.*
> *His dominion is an everlasting dominion*
> *Which will not pass away;*
> *And His kingdom is one*
> *Which will not be destroyed.*
>
> *As for me, Daniel, my spirit was distressed within me, and*
> *the visions in my mind kept alarming me.* (Dan. 7:13-15)

Since this prophetic passage, like all such passages in the Bible, is sequential,[3] Christ's coming in glory (vs. 13-14) will come after the saints' appointed season of reign (v. 12). It is unusual that Scofield does not attribute these verses to Christ's second coming,[4] especially when Jesus does in the first three gospels and John does so in Revelation. It was Jesus' quoting of this verse to the Sanhedrin that brought forth their death sentence against him on charges of blasphemy. Responding to the high priest's questioning if He was the Christ, the Son of the Blessed One, Jesus said: ". . . *'I am; and you shall see the Son of Man sitting at the right hand of power, and coming with the clouds of heaven"* (Mark 14:62).

Daniel's vision ends with verse 15. In summary, the vision's chronology is: (1) the reign of the first three beasts (vv. 1-6), (2) the rise of the fourth beast and the Antichrist (vv. 7, 8), (3) the judgment and destruction of the fourth beast and the Antichrist (vv. 9-11), (4) the rest of the beasts are granted an extension of life for a season and a time (v. 12), and (5) the second coming of Christ (vv. 13, 14). The remainder of Daniel 7 deals with the angel's interpretation of the vision to Daniel.

Some will argue, including C.I. Scofield, that verse 22 of Daniel 7 refers to Christ at His second coming. If so, Christ's second coming must be at the end of the tribulation when He slays the Antichrist.

> *I kept looking, and that horn was waging war with the saints and overpowering them until the Ancient of Days came, and judgment was passed in favor of the saints of the Highest One, and the time arrived when the saints took possession of the kingdom.* (Dan. 7:21-22)

But if we put these verses in context with the entire chapter, we can conclude only that Daniel is talking about God the Father here, not Christ. Daniel previously refers to the Ancient of Days twice (vv. 9 and 13). Both times he is referring to God the Father. Here he is also referring to God the Father. Tying verse 22 into verse 9, Daniel saw the Ancient of Days come and take his seat. The books are opened and judgment is passed in favor of the saints of the Highest One.[5] The beast is then destroyed with fire. As Daniel writes:

> *But the court will sit for judgment, and his dominion will be taken away, annihilated and destroyed forever.*
>
> *Then the sovereignty, the dominion, and the greatness of all the kingdoms under the whole heaven will be given to the people of the saints of the Highest One; His kingdom will be an everlasting kingdom, and all the dominions will serve and obey Him.* (Dan. 7:26, 27)

Jesus' Discourse of the End Times

Other evidence that the Lord's second coming will not take place at the end of the Great Tribulation is found in Christ's end-times discourse on the Mount of Olives. We will take a look at His accounts in both Matthew 24 and Mark 13.

In Matthew 24, Jesus' account of the end times can be divided into three parts: In verses 4 through 14, He discusses the time from the beginning of birth pangs (see chapter 1) to the end of the age; in verses 15 through 28, He speaks about the time from the Abomination of desolation to His second coming; and in verses 29 through 31, He speaks of a time from the end of the Great Tribulation to His second coming.

Posttribulationalists insist Jesus' words in Matthew 24 should be interpreted sequentially by pointing out that Christ placed His second coming and the rapture after the Great Tribulation at the end of the age. This makes complete sense. But let's take this assertion a step further by applying it to verses 15 through 27. First, observe verses 15 through 22:

> *Therefore when you see the Abomination of Desolation which was spoken of through Daniel the prophet, standing in the holy place (let the reader understand), then let those who are in Judea flee to the mountains; . . . for then there will be a great tribulation, such as has not occurred since the beginning of the world until now, nor ever shall.*

> *And unless those days had been cut short, no life would have been saved; but for the sake of the elect those days shall be cut short.* (Matt. 24:15, 16, 21, 22)

We can grasp some important points from the sequence Jesus lays out. First, he describes the Abomination of Desolation (v. 15). He then describes the flight from Judea after it (vv. 16-20). In verse 21 he describes the Great Tribulation that follows, while in verse 22, he describes the tribulation's very abrupt ending. Verse 22 shows God will intervene to cut the Great Tribulation short. What is crucial to note though, is after describing the end of the tribulation, Jesus says:

> *Then if anyone says to you, "Behold, here is the Christ," or "There He is," do not believe him.*

> *For false Christs and false prophets will arise and will show great signs and wonders, so as to mislead, if possible, even the elect.*

> *Behold, I have told you in advance.*

> *If therefore they say to you, "Behold, He is in the wilderness," do not go forth, or, "Behold, He is in the inner rooms," do not believe them.*

> *For just as the lightening comes from the east, and flashes*
> *even to the west, so shall the coming of the Son of Man be.* (Matt.
> 24:23-27)

The word *then* used in verse 23 comes from the Greek word *tote*, which literally means "at the time that" or "then," and denotes succession. It comes from the root word *hote*, which means "after that." Jesus explicitly told His disciples that if after the tribulation (of verses 15-22), *"anyone says to you, Behold here is the Christ, . . . do not believe him."* He did not place His second coming at the end of the Great Tribulation!

Jesus said certain events would take place after the end of the tribulation and before His return (the religious deception of verses 23-26). The deception Jesus is talking about in verses 23-26 must be the last, great religious deception Satan will perform on earth after he is released from the bottomless pit at the end of time (Rev. 20:7-10). Chronologically, this final deception occurs after the Great Tribulation.

We must look at why Jesus, in His chronology, didn't mention a kingdom reign of the saints. His discourse jumped straight from the end of the tribulation (v. 22) to Satan's final deception (v. 23) upon his release from the abyss. I believe He didn't mention it because, just as He knew His disciples expected Him to set up a visible kingdom on earth at His first coming, He knew they would also expect Him to set up a visible kingdom on the earth at His second. Any talk of a saints' kingdom connected with the events of His second coming would only further fuel such speculation.

Jesus' reluctance to discuss the details of the kingdom period is also shown in the book of Acts. Consider the following conversation He had with His disciples prior to ascending to the Father's right hand:

> *And so when they had come together, they were asking Him,*
> *saying, "Lord, is it at this time You are restoring the kingdom to*
> *Israel?"*
>
> *He said to them, "It is not for you to know times or epochs*
> *[seasons] which the Father has fixed by His own authority."*
> (Acts 1:6, 7)

Jesus told His disciples it was not for them to know times or epochs fixed by the Father; this explains why He excluded mentioning the kingdom reign in His discourse on the Mount of Olives. The word *epochs* comes from the Greek word *kairos*, which literally means "an occasion," a "short time," or "a season." The King James translates it as "seasons." It is key to note that Jesus refers to the kingdom period as a "season," just as Daniel refers to it as a "season" (Dan. 7:12).

Let us now look carefully at Jesus' following words:

> *But immediately after the tribulation of those days the sun will be darkened, and the moon will not give its light, and the stars will fall from the sky, and the powers of the heavens will be shaken, and then the sign of the Son of Man will appear in the sky, and then all the tribes of the earth will mourn, and they will see the Son of Man coming on the clouds of the sky with power and great glory.* (Matt. 24:29, 30)

As the text shows, the sun being darkened, the moon not giving its light, and the stars falling from the sky are signs that precede the Lord's coming. Jesus said these cataclysms would occur after the tribulation. But if Jesus' second coming (when He slays the Beast) brings the tribulation to a close, a clear contradiction exists; for then these phenomena would have to occur not only after the tribulation but after, not before, His second coming. This is impossible. Either Jesus has the chronology all wrong, or His second coming is not at the end of the tribulation.

Mark put Jesus' account this way:

> *But in those days, after that tribulation, the sun will be darkened, and the moon will not give its light,*

> *An the stars will be falling from heaven, and the powers that are in the heavens will be shaken.*

> *And then they will see the Son of Man coming in the clouds with great power and glory.* (Mark 13:24-26)

Jesus' words in Mark are clear: there will be days after (the end of) the tribulation, and in those days the sun will be darkened, the moon will not give its light, the stars will fall from heaven, and after these things, Jesus Himself will come back. There is no way we can misinterpret this. The tribulation will have an abrupt end (Matt. 24:22). But Jesus' second coming will not bring it about. Intervening days must come after the Great Tribulation and before the Son of Man coming in power.

Distinctions Between the Tribulation and The Days Before Christ's Coming

There is more evidence to support the idea that Christ's second coming will not come at the end of the tribulation. Take for instance the vast difference between the days of the Great Tribulation and Jesus' own description of the days before His coming. Both Jesus and Daniel describe the Great Tribulation as a time of extreme distress *"such as has not occurred since the beginning of the world until now, nor ever shall"* (Matt. 24:21). It will be so terrible that unless it *"had been cut short, no life would have been saved"* (v. 22). Even so, Jesus says the coming of the Son of Man will be just like in the days of Noah.

> *For as in those days which were before the flood they were eating and drinking, they were marrying and giving in marriage, until the day that Noah entered the ark,*
>
> *and they did not understand until the flood came and took them all away; so shall the coming of the Son of Man be.* (Matt. 24:38-39)

Instead of a time of extreme tribulation, Jesus describes the days prior to His return as a time of relative peace, with people going about their everyday business; eating and drinking, marrying and giving in marriage, working in the field and grinding at the mill. Paul gives further evidence to this in his first letter to the Thessalonians:

> *For you yourselves know full well that the day of the Lord will come just like a thief in the night.*
>
> *While they are saying, "Peace and safety!" then destruction will come upon them suddenly like birth pangs upon a woman with child; and they shall not escape.* (1 Thess. 5:2-3)

Paul says the Day of the Lord will come, not after the drastic calamity of the seven year tribulation, but after a peaceful season on the earth. Judging from Jesus' words, *"But immediately after the tribulation of those days the sun will be darkened, and the moon will not give its light"* (v. 29), this season will likely be of short duration, at least in God's eyes. I believe many who survive the tribulation will live through this period to witness the Son of Man coming in glory.

Jesus' Coming at the End of the World

George Eldon Ladd, in *The Meaning of the Millennium*, writes, "I admit that the greatest difficulty to any premillennialism is . . . most of the New Testament pictures the consummation as occurring at Jesus' *parousia* [Second Coming]."[6] The scriptures pointing to Jesus' second coming at the end of the world are the strongest evidence of an amillennial eschatology. I am convinced they are the scriptures that led Augustine, the medieval Church, and the great reformers Martin Luther and John Calvin to reject the idea of an earthly millennial reign of Jesus Christ. These scriptures prove Christ's return will come on the *last day* and will bring about, in quick succession, the resurrection of the dead, the last judgment, the destruction of the world as we know it, the creation of the new heavens and the new earth, and the inauguration of the Father's eternal Kingdom.

Jesus' teaching on the resurrection in John 6, combined with Paul's teaching on the resurrection in First Thessalonians and First Corinthians, proves the resurrection will occur when Jesus comes again on the last day.

Regarding the last judgment, Jesus' parable of the sheep and the goats in Matthew 25 proves the last judgment and the initiation of the eternal state of man will come at the time of Christ's second coming. In this parable all unbelievers are condemned to the eternal fire, while all believers are received into everlasting life in the kingdom prepared for them from the foundation of the world. As we have seen, eternal life here cannot possibly mean physical, mortal life in an earthly millennial kingdom. In addition, the verdicts of this last judgment completely eliminate the need for any further future judgments.

That the present heaven and earth will be destroyed when Jesus comes back, and will be followed by the creation of the new heavens and new earth, is proven by Peter in his Second Epistle:

> *But the day of the Lord will come like a thief, in which the heavens will pass away with a roar and the elements will be destroyed with intense heat, and the earth and its works will be burned up.*

> *Since all these things are to be destroyed in this way, what sort of people ought you to be in holy conduct and godliness, looking for and hastening the coming of the day of God, . . .*

> *But according to His promise we are looking for new heavens and a new earth, in which righteousness dwells.* (2 Pet. 3:10-13)

The destruction of the world is also implied throughout Matthew when Jesus talks about His second coming at the end of the age (Matt. 13:39, 40, 49; Matt. 24:3; Matt. 28:20). The Greek word for *age* in these verses, *aion*, is defined by *Strong's Concordance* as "an age" by implication, "the world." The King James Bible interprets these verses as " the end of the world." The end of this present evil age will be brought about by the destruction of our present world.

That Jesus' second advent will inaugurate the Father's kingdom (as well as the resurrection), and not His own kingdom on David's throne during the millennium, is shown by Paul in his first letter to the Corinthians:

> *For as in Adam all die, so also in Christ all shall be made alive.*
>
> *But each in his own order: Christ the first fruits, after that those who are Christ's at His coming, then comes the end, when He delivers up the kingdom to the God and Father, when He has abolished all rule and authority and power.*
>
> *For He must reign until He has put all His enemies under His feet.* (1 Cor. 15:22-25)

Premillennialists claim verse 25 refers to Christ's rule during the millennial kingdom when He will put all his enemies under His feet. What they fail to realize, though, is that Paul was referring to David's words in the 110th Psalm: *"The Lord says to my Lord: 'Sit at My right hand, Until I make Thine enemies a footstool for Thy feet' "*(Psalm 110:1). David clearly shows Christ will reign, seated at the right hand of God in heaven, until all His enemies have been put under his feet. Then comes the end, when He delivers up the kingdom to God the Father. The author of Hebrews shows it even clearer when he writes:

> *But He, having offered one sacrifice for sins for all time, sat down at the right hand of God,*
>
> *Waiting from that time onward until His enemies be made a footstool for His feet.* (Heb. 10:12, 13)

The final evidence that the Father will receive the kingdom from Jesus at His second coming is given in Jesus' parable of the wheat and the tares, when He says that at the end of the age, the righteous sons of the kingdom *"will shine forth as the sun in the kingdom of their Father"* (Matt. 13:43).

With the abundance of evidence in the New Testament saying Christ's second advent will come at the end of this present evil world, and not at the beginning of some earthly millennial reign, is there any wonder why the Church, since Augustine, has accepted the doctrine of amillennialism? Their acceptance of this doctrine is based on a literal interpretation of these scriptures. Dispensationalists cannot say they are the only ones who interpret scripture literally.

Now we will see what awesome intervention of God—if not the second coming of Jesus Christ—will bring about the conversion of the Jews, the destruction of the Antichrist, the termination of the Great Tribulation, and the ushering in of the kingdom of Christ's Bride.

The Sword of the Spirit

Paul, in writing to the Thessalonians about the destruction of the Antichrist, declares:

> *And then that lawless one will be revealed whom the Lord will slay with the breath of His mouth and bring to an end by the appearance of His coming* [presence]. . . . (2 Thess. 2:8)

This verse is a parallel scripture to John's words in Revelation 19. Paul appears to be telling the Thessalonians that Jesus will destroy the Antichrist at His second coming. Be that as it may, we have seen there is strong biblical evidence supporting Jesus will come, not at the end of the Great Tribulation, but at the end of the world after His Bride has reigned for an appointed season of time.

For this reason Paul must be referring to something besides Christ's second advent when portraying the beast's destruction. The Greek word for "coming" in this verse is *parousia*. It stresses the actual personal presence of one who has arrived. *Parousia* is a word commonly used to describe the second coming of Christ. Still, it is no way unique to Jesus' coming. For instance, the same word is used to tell of the Antichrist's coming in the activity and power of Satan (2 Thess. 2:9). Nor does the New Testament always translate it as "coming." It is twice translated as "presence" (2 Cor. 10:10, Phil. 2:12). Paul exhorts the Philippians in the faith, reminding them they have always obeyed, not only in his presence (*parousia*), but even more in his absence. In fact, the New American Standard Bible notes that in 2 Thessalonians 2:8, *parousia* can be translated as "presence."

The word "appearance" in this verse comes from the Greek word *epiphaneia*—another word used to describe Jesus' second coming. It literally means "manifestation," an "appearing," or "brightness." In this verse, Paul says it is the Lord who will slay the Antichrist with the breath of His mouth, bringing him "to an end by the appearance (manifestation) of His coming (presence)." But here Paul does not mention Jesus specifically by name as he does throughout the rest of 2 Thessalonians.

When comparing the symbolism Paul uses in this verse to other scriptures describing Him, I believe Paul in 2 Thessalonians 2:8 is talking about the Holy Spirit, the Spirit of Jesus, who by coming in the full manifestation of His presence will slay the Antichrist. Note how Paul says the Lord slays the Antichrist with *"the breath of His mouth."* In John, Jesus breathes on His disciples and says *"Receive the Holy Spirit"* (John 20:22). In Revelation, John says that out of His mouth comes a *"sharp sword, . . . and the rest were killed with the sword which came from the mouth of Him who sat on the horse . . ."* (Rev. 19:15, 21). In Ephesians, Paul calls the word of God *"the sword of the Spirit"* (Eph. 6;17).

In Zechariah and Ezekiel (Ezek. 39:29), *"the Spirit of grace and supplication"* is poured out over Israel at their conversion. While in Daniel, *"a river of fire was flowing and coming out from before Him"* who sat on the throne, *"until the beast was slain . . . and given to the burning fire."* In the gospels, John the Baptist says Jesus *"will baptize you with the Holy spirit and fire"* (Matt. 3:11), while in Acts, *"tongues of fire"* came down on the apostles at Pentecost (Acts 2:3). Most importantly, Paul writes to the Corinthians: *"Now the Lord is the Spirit; and where the spirit of the Lord is, there is liberty"* (2 Cor. 3:17).

It is the full manifestation of the Holy Spirit, the awesome manifestation of God's Shekinah Glory, who will come in power to destroy the Antichrist. Just as Jesus will identify Himself with His saints as they battle against the Beast in the heavenly realm, so also will He identify Himself with His spirit[7]—as portrayed in 2 Thessalonians and Revelation 19—as He annihilates the Man of sin at the end of the tribulation.

God will intervene in a mighty way to cut short the Great Tribulation and to inaugurate the kingdom of His saints. He will do so by pouring out His glorious Holy Spirit—the Spirit of Truth, the Spirit of Jesus—over the surface of the earth. The world is now ready for the reign of the saints of the Most High. It is ready for the Kingdom of the Bride.

Notes

1. Scofield, 908.

2. Despite God's judgment on them, the United States and Russia will have a remnant in the kingdom age. Even though Germany lay in utter ruins after World War II, look at her now.

3. Entire books and chapters are not necessarily sequential. Individual passages within them are almost always sequential.

4. Scofield, 908.

5. This judgment of God the Father at the end of the Great Tribulation is the reason why John refers to Armageddon as "the war of the great day of God, the Almighty" (Rev. 16:14).

6. Taken from *The Meaning of the Millennium* edited by Robert G. Clouse, pp. 189–190. © 1977 InterVarsity Christian Fellowship of the USA. Used by permission of InterVarsity Press, P.O. Box 1400, Downers Grove, IL 60515.

7. Speaking of His Spirit, Jesus told His disciples, "Lo, I am with you always, even to the end of the age" (Matt. 28:20).

11
THE GLORY AND
THE BRIDE

The supernatural intervention of the Almighty will bring the Great Tribulation to its close and usher in the Kingdom of Christ's splendorous Bride. Yes, the time has come for Christ's Bride, His beloved Church and very body, to take possession of her kingdom. She will reign. And He will reign through her. And the miraculous outpouring of God's glory—the full manifestation of His Holy Spirit—will be the marvelous wonder that brings it about.

The Holy Spirit is the most special person of the Triune Godhead—the very glory of God Himself. Always in submission to the Father, always bearing witness and giving glory to Jesus, never exalting Himself, content to be third in line, the very instrument of the Father's love by which He touches a fragile, imperfect humanity. Of Him Jesus said: *"And whoever shall speak a word against the Son of Man, it shall be forgiven him; but whoever shall speak against the Holy Spirit, it shall not be forgiven him, either in this age, or in the age to come"* (Matt. 12:31). This is the one Stephen saw at his martyrdom with Jesus when *". . . he gazed intently into heaven and saw the glory of God, and Jesus standing at the right hand of God"* (Acts 7:55).

Today, Christians are the temples of the Holy Spirit. Every born-again believer has experienced different levels of His filling and different degrees of His power. Nevertheless, during the future appointed season of the Bride's reign, the manifested glory of God's Holy Spirit will cover the earth in a manner not experienced since the cloud of Yahweh's Shekinah Glory guided the children of Israel through the desert after their exodus from Egypt.

In Old Testament times, the glory of God dwelt in the Holy of Holies; first in the portable tabernacle erected by Moses during Israel's forty-year trek through the wilderness, and after that, in King Solomon's magnificent temple. His future return—rather, His full manifestation on the earth—will be a spiritual landmark: the first time in more than 2500 years when the glory of the Lord will be fully present in the world. The prophet Ezekiel witnessed the last departure of God's glory from

Solomon's temple in a vision from God during the Babylonian exile. Ezekiel saw the glory of the Lord departing from the temple via a series of steps: first, from the golden cherub (whose spread wings covered the ark of God) to the threshold of the temple; second, from the threshold through the temple's east gate; and last, from the temple and the city to the Mount of Olives east of Jerusalem.

> *Then the glory of the Lord went up from the cherub to the threshold of the temple, and the temple was filled with the cloud, and the court was filled with the brightness of the glory of the Lord. . . .*
>
> *Then the glory of the Lord departed from the threshold of the temple and stood over the cherubim.*
>
> *When the cherubim departed, they lifted their wings and rose up from the earth in my sight . . . and they stood still at the entrance of the east gate of the Lord's house. And the glory of the God of Israel hovered over them. . . .*
>
> *And the glory of the Lord went up from the midst of the city, and stood over the mountain which is east of the city.* (Ezek. 10:4, 18, 19; Ezek. 11:23.)

Ezekiel not only witnessed the departure of God's glory from Solomon's original temple, but in another vision he witnessed His impending return to the new temple; His final earthly place of habitation. Regarding His return after the Great Tribulation to the future end times temple in Jerusalem, Ezekiel writes:

> *Then he [the angel] led me to the gate, the gate facing toward the east;*
>
> *and behold, the glory of the God of Israel was coming from the way of the east. And His voice was like the sound of many waters; and the earth shone with His glory. . . .*
>
> *And the glory of the Lord came into the house by the way of the gate facing toward the east.*
>
> *And the Spirit lifted me up and brought me into the inner court; and behold, the glory of the Lord filled the house.*
>
> *Then I heard one speaking to me from the house, while a man was standing beside me.*

> *And He said to me, "Son of man, this is the place of My*
> *throne and the soles of my feet, where I will dwell among the sons*
> *of Israel forever. . . . " (Ezek. 43:1-2, 4-7a)*

Premillennialists try to say these verses refer to Christ's entrance into the temple to take up His seat on the throne of David. This is why they say Jesus will return through the temple's east gate. Yet, in Old Testament times, David's throne was never in the temple. And although Ezekiel goes into great detail describing the future kingdom temple, its sacrificial altar and all that is in it, he says nothing of an actual, physical throne. Rather, the temple throughout the Bible is described as God's footstool (1 Chron. 28:2), the resting place of His feet, just as Ezekiel implies here. Since it is the dwelling place of God's glory, symbolically it represents His throne, even as heaven is the Father's throne. The prophet Isaiah inscribed the Lord's words: *"Heaven is My throne, and the earth is My footstool"* (Isa. 66:1). Furthermore, Ezekiel states the visions were like previous visions he saw involving the glory of the Lord (Ezek. 43:3). We know it was the glory of God, not Jesus, that inhabited the temple in Old Testament times. Jesus, recognizing the temple as the dwelling place of the Holy Spirit, said: *"And he who swears by the temple, swears both by the temple and by Him who dwells within it"* (Matt. 23:21).

The idea of a "kingdom reign" by the Holy Spirit is not a new one. According to Walvoord, the twelfth-century Roman Catholic writer Joachim of Floris held the view that the millennium "begins and continues as a rule of the Holy Spirit."[1] Although He will not rule for a millennia, He will reign—with and through His Bride—for the appointed season preceding Christ's second advent. And the marvelous thing about this future reign is that He will not be confined to the Holy of Holies, with a dividing wall to separate Him from the people because of their sinfulness. For Jesus, God's high priest, has "entered through the greater and more perfect tabernacle not made with hands," the one found in heaven, so that through Him we might have access to the heavenly Holy of Holies and "with confidence draw near to the throne of grace."[2]

Rather than remaining in the holiest place, the glory of God will flow like water from the temple throughout the land. This analogy is no small coincidence, for when speaking of the Holy Spirit, Jesus said, *"but the water that I shall give . . . shall become a . . . well of water springing up to eternal life"* (John 4:14). Ezekiel describes this in the chapter 47 of his book, telling how the water flowed *"from the threshold of the house [the temple] toward the east,"* and how at a distance of a thousand cubits from the house there was *"water reaching the ankles"* (Ezek. 47:3). And how at another thousand, there was *"water reaching the knees"* (Ezek. 47:4). And how at another, it was *"reaching the loins"* (Ezek. 47:4). Until finally at the last thousand cubits *"it was a river that I could not ford, for the water had risen, enough water to swim in, a river that could not be forded"* (Ezek. 47:5). These waters of the Spirit will flow out into all the earth, healing the physical waters God will smite during the Great Tribulation, those turned to blood via the trumpets and the bowls of His wrath as well as those contaminated from the pestilence of nuclear fallout brought on by Armageddon. As told in Ezekiel:

> Then he said to me, *"These waters go out toward the eastern region and go down into the Arabah; then they go toward the sea, being made to flow into the sea, and the waters of the sea become fresh [lit., healed].*
>
> *And it will come about that every living creature which swarms in every place where the river goes, will live. . . . "* (Ezek. 47:8, 9)

These waters of the glory of God will flow everywhere, so that the prophet Habakkuk proclaims:

> For the earth will be filled
> With the knowledge of the glory of the Lord,
> As the waters cover the sea. (Hab. 2:14)

What a glorious time it will be when the Spirit of God's glory gushes out over the face of the earth, anointing His reigning Bride! And happening in congruence with it will be an event long hoped for by His church: the binding of Satan.

Satan Bound for a Thousand Years

After the glorious fire of God's Holy Spirit consumes both the Antichrist and the False Prophet, casting them into the burning lake of fire and brimstone, John the Revelator states that the devil will be bound for *"a thousand years."*

> And I saw an angel coming down from heaven, having the key of the abyss and a great chain in his hand.
>
> And he laid hold of the dragon, the serpent of old, who is the devil and Satan, and bound him for a thousand years, and threw him into the abyss, and shut it and sealed it over him, so that he should not deceive the nations any longer, until the thousand

years were completed; after these things he must be released for a
short time. (Rev. 20:1-3)

These verses on the binding of Satan have perplexed Bible scholars
throughout the centuries. Saint Augustine provided a thorough commentary on it in *The City of God*.[3] Traditional amillennial eschatology
derived from Augustine applies a symbolic meaning to these thousand
years, saying they are the "complete time" from Christ's first coming to
His second advent. On the contrary, premillennialists claim the thousand years of Satan's binding will occur concurrently with an earthly
millennial reign of Christ. In any sense, we can conclude that during the
saints' reign on the earth, Satan will be bound in the abyss, a place the
King James Bible translates as the *"bottomless pit."*

The key to interpreting the first six verses of Revelation 20—which
are divided into two parts, verses 1-3 describing the thousand years of
Satan's binding, and verses 4-6 describing the thousand-year reign of
Christ and His saints—depends on two things. First, should the
thousand years in each case be interpreted as a literal, absolute, earthly
duration? And second, do the thousand years in each case describe the
same time period or could they be describing two separate and
nonconcurrent epochs?

Based on the symbolism underlying the Book of Revelation, having
the thousand years symbolize both the complete period of Satan's
binding and the complete period of Christ's reign through the church
from His first to His second advent seems like a reasonable interpretation. Augustine even pondered whether the thousand years in each case
could be two separate periods "so that," as he puts it, "both parties have
their thousand years, that is, their complete time, yet each with a
different actual duration appropriate to itself."[4]

Still, we must go back and ask if it is even possible to interpret the
millennia in each case as literal thousand year periods. The keys to
determining this, which in turn will also resolve whether the two time
frames are one and the same (or whether they are separate and distinct),
lies in determining (1) where each event—the binding of Satan and the
reign of Christ—will take place, and (2) where John was when he saw
each vision.

Obviously, if it could be proved that while on the island of Patmos,
John saw Satan bound in the earth during the same thousand year period
of Christ's reign, and that in fact Christ does reign from the earth, then
a literal, earthly millennial reign of Christ would be proved beyond
doubt.

Einstein's Answer

The premillennial interpretation of Revelation 20—that it describes a single, literal thousand-year period on earth—is based on the classical assumption of the absolute character of time.[5] The establishment at the turn of the twentieth century of Einstein's Special and General Theories of Relativity, however, found "that space and time have no absolute significance."[6, 7]

Consider the following quotes from two separate articles on relativity: (1) "Whenever two observers are associated with two distinct inertial frames of inference in relative motion to each other, their determinations of time intervals and of distances between events will disagree systematically, without one being 'right' and the other 'wrong.' "[8] And (2) "In referring to the time [duration] of an event, it is always understood that the time is indicated by the clock at the point where the event occurs."[9]

Now think of our earth as nothing more than an inertial reference frame traveling through space with different modes of motion—rotational motion about its axis and circular motion about the sun. Also, think of heaven as an inertial reference frame. Regardless of whether heaven as God's throne is stationary in space or moving, it is fair to assume its motion (or nonmotion) is much different than the earth's.

Based on these observations and the notion of relativity, we must conclude the "clocked time"[10] of an event occurring in heaven will significantly differ from the "clocked time" of the same event taking place on earth, or any other place in the universe for that matter. In addition, an observer viewing and timing an event from heaven will observe a far different "clocked time" than an observer viewing and timing the same event from the earth, regardless of where the clocked event takes place.

Now let's relate all of this to the questions of where was John and where do the two events take place? Once again, the only way we can reasonably conclude the thousand years in Revelation 20 refer to a single, literal thousand year period on earth during which Jesus will reign and the devil will be bound, is by (1) proving the binding of Satan and the reign of Christ both occur on earth, and by (2) proving John was on the earth when he observed the vision.

The second point, however, can never be proven. John was not on the earth when he saw the vision. (Or, at least his spirit wasn't.) Revelation chapter 4 tells us:

> *After these things I looked, and behold, a door standing open*
> *in heaven, and the first voice which I had heard, like the sound*
> *of a trumpet speaking with me, said, "Come up here, and I will*
> *show you what must take place after these things."*
>
> *Immediately I was in the Spirit [or, in spirit]; and behold,*
> *a throne was standing in heaven. . . .* (Rev. 4:1, 2a)

John, whether in the body or out of the body (cf. 2 Cor. 12:2), was in heaven when he saw his revelations. He was in a different reference frame where time has a totally different meaning.

Now to address the first point—do Satan's binding and Christ's reign occur on the earth? Satan's binding is obvious. The text shows he will be bound in the abyss, the bottomless pit, for a thousand years. This cannot be in the earth. For one thing, since Satan is a spirit, he must be bound in the spiritual domain. In addition, a bottomless pit in our earth is physically impossible: it would come out the other side.

Regarding the thousand years of Christ's reign, it will surely happen someplace else other than the abyss. Therefore, according to relativity, it doesn't have to occur simultaneously with the thousand years of Satan's binding.[11] In chapter 13 we will see that Christ's reign will occur not on earth, but in heaven. In this case, since neither of the "thousand-year" occurrences envisioned by John will take place on earth, the elapsed time on the earth during those events need not be a thousand years. Because of the abstract dimension relativity adds to our concept of time, the German mathematician Hermann Minkowski stated in 1909, "From now on, space by itself and time by itself are mere shadows, and only a blend of the two exist in its own right."[12]

Yes, Satan will be bound in his place, the abyss, for one thousand years. And during this period, the saints, undeceived by his wiles, will rule the nations for their own appointed season of time.

The Glorious State of the Earth

Because of the outpouring of God's glory and the binding of Satan, during the righteous rule of the saints the world will experience a new era of peace never before known. Throughout it the peoples will go up to the mountain of the house of the Lord in Jerusalem to worship the Lord of hosts. Regarding these future days, the prophet Isaiah writes:

> *Now it will come about that*
> *In the last days, ...*
> *the law will go forth from Zion,*

> *And the word of the Lord from Jerusalem.*
> *And He will judge between the nations,*
> *And will render decisions for many peoples;*
> *And they will hammer their swords into plowshares,*
> *and their spears into pruning hooks.*
> *Nation will not lift up sword against nation,*
> *And never again will they learn war.* (Isa. 2:2-4)

The nations of the earth will take all of the weapons and materials of war they used to destroy the world during the Great Tribulation and will turn them into plowshares and pruning hooks—instruments of peace. Nation will not rise up against nation and "never again will they learn war." There will be a Utopia of peace on the earth, a period of tranquillity that even this generation's most ardent nuclear disarmament advocates can't possibly fathom. So harmonious a time for the whole creation will this season of the earth be that Isaiah wrote:

> *And the wolf will dwell with the lamb,*
> *And the leopard will lie down with the kid,*
> *And the calf and the young lion and the fatling together,*
> *And a little boy will lead them.*
> *Also the cow and the bear will graze;*
> *Their young will lie down together;*
> *And the lion will eat straw like the ox.*
> *And the nursing child will play by the hole of the cobra,*
> *And the weaned child will put his hand on the viper's den.*
> (Isa. 11:6-8)

The earth's entire ecosystem will experience a previously unknown aura of peace, harmony, and tranquillity. During this future season, all of God's creation will rest while the nations *"resort to the root of Jesse"* (Isa. 11:10), Jesus Christ. They will stream to *"the house of the God of Jacob"* (Isa. 2:3), the glorious resting place of His Spirit, so that He may teach them regarding His ways. And as Isaiah writes, *"the earth will be full of the knowledge of the Lord as the waters cover the sea"* (Isa. 11:9b).

The Feast of Booths

Zechariah prophesied that during this time all the nations of the world would go up to Jerusalem to celebrate the Feast of Booths: *"Then it will come about that any who are left of all the nations that went against Jerusalem will go up from year to year to worship the King, the Lord of hosts, and to celebrate the Feast of Booths"* (Zech. 14:16).

The Feast of Booths, or Feast of Tabernacles, is one of the main Jewish feasts. Called Sukkoth by the Jews, it is a reminder that the children of Israel wandered in the wilderness after the Lord led them out of Egypt, pitching tents or temporary booths along the way. By partaking in it, the celebrant declares faith in God that, just as He guided His children in that physical earthly desert, delivering them to a land flowing with milk and honey, He will keep his promise of guiding us to our permanent home in the promised land of heaven.[13] The Lord's instructions to Moses on how to celebrate the feast are found in the book of Leviticus.

> *Speak to the sons of Israel, saying, "On the fifteenth of this seventh month is the Feast of Booths for seven days to the Lord. . . .*
>
> *Now on the first day you shall take for yourselves the foliage of beautiful trees, palm branches and boughs of leafy trees and willows of the brook, and you shall rejoice before the Lord your God for seven days. . . .* (Lev. 23:34, 40)

Notice in Zechariah that rather than just the nation of Israel, all the nations of the world go up to celebrate the Feast of Booths at Jerusalem. What a proper feast it will be to celebrate the Lord of Hosts after the Great Tribulation and throughout the kingdom period of the saints! It will bring to mind how God guided both the Church and Israel through the wilderness of the Great Tribulation by providing them with safe, temporary sanctuaries. And when the citizens of Israel, after their deliverance, are again branches on the olive tree, which is the true spiritual Israel, they will celebrate this feast as members of God's Church. The Church's celebration of the Feast of Booths is portrayed in the following vision from Revelation:

> *After these things I looked, and behold, a great multitude, which no one could count, from every nation and all tribes and peoples and tongues, standing before the throne and before the Lamb, clothed in white robes, and palm branches were in their hands;*
>
> *and they cry out with a loud voice, saying, "Salvation to our God who sits on the throne, and to the Lamb."*
>
> *And all the angels were standing around the throne and around the elders and the four living creatures; and they fell on their faces before the throne and worshipped God,*

*saying, "Amen, blessing and glory and wisdom and thanks-
giving and honor and power and might, be to our God forever
and ever. Amen."*

*And one of the elders answered, saying to me, "These who are
clothed in the white robes, who are they, and from where have
they come?"*

*And I said to him, "My lord, you know." And he said to me,
"These are the ones who have come out of the great tribulation,
and they have washed their robes and made them white in the
blood of the Lamb.*

*For this reason, they are before the throne of God; and they
serve Him day and night in His temple, and He who sits on the
throne shall spread His tabernacle over them."* (Rev. 7:9-15)

John's vision is a dual vision—one which contains elements of both
heaven and earth. John saw the great multitude standing before God's
throne. At the same time, he also saw the angels of heaven standing
around the throne, around the four living creatures, and around the
elders. Nevertheless, note that the angels are not standing around the
great multitude.

Regarding the multitudes clothed in white robes, one of the elders
tells John, "These are the ones who [have] come out of the great
tribulation, and they [have] washed their robes and made them white in
the blood of the Lamb." Lindsey says the multitude are believers
martyred during the tribulation[14] although there is nothing in the vision
to indicate this. The single fact they have come out of the Great
Tribulation implies they have survived the Great Tribulation and are
now standing, rejoicing, before God's throne.

Furthermore, elsewhere in Revelation John clearly distinguishes
the temple of God *"which is in heaven"* (Rev. 11:19; Rev. 14:17; Rev.
15:5) from the temple on earth. Here he makes no distinction. If we
consider also that the earthly temple is the throne of God's Spirit (Ezek.
43:7), then John must be referring to the temple on earth. That the
surviving multitudes are waving palm branches shows they are in
Jerusalem's temple rejoicing before the Lord's throne while celebrating
the Feast of Booths (cf. Lev. 23:40).

The white robes symbolize Christ's bride having clothed herself in
fine linen, bright and clean (Rev. 19:7, 8). Since the throne of God and
He who sits on it, and the Lamb in its center, refer to a heavenly throne
room, the multitude in this vision (though on the earth) are standing

before the Father's heavenly throne just as Christ's Church does today. As the author of Hebrews writes: *"Let us therefore draw near with confidence to the throne of grace, that we may receive mercy and may find grace to help in time of need"* (Heb. 4:16).

There is quite a contrast between John's and Zechariah's visions of the Feast of Booths. In John's vision, the multitudes are obviously in love with the Lamb and *"serve Him day and night in His temple"* (notice that in heaven there is no night, cf. Rev. 22:5). They are continually celebrating before the Lord. He is their shepherd and guides them to the springs of the water of life while wiping away their every tear (Rev. 7:17). He covers them with His tabernacle (Rev. 7:15).

In Zechariah, however, the nations are referred to as those *"who are left of all the nations that went against Jerusalem,"* who go up from *"year to year"* to worship the King—some, it seems, more to avoid the plague of drought for not celebrating the feast than to honor Him. Zechariah's writing style reflects how he is an Old Testament prophet under the law, while John's reflects how he is a New Testament saint under grace; one who personally knows and loves the Lord Jesus. Zechariah also demonstrates how after the tribulation and during the kingdom period of the saints, skeptics and unbelievers will be left on the earth. There will be doubters, who despite all that has happened during the tribulation, will still not believe.

The glorious thing about John's vision though, is that it shows the great majority of Christians who experience the tribulation will survive. Rather than being martyred and killed by the Antichrist, they will live to rejoice in the glory of God's earthly kingdom.

The Kingdom Temple

It is obvious that Jerusalem and the temple will play a key role during the reign of Christ's bride. This future glorious dwelling place of God's Holy Spirit is described exclusively in Ezekiel, chapters 40 through 46. Many dispensational scholars contend this temple is different from the tribulation temple—the one the Antichrist will desolate—and is to be built during the Kingdom period.[15] This is difficult to prove from scripture. If this temple is a different temple, we need to ask: What will happen to the temple of the tribulation period? Will it be destroyed? If so, it is not predicted by prophecy.

In all likelihood they will not be different temples; the future temple the Jews will build as a result of their covenant with the Antichrist prior to the tribulation and the Kingdom temple Ezekiel describes must be one and the same. We can be sure that the Orthodox Jews of today know the significance of Ezekiel's prophecy. When they do build another temple, they undoubtedly will follow the pattern described in Ezekiel's writings (Ezek. 40:5, 43:17).

Another reason the temples are the same is because an angel appeared to Ezekiel holding a measuring rod and proceeded to measure the temple (Ezek. 40:3). Meanwhile, a similar scene occurs in Revelation where an angel appears to John and tells him to measure the temple of God; a temple obviously built before the forty-two-month Great Tribulation. *"And there was given me a measuring rod like a staff; and someone said, 'Rise and measure the temple of God, and the altar, and those who worship in it' "* (Rev. 11:1).

Since the temple that the Antichrist will desecrate during the tribulation and Ezekiel's kingdom temple are one and the same, the significance behind the 1,290 days that Daniel mentions—*"And from the time that the regular sacrifice is abolished, and the abomination of desolation is set up, there will be 1,290 days"* (Dan. 12:11)—could be that from the end of the Great Tribulation up until the 1,290th day, the temple will be cleansed, just as the prior temple was after the abomination of desolation of Antiochus Epiphanes, the Syrian king who slaughtered a sow in the holy place around the year 170 B.C.

As for the 1,335th day—*"How blessed is he who keeps waiting and attains to the 1,335 days!"* (Dan. 12:12)—on that day (measured from the Abomination of Desolation) the festive celebration of the Feast of Booths described in the book of Revelation will most likely take place in the glorious temple of God.

Animal Sacrifices During the Kingdom Period?

Ezekiel's writings raise another baffling question for prophetic commentators. He graphically illustrates the future practice of animal sacrifice according to the Mosaic Law—a system that the New Testament teaches has been made obsolete by Christ's New Covenant (Heb. 8:13). This poses no dilemma for dispensationalists, who claim mankind will revert back to the law of Moses during the Millennium. The following excerpt taken from the prophetic literature of a Colorado-based Messianic Synagogue (whose prophetic teachings are rooted in dispensationalism) typifies this belief: "The mortals that live during the Millennial are not redeemed by Christ's crucifixion. Therefore the sacrifices will be reinstituted." In most Christians' eyes, this statement belittles the price Christ paid on the cross.

The only answer to the irony Ezekiel presents is that the sacrifices he predicts will be those performed by the Jews in the first half of the tribulation before the Antichrist puts a stop to sacrifice and grain offering (Dan. 9:27). If the Jews are going to rebuild their temple, they will do so for the purpose of carrying out animal sacrifices according to the law. Ezekiel's chapters provide them instructions on how to perform them.

Another reason these sacrifices likely will occur during the first half of the tribulation is that the events in the book of Ezekiel do not appear to be sequential. In chapter 44, an angel instructs Ezekiel that the gate through which the glory of God enters—an event that marks the end of tribulation, the conversion of the Jews and the start of the kingdom period—is to be kept shut:

> *Then He brought me back by way of the outer gate of the sanctuary, which faces the east; and it was shut.*
>
> *And the Lord said to me, "This gate shall be shut; it shall not be opened, and no one shall enter by it, for the Lord God of Israel has entered by it; therefore it shall be shut."* (Ezek. 44:1–2)

Nevertheless, in chapter 46 where the animal sacrifices are described, this same gate is opened.[16]

> *Thus says the Lord God, "The gate of the inner court facing east shall be shut the six working days; but it shall be opened on the Sabbath day, and opened on the day of the new moon. . . . but [on the six working days] the gate shall not be shut until the evening. . . .*
>
> *And when the prince provides a freewill offering, a burnt offering, or peace offerings as a freewill offering to the Lord, the gate facing east shall be opened for him.* (Ezek. 46:1, 2b, 12a)

This indicates the sacrifices described in chapter 46 will occur before the glory of God enters the temple, before the Jews come to know their Messiah and before the eastern gate is shut for good.

As to why God will have Israel reinstitute these sacrifices before their salvation, we can only speculate that they will have a purpose in pointing the Jews towards Jesus Christ. Remember that the Law is described as *"a shadow of the good things to come"* (Heb. 10:1). The Jews, since they failed to see Christ as the true Passover Lamb and as the fulfillment of the law, now no longer have the practiced law (the carrying out of animal sacrifices) to direct them to Christ. For this reason, God will use the symbolism behind and the futility of a system of animal sacrifices to point His chosen people towards the truth of the Messiah as the Lamb of God.

Zechariah's Feast of Booth's passage indicates there will still be temple sacrifices after the conversion of the Jews (Zech. 14:20-21), just as there were in Jesus' time. As seen in the Acts of the Apostles, temple worship played a major role in the lives of the Jewish disciples. Obviously with such a large number of Jewish Christians entering the Kingdom of God all at once after Israel's conversion, it will be difficult for them to immediately give up the practice of animal sacrifice. Paul, well into his Christian life, even went through a Jewish purification rite and would have offered a temple sacrifice for himself, had unbelieving Jews not prevented him (Acts 21:26). But to say, as dispensationalists teach, that the whole earth will revert back to Judaism and the Mosaic law during the kingdom period goes against everything the New Testament teaches and against everything Christ accomplished on the cross.

The sacrifices offered during the kingdom period will not be for the remission of sin. Nor will they be prerequisites for entering into the presence of God's glory. They will be for celebrating before the King. Jesus Himself went up to celebrate the Feast of Booths in Jerusalem (John 7:2-10), and we all know He had no sin that required propitiation. The Feast of Booths will be a continual celebration before the Lord—a celebration of the marriage supper of the Lamb and His victorious Bride.

Notes

1. John F. Walvoord, "The Millennial Issue in Modern Theology," *Bibliotheca Sacra*, 106:152, January, 1948, cited in Pentecost, 384.

2. Quotes are from Heb. 9:11, Heb. 10:14, and Heb. 4:16.

3. St. Augustine, *The City of God,* Book 20, ch. 8, 722-724. Used by permission.

4. *Ibid,* 732.

5. Absolute time says that "if a certain physical process takes, say, one hour as determined in one inertial frame of reference, it will take precisely one hour with respect to any other inertial frame; and if two events are observed to take place simultaneously by an observer attached to one inertial frame, they will appear simultaneous to all other inertial observers. . . . The idea that a universal time can be used indiscriminately by all, irrespective of their

[each person's] varying states of motion—that is, by a person at rest at his home, by the driver of an automobile, and by a passenger aboard an airplane—is so deeply ingrained in most people that they do not even conceive of alternatives. It was only at the turn of the 20th century that the absolute character of time was called into question, ..." From Peter G. Bergmann, "Relativity," in *Encyclopaedia Britannica*, 15th ed. (1990), 26:531.

6. Quote in text is from H. B. Phillips, "Relativity," *Encyclopedia Americana*, 1979.

7. "In classical physics it was assumed that all observers anywhere in the universe, whether moving or not, obtained identical measurements of space and time intervals. According to relativity theory, this is not so, but their results depend on their relative motions." From Bergmann, 581.

8. Bergmann, 583.

9. Phillips, 338.

10. By "clocked time" I mean the elapsed, measured time.

11. "Einstein demonstrated that if each observer [i.e. two observers in two different inferential reference frames] applied the same method of analysis to his own data, then events that appeared simultaneous to one would appear to have taken place at different times to observers in different states of motion. Thus, it is necessary to speak of relativity of simultaneity." From Bergmann, 583.

12. Phillips, 337.

13. Martha Zimmerman, *Celebrate the Feasts* (Minneapolis: Bethany House Publishers, 1981), 162.

14. Lindsey, *The Rapture*, 19-20, 147.

15. Which in dispensational theology is Christ's earthly millennium.

16. In Ezekiel 44:1, the shut gate facing east is described as the outer gate of the sanctuary. According to Ezek. 41:21-23 and Ezek. 44:16, 17, 27, the sanctuary is made up of the inner court and the nave (i.e., the holy of holies). Also, in Ezekiel 43:4, 5, the Glory of God comes into the house by the way of the gate facing east and fills the inner court (implied). Therefore, the gate of Ezek. 44:1 can also be described as the outer gate of the inner court, that is, the outer gate of the wall dividing the inner court from the outer court. In Ezek. 46:1, the gate described is the gate of the inner court facing east. This has to be the same gate described in Ezekiel 44:1, which is to be forever shut after the glory of God enters.

12

THE WEDDING FEAST
OF THE BRIDE

The Marriage Supper of the Lamb

Jesus during the sermon on the mount proclaimed: *"Blessed are the meek; for they shall inherit the earth"* (Matt. 5:5). The Apostle Paul in his epistle to the Corinthians asked: *"Or, do you not know that the saints will judge the world?"* (1 Cor. 6:2a). The prophet Daniel in his apocalypse declared: *"Then the sovereignty, the dominion, and the greatness of all the kingdoms under the whole heaven will be given to the people of the saints of the Highest One"* (Dan. 7:27a). And finally, the Son of God in the book of Revelation proclaimed:

> *And he who overcomes, and he who keeps My deeds until the end to him I will give authority over the nations;*
>
> *And he shall rule them with a rod of iron, as the vessels of the potter are broken to pieces, as I also have received authority from My Father; . . .* (Rev. 2:26-27)

Christ's Bride, victorious over the Antichrist and reigning upon the earth, has prepared herself for her Bridegroom. In the Book of Revelation, a great multitude, with a sound like many waters and like mighty peals of thunder, cried out:

> *Let us rejoice and be glad and give glory to Him, for the marriage supper of the Lamb has come and His bride has made herself ready. . . .*
>
> *And he said to me, "Write, Blessed are those who are invited to the marriage supper of the Lamb." And he said to me, "These are true words of God."* (Rev. 19:7,9)

These words signify that the marriage supper of the Lamb—Christ's great wedding feast—has come. The angel's proclamation in Revelation places the start of the marriage supper at the end of the Great Tribulation and at the defeat of the Antichrist. Thus, the celebration of the wedding feast is coincident with and representative of the reign of Christ's Bride on the earth. The Bride of Christ, *"having no spot or wrinkle or any such thing; but . . . holy and blameless"* (Eph. 5:27), has prepared herself for the wedding feast. And what a glorious feast it will be!

Dispensationalists often draw analogies between Christ's coming for His Bride and the Hebrew marriage tradition of Jesus' day when trying to prove the validity of a pretribulation rapture.[1] But the simple fact remains: The wedding feast precedes the actual joining of the Bridegroom to the Bride on the wedding night—a blissful moment which will happen only when she is joined to Him at His second coming. This is illustrated in chapter 29 of Genesis:

> *Then Jacob said to Laban, "Give me my wife, for my time is completed, that I may go in to her."*
>
> *And Laban gathered all the men of the place, and made a feast.*
>
> *Now it came about in the evening that he took his daughter Leah, and brought her to him; and Jacob went in to her.* (Gen. 29:21-23)

Before the two become one on their wedding night, Christ is the Bridegroom and the Church is the Bride. Only after that sweet night—when Jesus comes back and she is raptured into His presence—are they truly husband and wife.

This is illustrated at the marriage supper where the church is referred to as the Bride of the Lamb. Paul further describes her as a virgin waiting for her Bridegroom's coming (2 Cor. 11:2). Only after the consummation, when Jesus comes back for her and she finds her home in the new heavens and the new earth, is she exclusively referred to as His wife (Rev. 21:9). Paul also portrays this in Ephesians when he writes:

> *For this reason a man will leave his father and mother and be united to his wife, and the two will become one flesh.*
>
> *This is a profound mystery—but I am talking about Christ and the church.* (Eph. 5:31, 32, NIV)

Nevertheless, until that time a multitude of saints from every nation will celebrate the wedding feast at God's temple in Jerusalem. They will celebrate the Bride's victory in the earth; a victory accomplished for her by her soon-coming Bridegroom.

The Parable of the Ten Virgins

Jesus spoke of the wedding feast in the gospel of Matthew. He did so in two intriguing parables—the one about the ten virgins, and the other about the King who gave a wedding feast for His son.

The parable of the ten virgins (Matt. 25:1-13) is a story portraying the future salvation of the Jews when they meet their Messiah. It talks about five wise virgins who brought oil for their lamps while waiting for the Bridegroom's arrival and of five foolish virgins who forgot their oil. Classical dispensationalism attributes this parable to the judgment of the Jewish remnant at the end of the tribulation.[2, 3]

What distinguishes this parable from New Testament passages on Christ's second coming is that both the believing wise virgins and the unbelieving foolish virgins anticipate meeting the Bridegroom, the Messiah (v. 1). Yet, only the five wise virgins, the ones who brought oil for their flasks, meet Him when He arrives and enter with Him into the wedding feast (v. 10). Also, even though they were left outside the door, destruction does not immediately come upon the five foolish virgins (vv. 11, 12). Finally, prior to meeting the bridegroom, the virgins are bridesmaids (Ps. 45:14), not the actual bride. They have no notion of their relationship to the Messiah as that of a bride to her bridegroom.

In this parable, the "meeting" of the bridegroom is an introduction rather than a rendezvous. The ten virgins are the Jewish people who anticipate meeting the Bridegroom, the Messiah. The bridegroom's delaying and the virgins' falling asleep symbolize how they missed their Messiah at His First Advent. The foolish virgins who forgot their oil, which symbolizes the Holy Spirit, are those Jews who because of their unbelief also will not meet the Lord Jesus after the Spirit's outpouring at the close of the seventieth week. The wise virgins who brought their oil are those Jews who will meet Him and will light their lamps by receiving the full outpouring of His Spirit.

After meeting the Bridegroom, the five virgins who were prepared enter with Him into the wedding feast. With Jesus in their lives, they will enter into the marriage supper of the Lamb. After that the door is shut. The Greek word for "door" in this parable is thura, which literally means a door or a gate. After the gate is shut, the five foolish virgins are not allowed to enter the wedding feast.

> *And while they [the foolish virgins] were going away to make the purchase, the bridegroom came, and those who were ready went in with him to the wedding feast; and the door was shut.*

> *And later the other virgins also came, saying, "Lord, lord, open up for us."*
>
> *But he answered and said, "Truly I say to you, I do not know you."* (Matt. 25:10-12)

The shutting of the gate in this parable might well symbolize the shutting of the temple sanctuary's east gate in Ezekiel (Ezek. 44:1). After the glory of God's outpouring and His entering of the temple sanctuary via the east gate—the event that marks the start of the marriage supper and kingdom period—only those Jews who have met Jesus as their Messiah will be allowed to enter the wedding feast. The gate will be shut on all the rest.

This is a difficult parable, but if true it predicts exactly what Daniel prophesied in chapter 9 of his book: the salvation of the Jews will be fulfilled in the seventieth week, the time frame of the tribulation. For those Jews who miss this last appointed meeting with their Messiah, sad to say, there will be no other chance.

The Inheritance of Israel

With their conversion into the body of Christ, the nation of Israel will finally receive the full blessings of God's promises made in the Abrahamic and Davidic Covenants—blessings that are now entered through the New Covenant in Jesus' blood. They will no longer be Israel solely according to the flesh, which in actuality is not truly Israel (Rom. 9:6, 8), but they will be Israel according to the promise, the children of promise—the true spiritual Israel that is the Church—who enter into the promises of God through faith in Jesus Christ (Rom. 4:13-17). As part of the Church, the olive tree of God, the nation of Israel will be complete partakers of the rich blessings bestowed upon Christ's Bride.

On top of this, the nation of Israel will obtain a unique geographical inheritance in the promised land. Matthew 25:32 clearly states that when Jesus comes back, there will be many nations on the earth. Israel, too, will be among them. Ezekiel predicts the geographical inheritance Israel will receive in Palestine in chapters 47 and 48 of his book. This will be all of the land God promised to Abraham's descendants in Genesis 15:18-21. Yet again, we need to realize it is the children of the promise—all who believe in Christ by faith—who are regarded as Abraham's descendants (Rom. 9:8). Therefore, those who are not Abraham's descendants according to the flesh—who are not Jews—but who are of the same faith as Abraham through belief in Jesus Christ

(Rom. 4:16), also will receive an inheritance in the holy land. For this reason Ezekiel instructs the native-born sons of Israel, the Jews:

> *And it will come about that you shall divide it [the holy land] by lot for an inheritance among yourselves and among the aliens who stay in your midst, who bring forth sons in your midst. And they shall be to you as the native-born sons of Israel; they shall be allotted an inheritance with you among the tribes of Israel.* (Ezek. 47:22)

This lone verse contains the ultimate solution to the Jewish-Palestinian problem—a solution that all of the war or terrorism or negotiation or subjugation or taking of land or dividing of land, will never accomplish. Only when the Jewish and Palestinian peoples are brothers and sisters in Christ will they ever dwell in harmony in the beautiful land. Only then.

The nation of Israel will hold a very special and exalted position among the nations in the saint's kingdom age. As the home of the holy city of Jerusalem—the center of the Christian faith—and as the guardian of the holy places, it will occupy a role among the nations much like Saudi Arabia does today as the guardian of Islam's holy cities of Mecca and Medina. In this future age, the fulfilled Jew will be loved and admired by all believers who come to worship the King at Jerusalem. For in Zechariah it says: *"Thus says the Lord of Hosts, 'In those days ten men from all the nations will grasp the garment of a Jew saying, "Let us go with you, for we have heard that God is with you" ' "* (Zech. 8:23).

The Parable of King's Wedding Feast

Jesus described another parable of the marriage supper to His disciples; that of a king who gave a wedding feast for his son. Just as the parable of the ten virgins applies to the Jewish people, this wedding feast parable applies to the Gentiles.

> *The kingdom of heaven may be compared to a king, who gave a wedding feast for his son. . . .*
>
> *Then he said to his slaves, "The wedding is ready, but those who were invited were not worthy.*
>
> *"Go therefore to the main highways, and as many as you find there, invite to the wedding feast."*
>
> *And those slaves went out into the streets, and gathered together all they found, both evil and good; and the wedding hall was filled with dinner guests.*

> *But when the king came in to look over the dinner guests, he saw there a man not dressed in wedding clothes, and he said to him, "Friend, how did you come in here without wedding clothes?" And he was speechless.*

> *Then the king said to the servants, "Bind him hand and foot, and cast him into the outer darkness; in that place there shall be weeping and gnashing of teeth."*

> *For many are called, but few are chosen.* (Matt. 22:2, 8-14)

Verses 3 through 7, which are not shown here, deal with the Jews who rejected the King's initial invitation by spurning and crucifying Christ at His first coming. They also describe how in retaliation, the King sent armies to destroy *"those murderers"* and their city (v. 7). This signifies the Roman army under Titus destroying Jerusalem in 70 A.D.

After deeming those first invited as unworthy, slaves who are the heralds of the gospel go out and gather all they find, both good and evil, into the wedding hall until it is brimming with guests. This illustrates how *"the wedding feast"* reign of the Bride will be a time of great evangelism on the earth; a time when the *"gospel of the kingdom shall be preached in the whole world for a witness to all the nations"* (Matt. 24:14). It also shows how both good and evil, both believers and unbelievers, will enter the Wedding Feast. When the King arrives, the man not wearing wedding garments—the one who has not been redeemed by Christ—is asked by the King: *"Friend, how did you come in here without wedding clothes?"* Unable to answer, the King commands His servants to bind him hand and foot and cast him into outer darkness. This symbolizes how at the end of the age, the Son of Man will send forth His holy angels to weed out of His kingdom the tares from amongst the wheat (Matt. 13:36-43).

What needs to be realized about this parable is that many without wedding clothes (those not redeemed) entered the wedding hall. Still, only one individual was singled out by the King when He arrived for not wearing them. The rest must have changed garments during the feast. This implies that many will be saved during the marriage supper. The King cares only if the guests have on wedding clothes when He arrives. He really does not care if the guests put them on before or during the feast. Even though those waiting until this last moment are taking a tremendous risk, the parable, nevertheless, illustrates the unsurpassable grace of God who will bring souls into His Kingdom right up until the very instant prior to His Son's return.

From the two wedding feast parables, it might be asked why the nonbelieving Gentiles are allowed to enter the wedding feast while the nonbelieving Jews are not. The simplest answer is that the nonbelieving Jews, by rejecting Christ's perfect sacrifice on the cross, will want to continue sacrificing animals in the temple for the purpose of atonement, outraging God. If allowed to do so, they would become a tremendous obstruction to the celebration of the marriage supper. The nonbelieving Gentiles will cause no such problem. Thank God, countless Jews will not fall into this category but will come to know Jesus Christ as their Messiah!

All in all, the wedding feast will be a time for celebrating and rejoicing. It will be a time to celebrate the Bride's victory in the world and to rejoice over her marriage to the King. It will be a time to anticipate their soon, imminent, joining on their wedding night—their rapture at His second coming.

Christ's resplendent Bride has made herself ready. This is the Bride for whom Jesus is coming—a united, overcoming Bride without sect or denomination; a mature, splendorous, and conquering Church whose raiment is white, *"having no spot or wrinkle or any such thing; but . . . holy and blameless"* (Eph. 5:27); a Bride adorned with the Spirit of God, winning over the multitudes to Jesus Christ—and reigning upon the earth. Jesus will not return for anything less, for He is too glorious a Bridegroom indeed.

At the same time, a chronology placing Jesus' second advent after His Bride has reigned on the earth for a season of unspecified duration is the only eschatology that places Jesus' second coming at the consummation of the age on the last day, while leaving the exact day and hour of His return a mystery. This can't be said of the premillennial position. Placing Jesus' second advent at the end of the Great Tribulation allows it to be traced from either the beginning of Daniel's seventieth week or the abomination of desolation. In fact, Lindsey is bold enough to say that from the signing of the Antichrist's protection treaty with Israel— beginning Daniel's seventieth week—there "will be exactly . . . 2,520 days, until the second coming of Jesus the Messiah." [4] He predicts this even though Jesus clearly said: *"But of that day and hour no one knows, not even the angels of heaven, nor the Son, but the Father alone"* (Matt. 24:36). At the completion of the Bride's reign and at a time known only to the Father, Jesus will come back to receive His beloved for Himself.

Satan Loosed After His 1000 Years

Near the consummation of this world and the completion of the Lamb's marriage supper, at a far away place in another dimension of time and space, the thousand years of Satan's imprisonment will draw to a close. When he is released from the abyss, the devil will go forth to deceive the nations once more.

> *And when the thousand years are completed, Satan will be released from his prison,*
>
> *and will come out to deceive the nations which are in the four corners of the earth, Gog and Magog, to gather them together for the war; the number of them is like the sand of the seashore.*
>
> *And they came up on the broad plain of the earth and surrounded the camp of the saints and the beloved city. . . .* (Rev. 20:7-9a)

Predicting this last great deception would take place after the Great Tribulation, Jesus warned:

> *Then if anyone says to you, "Behold, here is the Christ," or "There He is," do not believe him.*
>
> *For false Christs and false prophets will arise and will show great signs and wonders, so as to mislead, if possible, even the elect.*
>
> *Behold, I have told you in advance.*
>
> *If therefore they say to you, "Behold, He is in the wilderness," do not go forth, or, "Behold, He is in the inner rooms," do not believe them.*
>
> *For just as the lightening comes from the east, and flashes even to the west, so shall the coming of the Son of Man be.* (Matt. 24:23-27)

Jesus is evidently referring to the inner rooms of the temple in verse 26. He warns that if anyone says " *'Behold, He is in the inner rooms* [of the temple], *'do not believe them.* "In spite of his impending defeat, Satan will attempt to deceive the world's inhabitants one last time, especially those who still will not believe in Jesus Christ. He will entice them to rebel against the saints of the Highest One and will lead them out to war.

The unbelieving of the earth will gather together for war from the far corners of the globe, from Gog and Magog, to *"the camp of the saints and the beloved city.* "They will come to Israel and Jerusalem, the center of the Christian faith. Once again, Jerusalem will come under siege from the nations of the world. The prophet Joel prophesied about this final great gathering for battle in the *"valley of decision"* when he wrote.

> Proclaim this among the nations:
> Prepare a war; rouse the mighty men!
> Let all the soldiers draw near, let them come up!
> Beat your plowshares into swords,
> And your pruning hooks into spears; . . .
> Let the nations be aroused
> And come up to the valley of Jehoshaphat,
> For there I will sit to judge
> All the surrounding nations. . . .
> Put in the sickle, for the harvest is ripe. . . .
> Multitudes, multitudes in the valley of decision!
> For the day of the Lord is near in the valley of decision. (Joel
3:9-10a, 12-13a, 15)

Joel's passage is a specific reference to the final climactic second battle of Gog and Magog that will follow the kingdom reign of the Bride. There is no way this battle can be a description of Armageddon, which occurs at the close of the tribulation. For before Joel's battle, the nations will *"beat their plowshares into swords and their pruning hooks into spears,"* the exact opposite of what will happen after the saints triumph over the Antichrist and possess the kingdom on earth (Isa. 2:4). The climate of the world leading up to and throughout the Great Tribulation is characterized by war and rumors of war (Matt. 24:6, 7), until its climax at Armageddon. The globe's western and eastern powers will be armed with a great array of nuclear and conventional weapons. Prior to Armageddon there will be no need to beat plowshares into swords and pruning hooks into spears. Only before the second battle of Gog and Magog, at the end of the saints' righteous reign, when there are no weapons of battle, will the world's rebellious nations need to transform their instruments of peace into instruments of war.

Whereas in Revelation 16 the place of battle is called Armageddon, which translated means "a place of slaughter," in Joel the nations are gathered together to the valley of Jehoshaphat, which literally means "Yahweh judges." The purpose of this battle will be to gather the nations together for judgment, for the prophet says, *"the day of the Lord is near in the valley of decision."* Oh how that valley will truly be a place of decision! The unsaved of the world will gather there, and this will be their last opportunity to make the decision to receive Jesus Christ.

The Plundering of Jerusalem

The prophet Zechariah describes the capture of Jerusalem, the city of the saints, during this final battle when he writes:

> *Behold, a day is coming for the Lord when the spoil taken from you will be divided among you.*

> *For I will gather all the nations against Jerusalem to battle, and the city will be captured, the houses plundered, the women ravished, and half of the city exiled, but the rest of the people will not be cut off from the city.* (Zech. 14:1-2)

There are several reasons why the battle described here is different from the one described in Zechariah 12:2-9 and 14:12-15, passages that describe the Battle of Armageddon prior to Israel's salvation. The commonalties between Zechariah 12:2-9 and Zechariah 14:12-15 indicate they are parallel passages. Both mention Judah fighting at Jerusalem (Zech. 12:6-8, 14:14). In both, the Lord's method of punishing the nations fighting against Jerusalem is strikingly similar: every horse is struck with blindness and every rider with madness (Zech. 12:4), while a great panic from the Lord falls on all of them (Zech. 14:13). Both passages are followed by events dealing with either the end of the Great Tribulation—the Holy Spirit's outpouring on the house of Israel (Zech. 12:10)—or the start of the kingdom period in Israel—the nation's celebrating the Feast of Booths at Jerusalem (Zech. 14:16).

In Zechariah 12, Jerusalem under siege is described as a cup that causes reeling to the peoples round about (Zech. 12:2). She is a heavy stone for all the peoples, one that severely injures all who lift her. The inhabitants of Jerusalem are described as once again dwelling on their own sites in Jerusalem (Zech. 12:6), while the clans of Judah describe the inhabitants of Jerusalem as a strong support for them through the Lord of Hosts (Zech. 12:5). Everything indicates Jerusalem during the Battle of Armageddon, despite being besieged, is an unconquerable stronghold against the enemy, a true bulwark. After the battle, spoil of gold and silver and wealth from the surrounding nations are gathered to her (Zech. 14:14).

In Zechariah 14:1-2, however, instead of being a cup that causes reeling or a strong bulwark, Jerusalem is captured before the Lord intervenes. Her houses are plundered, her women are ravished, and half the city is exiled.[5] Consequently, there is no possible way Zechariah 14:1-2 can be describing the same battle as Zechariah 12 and Zechariah 14:12-15. It must be a prophecy of a battle to take place after Armageddon. In Zechariah 14:1-2, spoil is not gathered from the nations to Jerusalem. After half of Jerusalem falls, the spoil already there is now taken from her.

Zechariah 14 begins with the Lord's promise to regain the spoil, for the nations of the earth will gather against Jerusalem. It will be captured, its houses will be plundered, and half the city will be exiled. Still, once again the Lord God will go forth to battle for His Bride. For as the prophet writes:

> *Then the Lord will go forth and fight against those nations, as when He fights on a day of battle.*
>
> *And in that day His feet will stand on the Mount of Olives, which is in front of Jerusalem on the east; and the Mount of Olives will be split in its middle from east to west by a very large valley, so that half of the mountain will move toward the north and the other half toward the south.*
>
> *And you will flee by the valley of My mountains, for the valley of the mountains will reach to Azel; yes, you will flee just as you fled before the earthquake in the days of Uzziah king of Judah. . . .* (Zech. 14:3-5a)

Premillennialists enthusiastically teach how this passage describes Jesus at His second advent standing on the Mount of Olives, causing it to split down the middle from east to west as the Jews who have just received Him as their Savior flee to safety through its midst. Astonishing as it may seem, these words do not portray Christ. The key to proving this idea lies at the end of verse 5, which says: "*. . . Then the Lord, my God, will come, and all the holy ones with Him!*" (Zech. 14:5b).

If verse 4 describes Jesus standing on the Mount of Olives, meaning He has already come, then why does Zechariah in verse 5 say, "*Then the Lord, my God, will come, and all the holy ones with Him!*"? The end of verse 5 is indisputably a reference to Jesus' second coming with His holy angels and departed saints. But if Jesus already came causing the earthquake in verse 4, why does Zechariah say He will come again after the earthquake (in verse 5)? Can you see this contradiction? Because of this we can only conclude that verse 4 is not talking about Jesus standing on the Mount of Olives.

But if it is not Jesus on the Mount, who is it? It can only be one other person. In the Old Testament it was the glory of God, not Jesus, who went before the Israelites to battle against their enemies. At the end of the tribulation, the glory of God, the Spirit of Jesus, will go forth to fight against the Antichrist. And finally here at the consummation, the divine glory of God—the Holy Spirit—will go forth to fight *"against those nations, as when He fights on a day of battle."* Departing from the temple's most holy place, He will stand on the Mount of Olives just as He did the last time He departed the temple during the Jew's Babylonian exile. *"And the glory of the Lord went up from the midst of the city, and stood over the mountain which is east of the city"* (Ezek. 11:23).

After the glory of God stands on the Mount of Olives and causes it to split, Jesus Christ and *"all the holy ones with Him"* will return to rescue His Bride. He *"shall be revealed from heaven with His mighty angels in flaming fire, dealing out retribution to those who do not know God and to those who do not obey the gospel of our Lord Jesus"* (2 Thess. 1:7b, 8). This verse in Second Thessalonians provides the meaning behind the fire John saw in Revelation, when he prophesied against the nations who rebel against the saints of the Most High: *"and fire came down from heaven and devoured them"* (Rev. 20:9b).

And after the Son of God comes:

> . . . *it will come about in that day that there will be no light; the luminaries will dwindle.*
>
> *For it will be a unique day which is known to the Lord, neither day nor night, but it will come about that at evening time there will be light.*
>
> *And it will come about in that day that living waters will flow out of Jerusalem, half of them toward the eastern sea and the other half toward the western sea; it will be in summer as well as in winter.*
>
> *And the Lord will be king over all the earth; in that day the Lord will be the only one, and His name the only one. . . .*
>
> *And the people will live in it, and there will be no more curse, for Jerusalem will dwell in security.* (Zech. 14:6-9, 11)

Zechariah 14:6-11 describes the New Heavens, the New Earth and the New Jerusalem, not the "millennium" as dispensationalists teach. In comparing this passage to Revelation chapters 21 and 22, we see that both predict (1) how the sun and the moon, the luminaries, will disappear (Zech. 14:6, Rev. 21:23), (2) how there will be no night (Zech. 14:7, Rev. 22:5), (3) how living waters will flow out of Jerusalem (Zech. 14:8, Rev. 22:1), (4) how in that day the Lord will be King over all the earth, and His name the only name (Zech. 14:9, Rev. 22:3) and (5) how there will be no more curse (Zech. 14:11, Rev. 22:3).

Oh, what a glorious day it will be when Jesus comes back! Zechariah's prophecy is one more proof that Jesus' second coming will bring about the consummation: the end of this world to be immediately followed by the creation of a new heavens and a new earth wherein righteousness will dwell.

The end of the saints' earthly kingdom is last described in chapter 12 of Daniel. For in it the angel speaks:

> *And there will be a time of distress such as never occurred since there was a nation until that time; and at that time your people, everyone who is found written in the book, will be rescued.*
>
> *And many of those who sleep in the dust of the ground will awake, these to everlasting life, but the others to disgrace and everlasting contempt.*
>
> *And those who have insight will shine brightly like the brightness of the expanse of heaven, and those who lead the many to righteousness, like the stars forever and ever.*
>
> *But as for you, Daniel, conceal these words and seal up the book until the end of time; many will go back and forth, and knowledge will increase.*
>
> *And one said to the man [angel] dressed in linen, who was above the waters of the river, "How long will it be until the end of these wonders?"*
>
> *And I heard the man dressed in linen, who was above the waters of the river, as he raised his right hand and his left toward heaven, and swore by Him who lives forever that it would be for a time, times, and half a time; and as soon as they finish shattering the power of the holy people, all these events will be completed.* (Dan. 12:1b-7)

The angel here is foretelling to Daniel three events and the time frames in which they will occur. In verse one he predicts the Great Tribulation and the salvation of the Jewish people. In verse two the angel describes the resurrection of the dead. In verse three he portrays the rapture—which includes the resurrection of the righteous—and the glorified state of the believers who are transformed by it. Jesus spoke similar words to depict the splendor of the transformed righteous after His second coming: *"Then the righteous will shine forth as the sun in the kingdom of their Father"* (Matt. 13:43a).

In verse 7, the angel answers the question: *"How long will it be until the end of these wonders?"* He answers it in two parts. In the first part, *"that it would be for a time, times and half a time* [three-and-one-half years]," he confirms the length of the Great Tribulation.

It is the verse's second part— *"and as soon as they finish shattering the power of the holy people"*—however, that is crucial to determining when the rapture and the resurrection will occur. The Hebrew word for "shattering" in this verse, *naphats*, literally means to "dash to pieces" or to "beat to sunder." The Hebrew word for power, *yad*, literally means "a hand" and indicates power or authority. These are important words because they do not allow the rapture or the resurrection to take place at or before the end of the Great Tribulation.

Yad is the same word Abraham used to describe the authority Sarah held over her maid Hagar: "Behold your maid is in your power (hand); do to her what is good in your sight" (Gen. 16:6). During the Great Tribulation the Antichrist will be in power, not the saints, and they will be "given into his hand (*yad*) for a time, times, and half a time (Dan. 7:25). He will wage war on them and will be overpowering them (Dan. 7:21). Yet, he will never completely subdue or shatter (*naphats*) them. He will only "wear them down" (Dan. 7:25)—the Chaldean word *bela* literally means "to afflict"—until they are ultimately victorious (Rev. 15:2) and the time arrives for them to take possession of the kingdom (Dan. 7:22).

Therefore, *"as soon as they finish shattering the power of the holy people"* can refer only to the end of a season when the saints have power on the earth, ultimately proving that Christ's Bride must reign on this planet. Her worldly reign will come to an end after the loosing of Satan, after the rebellion of the nations (Rev. 20:7-9) and after the rebels' capture and plunder of the holy city of Jerusalem (Zech. 14:1-3). It is only after *"they finish shattering the power of the holy people"* that all of the wonders the angel spoke of—the salvation of the Jews, the rapture, and the resurrection of the dead—will be completed. The kingdom of Christ's Bride will have come to an end. Her hand will have been broken—but only on the earth, for her jealous Bridegroom Jesus Christ, allowing it just for a moment, will return with great power and glory to rescue His beloved Bride. And along with Him, she shall *"possess the kingdom [of heaven] forever, for all ages to come"* (Dan. 7:18b). Amen.

Notes

1. Lindsey, *The Rapture*, 110-111.

2. Pentecost, *Things to Come*, 282-284.

3. Lindsey, *The Rapture*, 145.

4. Lindsey, *The Rapture*, 7.

5. This will likely happen to the unbelieving of the city.

13
THE LAST DAY:
THE DAY OF
THE LORD

The prophet Joel wrote about the approaching Day of the Lord:

> *The sun will be turned into darkness,*
> *And the moon into blood,*
> *Before the great and awesome day of the Lord comes.*
> *And it will come about that whoever calls on the name of the*
> Lord
> *Will be delivered;*
> *For on Mount Zion and in Jerusalem*
> *There will be those who escape,*
> *As the Lord has said,*
> *Even among the survivors whom the Lord calls.* (Joel 2:31, 32)

As the Apostle Paul said, the Day of the Lord will come like a thief in the night, bringing with it swift destruction. It will be just as in the days of Noah: *"For in those days which were before the flood they were eating and drinking, they were marrying and giving in marriage, until the day that Noah entered the ark, and they did not understand until the flood came and tool them all away; so shall the coming of the Son of Man be"* (Matt. 24:38, 39).

But, for those of us not in darkness, Jesus promised that day will not overtake us like a thief, for we are sons and daughters of the light. Michelangelo's fresco masterpiece *The Last Judgment*, in the Vatican's Sistine Chapel is, more than any historical artistic work, the most awesome depiction of that great and glorious day. But, in contrast to Michelangelo's inspiration behind *The Last Judgment*, which was his fear of being judged unworthy on the day of resurrection,[1] the real greatness of the last day will be in the astonishing joy that accompanies the greatest marriage in history: the joining of the great Son of God to His eternal Bride.

What a day of startling paradoxes it will be! It will be a day of terrifying grief for those who do not know God, and in spite of its frightening awe, a day of unsurpassed exhilaration for those longing for His return. It will be a time of perfect and everlasting union, but also one of total and final separation. The blissful and eternal union will be of the Bridegroom to the Bride. The ultimate separation will be of the ungodly from the one true God whom they refused to believe. It will usher in resurrected life for the redeemed, and unending death for the damned. It will originate a brilliant new creation, and lock the door on an everlasting destruction. Thick darkness and radiant light both will be its canopies. It will be a day of shocking disparities. Evil will be forever destroyed, as everlasting truth is ushered in for the future, eternal ages. Time as we know it will end. Eternity as we can only dream of will begin. It will be on that day as the prophet Zechariah writes, *"the Lord will be king over all the earth; in that day the Lord will be only one, and His name the only one"* (Zech. 14:9).

The Day of Judgment

Starting with Augustine, the terms the "Last Day" and the "Day of Judgment" have been used extensively in classic amillennial thought to describe the Day of the Lord. Augustine wrote about the day of judgment in *The City of God*. To him, the day of judgment, the day of the Lord, and the last day were all one and the same, and concurrent with it would be the resurrection of the dead (p. 714).

Regarding Jesus' parable of the wheat and the tares (Matt. 13:36-43), Augustine wrote: "He [Jesus] did not name the judgment or the day of judgment, but indicated it much more clearly by describing the circumstances [of it], and foretold that it should take place in the end of the world."[2] Likewise, the saint called Jesus' parable of the sheep and goats (Matt. 25:31-46), "the passage which speaks of the separation of the good from the wicked by the most efficacious and final judgment of Christ."[3]

Augustine's emphasis of the last day as the ever-approaching Judgment Day affected the Church's attitude toward if for centuries to come. As Althaus writes: "The medieval church . . . spoke of the Last Day. It placed the emphasis, however, completely on its significance for the individual as the day of judgment."[4] This societal mind-set explains Michelangelo's inspiration behind *The Last Judgment* as one born out of fear, rather than one born out of hopeful expectation.

Martin Luther brought back to the church a renaissance of hope in its concept of the last day. Says Althaus: "The Middle Ages feared the Day of Wrath but Luther desires the coming of Jesus. . . . [Thus,]

Luther can call it 'the most happy Last Day.' Therewith, the early Christian attitude toward the Last Day was renewed and brought back to life."[5] His statement is so true. For Christians today who know and love Jesus Christ, it is the day for which our hearts yearn.

The Day of His Return

On the last day, the Lord Himself will return for His beloved Bride, *"descending from heaven with a shout; with the voice of the archangel, and with the trumpet of God"* (1 Thess. 4:16). As also told in the gospel of Matthew:

> *and then the sign of the Son of Man will appear in the sky, and then all the tribes of the earth will mourn, and they will see the Son of Man coming on the clouds of the sky with power and great glory.*
>
> *And He will send forth His angels with a great trumpet and they will gather together His elect from the four winds, from one end of the sky to the other.* (Matt. 24:30, 31)

Every Christian earnestly longs for this moment—the instant when we are reunited with our beautiful Lord, Jesus Christ. Jesus, not in humility as at His first coming, but in the eternal glory that He shares with the Almighty Father; not in weakness of the flesh, but in the eternal might and power of His everlasting majesty, His glory radiating brighter than the morning star. The Apostle John best describes the beauty and mystery of the moment when he writes:

> *Beloved, now we are children of God, and it has not appeared as yet what we shall be. We know that, when He appears, we shall be like Him, because we shall see Him just as He is.*
>
> *And everyone who has this hope fixed on Him purifies himself, just as He is pure.* (1 John 3:2-3)

Can you comprehend this awesome truth? In the twinkling of an eye, we will be like Him in every way; perfect, glorious, and imperishable, never again to taste of sin and death. We will be united with Him in the perfection of our future resurrected bodies—bodies that neither age, nor hurt, nor fail—never to be separated again. Saint Paul describes this final blessed bodily state when he writes to the Corinthians:

> *So also is the resurrection of the dead. It is sown a perishable body, it is raised an imperishable body;*

it is sown in dishonor, it is raised in glory, it is sown in weakness, it is raised in power;

it is sown a natural body, it is raised a spiritual body. If there is a natural body, there is also a spiritual body . . .

And just as we have borne the image of the earthly, we shall also bear the image of the heavenly.

Now I say this, brethren, that flesh and blood cannot inherit the kingdom of God; nor does the perishable inherit the imperishable.

Behold, I tell you a mystery; we shall not all sleep, but we shall all be changed,

in a moment, in the twinkling of an eye, at the last trumpet; for the trumpet will sound and the dead will be raised imperishable, and we shall be changed.

For this perishable must put on the imperishable, and this mortal must put on immortality.

But when this perishable will have put on the imperishable, and this mortal will have put on immortality, then will come about the saying that is written, "Death is swallowed up in victory.

O DEATH, WHERE IS YOUR VICTORY? O DEATH, WHERE IS YOUR STING?" (1 Cor. 15:42-44, 49-55)

How magnificent will be the Lord's second coming and the transformation it will bring! Such splendor is beyond comprehension. The Bridegroom's appearance is an utter bliss we can only joyfully anticipate.

The Resurrection of the Last Day

Althaus writes, "The hope of the early church centered on the resurrection on the Last Day."[6] Martha, sister of Mary, reflected this hope at the onset of the Christian faith when she spoke to Jesus about her dead brother Lazarus, *"I know the he will rise again in the resurrection on the last day"* (John 11:24).

Martha's knowledge of the resurrection reflects how belief in the raising of the dead was common within the Judaism of Jesus' lifetime. Resurrection was one of the primary teachings of the Pharisees (Acts

23:6-8). Nonetheless, Martha most likely learned more about it from Jesus' own teaching on the subject. Four times in the sixth chapter of John's gospel, Jesus speaks of *"the resurrection on the last day."*

> *And this is the will of Him who sent Me, that of all that He has given Me I lose nothing, but raise it up on the last day.*

> *For this is the will of my Father, that everyone who beholds the Son and believes in Him, may have eternal life; and I Myself will raise him up on the last day. . . .*

> *No one can come to Me, unless the Father who sent Me draws him; and I will raise him up on the last day. . . .*

> *He who eats my flesh and drinks my blood has eternal life, and I will raise him up on the last day.* (John 6:39, 40, 44, 54)

Jesus' teaching on the last day exposes a major weakness in the theory of a pretribulation rapture and resurrection, which if true would have to occur on a day before the last day. This directly contradicts what Jesus said about when the resurrection of the dead will take place. The Lord clearly stated He would raise *"everyone who beholds the Son and believes in Him"* on the last day. Since He states this four times, we should believe Him.

The First Resurrection

Let us now tackle the major scripture obstacle that premillennialists use to contend the amillennial teaching of a literal, last-day-only resurrection. It is Revelation 20:4-6, the passage premillennialists say describes Christ's thousand-year reign on earth. In John's Apocalypse, the Apostle sees thrones and those who sit upon them.

> *And I saw thrones, and they sat upon them, and judgment was given to them. And I saw the souls of those who had been beheaded because of the testimony of Jesus and because of the word of God, and those who had not worshipped the beast or his image, and had not received the mark upon their forehead and upon their hand; and they came to life and reigned with Christ for a thousand years.*

> *The rest of the dead did not come to life until the thousand years were completed. This is the first resurrection.*

> *Blessed and holy is the one who has a part in the first resurrection; over these the second death has no power, but they*

will be priests of God and of Christ and will reign with Him for a thousand years. (Rev. 20:4-6)

Premillennial scholars constantly stress that any teaching about a single, all-encompassing resurrection of the dead on a final day of judgment is incorrect, since John makes a definite reference here to two resurrections separated by a thousand years. George Ladd writes in *The Blessed Hope:*

> Amillennialists deny that there are in fact two resurrections. They speak of the General Resurrection of all the dead. However, the teaching of two resurrections is a clear assertion of Scripture. . . . The Revelation speaks explicitly of a first resurrection at the beginning of the millennium, and then describes a second resurrection at the end of the millennium. . . . Any interpretation of this first resurrection which spiritualizes it and refuses to see a bodily resurrection of the same sort as the second resurrection does not do justice to the demands of the language. Two bodily resurrections are demanded.[7]

That John is talking about two bodily resurrections seems even more apparent when we consider the Greek verb *ezèzan* translated *"they came to life"* (Rev. 20:4-5) is never used in the New Testament for life after death except in bodily resurrection.[8]

Indeed, Augustine did foster the belief that the first resurrection of Revelation 20 was spiritual, a resurrection of the soul accomplished through faith in Christ, and that the second resurrection at the end of the "thousand years" was the general, bodily resurrection of all the dead. Nevertheless, I believe his teaching was based on his denial of an intervening earthly millennium. Augustine's belief in a single, general resurrection was based on his conviction that all the dead (righteous and wicked) would be raised on the last day at the judgment.

The scriptures do, however, give evidence that the bodily resurrections of the righteous and the wicked are separate and distinct, and that the resurrection of the righteous occurs first. Ladd cites how:

> Our Lord spoke of a resurrection of life (the first resurrection), and a resurrection of judgment (the second resurrection, John 5:29). He spoke of the resurrection of the just as though it was to be distinguished from the resurrection of the unjust (Luke 14:14). He spoke of those "that are accounted worthy to attain to . . . the resurrection of the dead" (Luke

20:35), indicating that it is a resurrection of some of the dead . . . a favored group who have been accounted worthy of [it]. . . . [9]

Premillennialists, by relying on the Revelation passage, separate these two resurrections by a period of a thousand years. They say the first resurrection will occur at the start of the Millennium when Jesus comes back, while the resurrection of the wicked will occur after the Millennium. Still, this contradicts Jesus' teaching of a last day only resurrection.

> *Do not marvel at this; for an hour is coming, in which all who are in the tombs shall hear his voice,*
>
> *and shall come forth; those who did the good deeds to a resurrection of life, those who committed the evil deeds to a resurrection of judgment.* (John 5:28, 29)

If Jesus' words are to be taken literally, the resurrection of the just and of the unjust must take place within an hour of each other on the last day.

The Dispensational View

Dispensationalists expand the premillennial concept of the first resurrection by teaching that it will occur in stages. The first phase will come at the rapture before the tribulation, when Christ returns for His church. The second stage—that of the tribulation martyrs and Old Testament saints—will occur after the tribulation. Dispensational theology is complicated even further when one considers those mortals who will live during a supposed earthly millennium. The deaths of the millennial-age believers would require also a post-thousand year resurrection of the righteous.

The theory of a pretribulation resurrection as a stage of the first resurrection can only be considered wishful thinking on the part of dispensationalists. The Greek word John used for the first resurrection is *protos*, which literally means "foremost (in time, place, order or importance)." In the chronology of Revelation, chapter 20, it occurs after the tribulation. If the posttribulation resurrection that John saw comes first, how then can a pretribulation resurrection precede it? It cannot. Why did John also not mention such an important event as a pretribulation rapture and resurrection of the Church in his Revelation passage? Because it simply does not exist. Ladd writes, "If in fact the first resurrection is divided into two parts . . . the Word of God ought to make this clear. The two stages of the first resurrection should be as clear as the fact of the two resurrections."[10]

Admittedly, I also believe the first resurrection will occur in two stages. But unlike dispensationalists, I believe both stages are described in Revelation 20:4-6. I also believe both stages, along with the second resurrection (the resurrection of the wicked), will occur on the last day.

The Thousand-Year Reign

The big question that needs to be answered about Revelation 20:4-6 before any interpretation can be given is, where does the scene take place? As mentioned in chapter 11, if it can be proven that this scene takes place on earth, the premillennialists have all the proof they need to support their view of a thousand-year earthly reign of Jesus Christ after His second coming. On the contrary, if it can be proven from these verses that the scene occurs in heaven, then the idea of an earthly millennium wherein Christ physically reigns will be disproved entirely.

The vision John saw will be fulfilled in heaven. The first indication that the scene will take place in heaven is by the presence of God the Father: "*. . . but they will be priests of God and Christ and will reign with Him for a thousand years.*" There is more proof still. The crucial key in determining where the scene takes place can be found by knowing the identity of two groups John saw: the ones who sat upon thrones, and of the rest of the dead who came to life after the thousand years were completed.

> *I saw thrones, and they sat upon them, and judgment was given to them. And I saw the souls of those who had been beheaded because of the testimony of Jesus and because of the word of God, and those who had not worshipped the beast or his image, and had not received the mark upon their forehead and upon their hand; and they came to life and reigned with Christ for a thousand years.*
>
> *The rest of the dead did not come to life until the thousand years were completed. This is the first resurrection.* (Rev. 20:4, 5)

The Ones Sitting Upon the Thrones

The style of John's writing implies he saw two separate groups of individuals in verse 4: a first group, those who are sitting upon the thrones, followed by a second, those who were beheaded for their testimony of Jesus and the word of God and who had not worshipped the Beast or his image. Ladd bears this out by writing:

John saw two groups of people: he saw thrones and people seated upon them to whom judgment was given. John says little about this first group because his main concern is with [the second,] those who have been slain by the Antichrist. . . .

The identity of the second group is clear. But who are contained in the first, undefined group? Only one possibility commends itself. They are the righteous who have died naturally, who have not been martyred. They are the saints in general, the "dead in Christ."[11]

I completely agree with Ladd on the identity of this first group seated on the thrones. They are the righteous who have died naturally in the Lord, the "dead in Christ" to whom judgment is given. Ladd, however, contends they will also come to life with the second group of martyrs before the thousand years, and that this constitutes the first resurrection.

Here I disagree with Ladd. In verse 4, it is obvious the martyrs will be resurrected before the thousand years. Verse 4, in the *New American Standard Bible,* is divided into two sentences. The first sentence describes the ones sitting on the thrones and their distinct role in the vision: *". . . and judgment was given to them."* The second sentence, which tells of the resurrection, describes the martyrs and their role: *"and they came to life and reigned with Christ for a thousand years."* Grammatically speaking, the martyrs are the "objects" John talks about in the second sentence. He does not even mention the ones sitting on the thrones. Consequently, it is the martyrs, not those sitting upon the thrones, who are subjects of his phrase, *"and they came to life."* By distinguishing the two groups and by stating that only the martyrs will be raised before the thousand years, John implies that those sitting upon the thrones, the *"dead in Christ,"* will not be resurrected at the start of the thousand years. Now let us address the question: Who are the rest of the dead who come to life after the thousand years are completed?

The Resurrection After the Thousand Years

Almost all premillennialists interpret the resurrection of the dead after "the thousand years" as the second resurrection: the resurrection of the wicked dead at the end of the millennium. Yet, if you read verse 5, by itself, this resurrection appears to be a part of the first resurrection, the resurrection of the righteous: *"The rest of the dead did not come to life until the thousand years were completed. This is the first resurrection"* (Rev. 20:5).

The *New International Bible* seemingly realized this problem and attempted to remedy it by incorrectly placing the first sentence of verse 5 in parentheses to make it appear only the martyrs of verse 4, and not the dead of verse 5, are referred to as having a part in the first resurrection.

> *And I saw the souls of those who had been beheaded because of their testimony for Jesus. . . . They came to life and reigned with Christ a thousand years.*

> *(The rest of the dead did not come to life until the thousand years were ended.) This is the first resurrection.* (Rev. 20:4b, 5, NIV)

At first glance this appears to make sense, for verse 6, a definite reference to the resurrected martyrs, says:

> *Blessed and holy is the one who has a part in the first resurrection; over these the second death has no power, but they will be priests of God and of Christ and will reign with Him for a thousand years.* (Rev. 20:6)

Nevertheless, John could not have been writing about the wicked being raised when he saw the rest of the dead come to life after the thousand years. The words *"come to life"* in verse 5 come from the Greek word *anazao*, which literally means "to recover life." *Anazao* comes from the Greek root word *zao*—meaning "to live"—used in verse 4 to describe the martyrs who come to life. Both are different forms of the Greek word for "life," *zoe*, used in John 5:29:

> *Do not marvel at this; for an hour is coming in which all who are in the tombs shall hear his voice,*

> *and shall come forth; those who did the good deeds to a resurrection of life [zoe], those who committed the evil deeds to a resurrection of judgment.* (John 5:28, 29)

The dead in Revelation 20:5 are raised to life (*anazao*), just as the martyrs in Revelation 20:4 (*zao*) and the righteous in John 5:29 (*zoe*) are raised to life. Nowhere do the New or Old Testaments mention that the wicked will be raised to life at the resurrection. They describe them as being raised to judgment, as in John 5:29 and Revelation 20:13, or *"to disgrace and everlasting contempt,"* as in Daniel.

> *And the sea gave up the dead which were in it, and death and Hades gave up the dead which were in them; and they were judged, everyone of them according to their deeds.* (Rev. 20:13)

> *And many of those who sleep in the dust of the ground will*
> *awake, these to everlasting life, but the others to disgrace and*
> *everlasting contempt.* (Dan. 12:2)

From the usage of the Greek word for "life" in the New Testament dealing with the resurrection, and from these scriptures describing the resurrection of the wicked dead, it becomes apparent the rest of the dead coming to life after the thousand years (Rev. 20:5) are a part of the first resurrection. To be more definitive, they are the righteous raised during the second stage of the first resurrection.

Now, let's take the entire passage in context by relating those raised to life at the end of the thousand years to the group sitting upon the thrones to whom judgment is given, a group we identified previously as the "dead in Christ," and whom we have asserted will not be resurrected with the martyrs at the beginning of the thousand years. In this context we can conclude only one thing. The two groups, the *"dead in Christ"* (v. 4), and the righteous raised after the thousand years (v. 5), are one and the same. Since they also are Christ's, it can be said of them as well:

> *Blessed and holy is the one who has a part in the first*
> *resurrection; over these the second death has no power, but they*
> *will be priest of God and of Christ and will reign with Him for*
> *a thousand years.* (Rev. 20:6)

Can you begin to see how the whole vision fits together? If the "dead in Christ" sitting on the thrones (who are raised after the thousand years) live and reign with Christ in their spirits for a "thousand years" prior to their bodily resurrection, what can we conclude about the location of their reign? It has to be in heaven. Only in heaven could all of the unresurrected saints of the past ages reign spiritually alongside Christ and the resurrected martyrs (raised prior to the thousand years), patiently awaiting their part in the first resurrection at the end of this heavenly millennium[12]—a millennium in paradise that will be completed at the moment of the Lord's second coming.

A Thousand Years as One Day

Some may now ask, how can a first resurrection with two stages separated by a thousand-year heavenly reign of Christ coincide with Jesus' promise to raise everyone who believes in Him on the last day? Remember from chapter 11 how Einstein's Theory of Relativity effects our concept of time. Einstein proved that time, like any other physical entity, is relative. It will vary in the physical realm depending on the frame of reference. And if it differs in the physical realm, how much more so will it when it transcends from the physical to the spiritual? Voicing Luther's opinion on this, Althaus writes:

> [Luther] knows that our earthly concepts and measurements of time are no long valid beyond death. For this reason, lapses of time such as we experience here are set aside. "Here you must put time out of your mind and know that in that world there is neither time nor measurement of time, but everything is one eternal moment." . . . Because our periods of time are no longer valid in God's eternity, the Last Day surrounds our life as an ocean surrounds an island. . . . everywhere the Last Day dawns in the great contemporaneity of eternity.[13]

This abstractness of time has been recorded in the near death experience. People who have reported these phenomena often describe visions of heaven where they claim the concept of time is completely different from what we experience on earth. Rebecca Springer, writing of such an experience in her book *Within the Gates,*[14] states "There was no measurement of time as we measure it here, although many still spoke in the mortal language of months, days, and years." Her encounter further validates how it is impossible to strictly equate a thousand-year duration in heaven to the passage of an equivalent thousand-year period on earth.

I am convinced the Apostle Peter was referring to this when he wrote:

> *But do not let this one fact escape your notice, beloved, that with the Lord one day is as a thousand years, and thousand years as one day.*

> *The Lord is not slow about His promise, . . . but is patient toward you, not wishing for any to perish but for all to come to repentance.*

> *But the day of the Lord will come like a thief, in which the heavens will pass away with a roar and the elements will be destroyed with intense heat, and the earth and its works will be burned up.* (2 Pet. 3:8-10)

Speaking in context of the last day—the day of the Lord and the day of judgment—and the promise of Christ's coming, Peter asserts that with the Lord, *"one day is as a thousand years and a thousand years as one day."* Since he is speaking of the last day, we can conclude that to the

Lord, the last day is as a "thousand years" and a "thousand years" as the last day. If you take Peter's statement and our notion of the relativity of heavenly time to earthly time, and place both in the context of Christ's thousand-year heavenly reign (occurring between two stages of the first resurrection) and Jesus' words that He will raise all believers on the last day, then you have solved the puzzle. All will be resurrected on the last day. The martyrs and the tribulation saints will come to life at the start of the last day (at the start of the thousand years in heaven), while the rest of the saints, the dead in Christ, will come to life at the end of the last day at the Lord's second coming (after the thousand years in heaven).

Consequently, according to relativity the saint's thousand-year reign with Christ must be a different time period than the thousand years of Satan's binding. Remember they occur in different places. The saint's reign with Christ is in heaven. Satan's binding is in the bottomless pit. Satan's thousand years will occur during the Kingdom reign of the Bride on earth and will be completed before the last day upon his release prior to the Second Battle of Gog and Magog (Rev. 20:7-9). Christ's thousand years begins with and ends on the last day.

Up until now, I have said a bodily resurrection of the martyrs will precede the resurrection of the "dead in Christ" at the Lord's second coming. We will look at scriptures that support this initial stage of the first resurrection next.

The Resurrection of the Martyrs

The Spanish Jesuit Ribera was the first to espouse the view that the first resurrection of Revelation 20 is a reign of the martyrs in the heavenly state. It will probably shock most futurists to also be told he was the first scholar in the modern era to return to the patristic, futuristic, interpretation of prophecy. Concerning him, Ladd writes:

> In 1590, Ribera published a commentary on the Revelation as a counter-interpretation to the prevailing view among Protestants which identified the Papacy with the Anti-christ.[15] Ribera applied all of Revelation but the earliest chapters to the end time rather than to the history of the Church. . . . On one subject, Ribera was not a futurist: he followed the Augustinian interpretation of the millennium in making the entire period between the cross and Antichrist. He differed from Augustine in making the 'first resurrection' to refer to the heavenly life of the martyrs when they would

reign in heaven with Christ throughout the millennium, i.e., the church age.[16]

Since verse 4 of Revelation 20 speaks of a reign of the martyrs, it is easy to see why Ribera was able to come to his interpretation.

Nonetheless, where Ribera believed the first resurrection is a depiction of the spiritual reign of the martyrs, a reign in their souls after physical death, I have shown it will be a bodily resurrection of all believers composed of two stages. In the first stage, Christ will raise up the Christian and Old Testament martyrs and all the saints who will die during the tribulation. This will occur at the outset of the last day before Christ's second coming. Such a "pre-Last Day" resurrection must also involve a bodily ascension of the raised martyrs since they will reign with Christ in heaven. Consequently, it must have support from scripture. The foundation for it comes from John's words in Revelation 20:4-6. Still, it has additional support. Take for instance the prophecy on Revelation regarding the two witnesses, who, after being killed with their corpses left lying in the streets for three-and-one-half days, are raised to life and taken up to heaven (Rev. 11:11-12).

Also, consider the verses describing the breaking of the fifth seal:

> *And . . . I saw underneath the altar the souls of those who had been slain because of the word of God, . . .*
>
> *and they cried out with a loud voice, saying, "How long, O Lord, holy and true, wilt Thou refrain from judging and avenging our blood on those who dwell on the earth?"*
>
> *and they were told that they should rest for a little while longer, until the number of their fellow servants and their brethren who were to be killed even as they had been, should be completed.* (Rev. 6:9-11)

The martyrs here are told to rest for a while longer until the number of their fellow brethren who are to be killed, as they have been, is complete. Hence, this scene occurs prior to the resurrection. The passage implies that after those still to be martyred in the future are killed, then all the martyrs will be raised from the dead. God's promise of their resurrection is conditional, not on the Lord's second coming, but on the last martyr being killed.

Consider also the following verse from Hebrews: *"Women received back their dead, raised to life again. Others were tortured and refused to be released, so that they might gain a better resurrection"* (Heb. 11:35, NIV).

What better resurrection were these martyrs striving for? While the immediate context suggests they were seeking the eternal resurrection available to all rather than the temporal one in the first part of the verse (cf. 1 Kings 17:23 and 2 Kings 4:36), a greater truth may be contained here. The author of Hebrews could not have meant those being tortured viewed their fate as means of achieving to the first resurrection. That would make salvation contingent on martyrdom. I believe the better resurrection for which they were striving is the first stage of the first resurrection, the resurrection of the martyrs.

In addition to the martyrs of the past, all who die in the Lord during the tribulation, whether they are martyrs or not, will partake in the martyr resurrection at the end of the age. This is clear from Revelation 20: *"And I saw the souls of those . . . who had not worshipped the beast or his image, and had not received the mark upon their forehead and upon their hand; and they came to life and reigned with Christ for a thousand years"* (Rev. 20:4). Compare these words to John's in Revelation 14 where, speaking of those who had not worshipped the Beast and his image nor received his mark, the Apostle proclaims:

> *Here is the perseverance of the saints who keep the commandments of God and their faith in Jesus.*
>
> *And I heard a voice from heaven, saying, "Write, 'Blessed are the dead who die in the Lord from now on!' " "Yes," says the Spirit, "that they may rest from their labors, for their deeds follow with them."* (Rev. 14:12, 13)

Revelation 20:4 illustrates the reward for those Christians who will die naturally during the terrible hardship of the Great Tribulation. It will be found in the divine privilege of being, along with the martyrs, the first believers to partake in the resurrection, and in the reigning with the Lord Jesus in heaven for a thousand years. What a beautiful blessing it will be for those servants of the Lord from every era who surrendered their lives even unto death!

First Fruits of the Resurrection

The first resurrection's initial stage can be seen in the first fruits of the resurrection Paul wrote about to the Corinthians. The idea of offering the first fruits of a harvest to God is common in the Bible. Here Paul appears to be assigning an order for those who will be raised:

> *But Christ has indeed been raised from the dead, the first fruits of those who have fallen asleep. . . .*

For as in Adam all die, so in Christ all will be made alive.

But each in his own turn: Christ, the first fruits; then, when he comes, those who belong to him.

Then the end will come . . . (1 Cor. 15:20, 22-24b, NIV)

In Paul's analogy, Christ is the firstfruits to God of those who have fallen asleep (v. 20). In the same way, the raised martyrs and the tribulation saints will be the firstfruits to Christ of those who sleep in Him. John could very well be portraying these when he saw the 144,000 of Revelation 14 standing with the Lamb upon the heavenly Mount Zion (cf. Heb. 12:22):

And I looked, and behold, the Lamb was standing on Mount Zion, and with Him one hundred and forty-four thousand, having His name and the name of His Father written on their foreheads. . . .

These are the ones who follow the Lamb wherever He goes. These have been purchased from among men as firstfruits to God and to the Lamb. (Rev. 14: 1, 4b)

This 144,000 is a different group than the one spoken of in Revelation chapter 7 (who we identified as Israel).[17] Since they follow the Lamb wherever He goes, they may well be the *complete* number of martyrs who, by their blood, will be purchased from among men as firstfruits to God and Christ. And since they are firstfruits, as Paul says in 1 Corinthians 15, they will be raised from the dead before those raised at Christ's second coming. And they shall live and reign with Him in His heavenly kingdom for a "thousand years" prior to His return.

Since the martyrs' rising from the grave will occur during the terrifying celestial signs preceding the day of the Lord (Matt. 24:29, Joel 2:31), it will be scarcely noticed by the inhabitants of the earth (cf. Matt. 27:51-53). And when the Lord descends from heaven with a shout at the end of that Day, these glorified overcomers will also return with Him (cf. 1 Thess. 3:13).

The Lord's Second Coming: The Rapture

With the martyrs' heavenly reign complete, the harvest at the end of the last day comes, consummating the end of the age when the Lord will return to rapture His Church. Concerning that blessed moment, the instant every Christian yearns for, the Apostle Paul writes:

> *But we do not want you to be uninformed, brethren, about those who are asleep, that you may not grieve, as do the rest who have no hope.* . . .
>
> *For the Lord Himself will descend from heaven with a shout, with the voice of the archangel, and with the trumpet of God; and the dead in Christ shall rise first.*
>
> *Then we who are alive and remain shall be caught up together with them in the clouds to meet the Lord in the air, and thus we shall always be with the Lord.*
>
> *Therefore comfort one another with these words.* (1 Thess. 4:16-18)

What a blessed hope we have knowing that some day we will be reunited with our loved ones who have gone before us. We will all be caught up together in the clouds to meet the Lord in the air. This will be the absolute climax of our faith: the Bride and the Bridegroom joined as one. And so we will always be with the Lord.

An Eschatology of the Last Day: Summary

No matter how much is said or written about the Day of the Lord, the day of Christ's coming will be a day beyond our wildest imaginations. Still, it is a day our hearts know will some day come to pass. Jesus, sitting at the right hand of power on the clouds of heaven and accompanied by His mighty angels, will come to receive His beloved Bride. As John the Revelator said, *"Behold, He is coming with the clouds, and every eye will see Him, even those who pierced Him; and all the tribes of the earth will mourn over Him. Even so. Amen"* (Rev. 1:7).

No one can hope to fully describe the events that will take place on that awesome day when mankind meets its maker. Even so, here is my attempt to chronologically summarize the events that will take place on the last day and in the days and hours immediately preceding it.

(1) With the saints' earthly reign complete as described in Daniel, chapter 12, Satan will be released from prison for a short time. He will once again go forth to deceive the nations and will start a rebellion among all who still have not come to believe in Jesus Christ. (Dan. 12:7, Rev. 20:7).

(2) Unbelievers from every nation will gather against the camp of the saints, the holy city of Jerusalem. The number of those who will gather against it are like the sand of the seashore (Rev. 20:8, 9 and Zech. 14:2.).

(3) The sun will then be darkened and the moon will not give its light; and stars will fall from the sky, and the powers of the heavens will be shaken (Matt. 24:29 and Joel 2:31).

(4) While the signs in the heavens are taking place, those who were martyred for their testimony of Jesus and the word of God, and those who had not worshipped the Beast or his image will be raised to life, signifying the start of the last day and the first resurrection (Rev. 20:4 and John 6:39, 40, 44, 54). The martyrs will reign with Christ in heaven for a thousand years throughout the duration of the last day (Rev. 20:4-6, 2 Pet. 3:7-10, and John 6:39, 40, 44, 54).

(5) The glory of God will then go forth from the temple to fight against those nations which are gathered against Jerusalem. In that day, His feet will stand on the Mount of Olives, (Ezek. 11:23 and Zech. 14:3-5). The Mount of Olives will be split in its middle from east to west by a large valley and the saints of Jerusalem will flee through the midst of it.

(6) Men and women will faint from fear and the expectation of the things coming upon the earth. Nevertheless, this is the time when Christians will lift their heads, for their redemption is near (Rev. 6:15, 16 and Luke 21:26, 28).

(7) The sign of the Son of Man will appear in the sky and all the tribes of the earth will mourn, and they will see the Son of Man coming on the clouds of heaven in power and great glory with all His holy ones, including the glorified martyrs who were raised at the beginning of the last day (Matt. 24:30; Rev. 1:7; 1 Thess. 3:13 and Zech. 14:5b). He will be revealed from heaven in blazing fire with His mighty angels (2 Thess. 1:7 and Rev. 20:9).

(8) He will send forth His angels to gather out of His kingdom all who commit lawlessness. The angels will bind the wicked hand and foot and will cast them alive into the fiery furnace that burns with brimstone. In that place there will be weeping and gnashing of teeth; one will be taken and one will be left (Matt. 13:41, 42; 22:11-13 and Luke 17:34-37).

(9) Satan is cast into the lake of fire (Rev. 20:10).

(10) The last trumpet will sound and the dead in Christ will rise first, then we who are alive and remain will be caught up together with them in the clouds to meet the Lord in the air (1 Thess. 4:16, 17; Matt. 24:31; Rev. 10:15–18 and John 6:39, 40).

(11) The saints will stand before the judgment (mercy) seat of Christ, each to receive their reward (2 Cor. 5:10). Within an hour of the first resurrection, the wicked dead will be raised—this is the second resurrection. They will stand before the throne of God's Son in judgment (Acts 17:31; John 5:28, 29; Rev. 20:11-13 and Matt. 25:31-46).[18]

(12) The righteous raised at the Lord's second coming will rise up in judgment against the unbelievers standing before the throne of Christ (Matt. 12:41-42 and Rev. 20:4a).[19]

(13) All who are not found written in the book of life are cast into the lake of fire (Rev. 20:15).

(14) The present heavens and the earth are destroyed by fire (2 Pet. 3:7. 10).

(15) God creates a new heaven and a new earth in which dwells righteousness (2 Pet. 3:13; Rev. 21, 22 and Zech. 14:6-11).

> And *"Behold, the tabernacle of God will be among men,*
> *and He shall dwell among them, and they shall be His people,*
> *and God Himself shall be among them, ... "* (Rev. 21:3)

And they shall live forever. Amen!

Notes

1. Robert John Clements, "Michelangelo," *The New Encyclopedia Britannica,* Macropædia, 15th ed.

2. St. Augustine, *The City of God,* translated by Marcus Dods, D.D. (New York: Random House, 1950), 715. Used by permission.

3. Ibid, 716.

4. Reprinted from *The Theology of Martin Luther* by Paul Althaus, copyright © 1966 Fortress Press, p. 419. Used by permission of Augsberg Fortress.

5. Ibid, 420-421.

6. Ibid, 413.

7. George Eldon Ladd, *The Blessed Hope* (Grand Rapids, MI: Wm. B. Eerdmans Publishing Co., 1984), 81. Used by permission of Wm. B. Eerdmans Publishing Co.

8. Quoted by Ladd in Clouse, 190.

9. Ladd, *The Blessed Hope,* 82.

10. Ibid, 81.

11. Ibid, 83.

12. Peter, James, and John witnessed a similar scene at Jesus' transfiguration on the Mount of Olives (Matt. 17:1-3). At the transfiguration, we see Jesus, in His eternal glory, present with Moses and Elijah. Moses, yet to be resurrected but still in glory, depicts the dead in Christ who have not been raised and who will reign with the Lord during the thousand years in heaven. Elijah, in the splendor of his glorified spiritual body, represents those who will come to life at the beginning of the thousand years. Peter and James depict the martyred saints, while John represents those who have gone to be with the Lord outside of martyrdom. What a beautiful analogy this is of John's vision.

13. Althaus, *The Theology of Martin Luther,* 416.

14. Rebecca Springer, *Within the Gates,* (Springdale: Whitaker House, 11984), 92.

15. Ribera, Ladd points out, also predicted the Antichrist would be a single evil person who would be received by the Jews and would rebuild Jerusalem, abolish Christianity, deny Christ, persecute the Church, and rule the world for three-and-a-half years.

16. Ladd, *The Blessed Hope,* 37-38.

17. Concerning this distinction Pentecost writes in *Things to Come:*

> It is commonly held that those in Chapter Seven are on earth and these [in Chapter Fourteen] in heaven, making Mt. Zion the heavenly city of Jerusalem. Those in Chapter Fourteen are said to be identified with the Lamb and those in Chapter Seven are not. Those in Chapter Seven are 'sealed' but those in Chapter Fourteen have 'the Father's name written in [their] foreheads.' (p. 299)

18. Revelation 20:13 depicts the second resurrection, which is also a bodily resurrection. The sea in these verses could be either literal or symbolic: i.e., those who perished at sea, or the dead from the (sea of) nations, will be raised up. Death represents the grave. That Hades gives up some of the dead is because the wicked who are alive at the Lord's second coming will be cast body and soul into hell prior to the judgment.

19. Augustine referred to Jesus' teaching on how the "men of Nineveh shall rise in the judgment with this generation, and shall condemn it: because they repented at the preaching of Jonah; and . . . a greater than Jonah is here" (Matt. 12:41). And how the "queen of the south shall rise up in the judgment with this generation, and shall condemn it: for she came from the uttermost

parts of the earth to hear the words of Solomon; and . . . a greater than Solomon is here" (Matt. 12:42). Says Augustine: "Two things we learn from this passage, that a judgment is to take place, and that it is to take place at the resurrection of the dead. For when He spoke of the Ninevites and the queen of the south, He certainly spoke of dead persons, and yet He said that they shall rise up in the day of judgment" (p. 714). I believe the judgment spoken of in these two passages is the enactment of the judgment given to "those sitting on the thrones" in Revelation 20:4a—when they come to life at the conclusion of the heavenly millennium after Jesus comes back to raise the dead at the end of the last day.

14
AN ETERNAL
LOVE STORY

[THE BRIDEGROOM]:
How beautiful you are, my darling,
How beautiful you are!
Your eyes are like doves behind your veil. . . .
Your lips are like a scarlet thread,
And your mouth is lovely.
Your temples are like a slice of a pomegranate
Behind your veil. . . .
Your two breasts are like two fawns,
Twins of a gazelle,
Which feed among the lilies. . . .

You are altogether beautiful, my darling,
And there is no blemish in you. . . .
You have made my heart beat faster, my sister, my bride;
You have made my heart beat faster with a single glance of
your eyes. . . .
How beautiful is your love, my sister, my bride!
How much better is your love than wine,
And the fragrance of your oils
Than all kinds of spices!
Your lips, my bride, drip honey; . . .
And the fragrance of your garments is like the fragrance of
Lebanon.
A garden locked is my sister, my bride,
A rock garden locked, a spring sealed up.
Your shoots are an orchard of pomegranates
With choice fruits, . . .
Nard and saffron, calamus and cinnamon,
With all the trees of frankincense,
Myrrh and aloes, along with all the finest spices. . . ."

[THE BRIDE]:

> *Awake, O north wind,*
> *And come, wind of the south;*
> *Make my garden breathe out fragrance,*
> *Let its spices be wafted abroad.*
> *May my beloved come into his garden*
> *And eat its choice fruits!*

(Song of Solomon 4)

As shown here in King Solomon's Song of Songs, so is the love between the Bridegroom and the Bride; how great is His love for her. Bill Hammond, author of the book *The Eternal Church*,[1] once stated, "the greatest longing and heart desire of Jesus is to receive His bride," to be eternally united with her, and to reign with her through the future ages.

Still, will He settle for a Bride who hasn't made herself ready? Will He receive a Bride who is divided and segmented? Will He come for a church that battles more within herself over doctrine than with the forces of darkness? Will He return for a church that compromises, one which the world mocks, or one that, through division, has no impact on the earth? Will he return for a church that is made up of more than 900 different denominations and sects, and has forgotten the Bridegroom's call—when He asked His Father to make them *"one, just as We are one; I in them, and Thou in Me, that they may be perfected in unity, that the world may know Thou didst send Me, and didst love them, even as Thou didst love Me"* (John 17:22b, 23)? I think not.

Christ will return only for a bride who is united, not for one that is divided. He will return for one Bride—one without division, sect, denomination, or any such thing, but is completely unified—one universal, catholic church comprising every nation, and tribe, and people, and language from the four corners of earth, including His first love, Israel.

He will return for a Bride who has learned the meaning of sacrifice—one who has learned to put the welfare of others before herself! For a Bride who has been tested through the fire of the tribulation as gold is tested, and refined as silver is refined (Zech. 13:9)—and who has emerged triumphant.

The Bridegroom will return only for a Bride who has conquered—for a Bride who, through the Spirit, has overcome the forces behind this evil world of darkness; for a Bride who has learned how to care for the humanity Christ died for; for one who has learned how to apply that most powerful of forces—love—to a royal reign over a creation He fashioned for her. He will return for a Bride who has ruled upon the earth and one who is prepared to reign with Him through the future aeons.

He will only come back for a Bride *"in all her glory, having no spot or wrinkle or any such thing; but . . . holy and blameless"* (Eph. 5:27)— one that is worthy to inhabit her eternal home, the New Jerusalem, as a Bride adorned in a garment of everlasting splendor (Rev. 21:2). Yes, Jesus will not settle for less, for He is too glorious a Bridegroom indeed.

Concerning the Bride and Her future home in the new heaven and the new earth, the new Jerusalem, an angel of the seven plagues of God spoke to the Apostle John and said:

> *Come here, I shall show you the bride, the wife of the Lamb.*
>
> *And he carried me away in the Spirit to a great and high mountain, and showed me the holy city, Jerusalem, coming down out of heaven from God, having the glory of God. Her brilliance was like a very costly stone, as a stone of crystal-clear jasper.*
>
> *It had a great and high wall, with twelve gates, and at the gates twelve angels; and names were written on them, which are those of the twelve tribes of the sons of Israel. . . .*
>
> *And the wall of the city had twelve foundation stones, and on them were the twelve names of the twelve apostles of the Lamb. . . .*
>
> *And the material of the wall was jasper; and the city was pure gold, like clear glass.*
>
> *The foundation stones of the city wall were adorned with every kind of precious stone. . . .*
>
> *And the twelve gates were twelve pearls; each one of the gates was a single pearl. And the street of the city was pure gold, like transparent glass.*
>
> *And I saw no temple in it, for the Lord God, the Almighty, and the Lamb, are its temple.*
>
> *And the city has no need of the sun or of the moon to shine upon it, for the glory of God has illumined it, and its lamp is the Lamb.*
>
> *And the nations shall walk by its light, and the kings of the earth shall bring their glory into it. . . .*

> *And there shall no longer be any night; and they shall not*
> *have need of the light of a lamp nor the light of the sun, because*
> *the Lord God shall illumine them; and they shall reign forever*
> *and ever.* (Rev. 21:9-24, Rev. 22:5)

Yes, this is the glory that awaits God's people—a glory that is eternal, in a place where time has no end and space has no boundaries, but where nature is resplendent and everything belongs to the all compassionate Creator. In this magnificent paradise, the Bride shall dwell with the Bridegroom. And together they shall reign forever. For it is written:

> *Behold, the tabernacle of God is among men, and He shall*
> *dwell among them, and they shall be His people, and God*
> *Himself shall be among them,*

> *and He shall wipe away every tear from their eyes; and there*
> *shall no longer be any death; there shall no longer be any*
> *mourning, or crying, or pain; the first things have passed away."*

> *And He who sits on the throne said, "Behold, I am making*
> *all things new.... Write, for these words are faithful and true.*

> *"... I am the Alpha and the Omega, the beginning and the*
> *end.... He who overcomes shall inherit these things, and I will*
> *be his God and he will be My son."* (Rev. 21:3-7)

Every man and woman has one of two eternal destinies. You can be as either the person at the wedding feast who did not wear his wedding garment and who was cast into outer darkness, into a place of *"weeping and gnashing of teeth"* (Matt. 22:11-13). Or you can be as the one who did wear them and of whom it is written:

> *Blessed are those who wash their robes, that they may have*
> *the right to the tree of life, and may enter by the gates into the city.*
> (Rev. 22:14)

God by nature is all-compassionate. It is written that He does not wish *"for any to perish, but for all to come to repentance"* (2 Pet. 3:9). By surrendering your life to the Bridegroom, God's only begotten Son Jesus Christ, you too can wash your robes and in the process become a part of the Bride. And when you do, you will joyfully join her in proclaiming:

> *And the Spirit and the bride say, "Come." And let the one*
> *who hears say, "Come." And let the one who is thirsty come; let*
> *the one who wishes take the water of life without cost....*

He who testifies to these things says, "Yes, I am coming quickly." (Rev. 22:17, 20a)

Even so, Maranatha! Come Lord Jesus!

Notes

1. N.p., n.d., quoted in Greenwald's tape "The Reigning Bride."

APPENDIX
THE ORIGIN OF
PRETRIBULATIONISM

Regarding the origin of the pretribulation rapture, Alexander Reese, in *The Approaching Advent of Christ* writes:

> Yet the undeniable fact is that this "any-moment" view of Christ's return only originated about 1830, when Darby gave forth at the same time the mistaken theory of the Secret Coming and Rapture; but all down the centuries there had existed Christians who longed for the Revelation of Christ, whilst expecting that Antichrist would [come] first.[1]

> All down the centuries the Church expected Christ's Coming after the arrival of Antichrist, according to the teaching of Christ and His Apostles. Only in 1830 did a school arise that treats with intolerance, and often with contempt, the attitude of those who had looked for Him in the manner just named. Not the slightest respect was paid to a view that held the field for 1,800 years.[2]

Another writer who attributed the beginnings of the pretribulation rapture teaching to Darby was Floyd E. Hamilton. In his book, *The Basis of Millennial Faith*, Hamilton writes:

> About a hundred years ago a man named J. N. Darby, founded a group of Christians who have become known as ... "The Plymouth Brethren." His followers, . . . particularly C. I. Scofield, author of the "Scofield Reference Bible," have popularized what we may call a new view of the events preceding and following the Coming of Christ.[3]

Much has been written on how Darby got his idea of a pretribulation rapture. The most popular explanation is described by J. Barton Payne, who in his book *The Imminent Appearing of Christ* writes:

For soon after 1830 a woman, while speaking in tongues, announced the "revelation" that the true church would be caught up to heaven before the tribulation and before Christ's return to earth. Irving was deposed from the ministry and died in 1834 . . . There the Irvingnite view received the enthusiastic support of Darby and others, ...[4]

Another place where we find the "tongues" origin is in Samuel P. Tregelles's book *The Hope of Christ's Second Coming* (1864). Tregelles, an early Brethren scholar writes:

I am not aware that there was any definite teaching that there would be a secret rapture of the Church at a secret coming, until this was given forth as an "utterance" in Mr. Irving's Church, from what was there received as being the voice of the Spirit. . . . It came not from Holy Scripture, but from that which falsely pretended to be the Spirit of God, while not owning the true doctrines of our Lord's incarnation in the same flesh and blood as His brethren, but without taint of sin.[5]

In his last sentence Tregelles is referring to the fact Edward Irving was dismissed from the ministry in 1832 for teaching Christ had a sinful nature. This is shown in Dave MacPherson's book *The Unbelievable Pre-Trib Origin*. MacPherson writes:

For several years Irving had also been teaching a doctrine which the Presbyterian General Assembly increasingly looked upon as heresy—that Christ had a sinful human nature.[6]

MacPherson concludes that the woman who gave the "utterance" these writers refer to was a young girl named Margaret Macdonald who lived Port Glasgow, Scotland. MacPherson, however, notes that Margaret did not receive her "pretrib" revelation via a message in tongues, but in a vision she had in the early part of 1830. Robert Norton, an eyewitness of the 1830 charismatic revival in western Scotland prefaces an account of her vision in his book *The Restoration of Apostles and Prophets; In the Catholic Apostolic Church* with the following statement:

Marvelous light was shed upon Scripture, and especially on the doctrine of the second Advent, by the revived spirit of prophecy. In the following account by Miss M. M. (Margaret Macdonald) . . . we have an instance; for here we first see the distinction between that final stage of the Lord's coming, when every eye will see Him, and His prior appearing in glory to them that look for Him.[7]

This is a definitive written report by an eyewitness that directly attributes the teaching of a two-stage coming of Jesus Christ to Margaret Macdonald's vision.

Margaret Macdonald was neither a member of Edward Irving's London congregation nor John Darby's Brethren. Both Darby and Irving, however, had direct or indirect contact with her. Edward Irving wrote a letter on June 2, 1830 that demonstrates how early and to what extent he knew of Margaret Macdonald's writings. In it he wrote:

> The substance Mary Campbell's and Margaret Macdonald's visions or revelations, given in their papers, carry to me a spiritual conviction and a spiritual reproof which I cannot express.[8]

MacPherson also presents Darby's complete written account, taken from his book the *Irrationalism of Infidelity* (1853), of his own visit to Port Glasgow. In it he described his visit to the Macdonald home, his encounter with the Macdonald brothers and Margaret, and his observation of their gift of tongues.

Although the evidence just presented strongly suggests it, most pretribulational scholars have denied their theory originated from a fifteen-year-old Scottish girl's vision. Nevertheless, almost all pretribulational scholars, Hal Lindsey included, will admit the development of the pretribulational teaching, and the dispensational method of interpretation on which it hinges, originated primarily from the works of John N. Darby.[9] What has been ignored, though, is that most mid-nineteenth century scholars credited its initial development not to Darby, but to Edward Irving.

Robert Baxter was one such early writer who attributed pretribulationalism to Irving. A regular attendant of Irving's church, he published a book in 1833 entitled *Narrative of Facts, Characterizing the Supernatural Manifestations in Members of Mr. Irving's Congregation, and Other Individuals, in England and Scotland, and Formerly in the Writer Himself.* Baxter writes:

> An opinion had been advanced in some of Mr. Irving's writings, that before the second coming of Christ, and before the setting in upon the world of the day of vengeance, emphatically so called in the Scriptures, the saints would be caught up to heaven like Enoch and Elijah; and would be thus saved from the destruction of this world, as Noah was saved in the ark, and as Lot was saved from Sodom.[10]

By 1833, when his book was published, Baxter was completely convinced the Irvingite movement in London was not of God.[11]

Besides Baxter, Norton was another early writer who credited the origin of the pretribulation rapture teaching to Irving.[12] A more modern scholar who also did was Iain H. Murray, who in his book *The Puritan Hope* writes:

> All the salient features of Darby's scheme are to be found in Irving. . . . At Albury and Irving's London congregation a curious belief, practically unknown in earlier Church history, had arisen, namely, that Christ's appearing before the millennium is to be in two stages, the first a secret "rapture" removing the Church before a "Great Tribulation" smites the earth, the second his coming with the saints to set up his kingdom. This idea comes into full prominence in Darby.[13]

From the historical evidence, it seems likely that the original early development of pretribulationalism came not from John Darby, but from Edward Irving, a man who taught the obvious heresy that our Lord Jesus Christ possessed a sinful human nature. The pretribulation rapture teaching was started by a man who was unsound in one of the most basic of Christian doctrines—the sinlessness of Jesus Christ. Even so, most of the born-again movement has openly embraced Edward Irving's position. Perhaps the Apostle Paul's words to Timothy are presently coming to pass:

> *For the time will come when men will not put up with sound doctrine. Instead, to suit their own desires, they will gather around them a great number of teachers to say what their itching ears want to hear.*
>
> *They will turn their ears away from the truth and turn aside to myths.* (2 Tim. 4:3,4, NIV)

All Christians should be aware of how the pretribulation rapture teaching originated 160 years ago. Unfortunately, most Christians are not that informed. Still, many in the church today are teaching the "doctrine" of a pretribulation rapture as if it were an indisputable truth. The simple truth is, it is not.

Notes

1. Reese, 227.

2. Reese, 240.

3. (Grand Rapids, MI: William B. Eerdmans Publishing co., 1942), 23-24, quoted in MacPherson, 21.

4. (Grand Rapids, MI: Wm. B. Eerdmans Publishing Co., 1962), 32.

5. London: Samuel Bagster & Sons, 1864), 35, quoted in MacPherson, 18-19.

6. MacPherson, 40.

7. (London: Bosworth & Harrison, 1861), quoted MacPherson, 47.

8. Margaret O. W. Oliphant, *The Life of Edward Irving* (London: Hurst and Blackett Publishers, 1865) quoted in MacPherson, 111.

9. Lindsey, 83-84, 173-174.

10. (London: James Misbet, 1833), 17, quoted in MacPherson, 95.

11. MacPherson, 98.

12. MacPherson, 87.

13. Murrays, 200, quoted in MacPherson, 33-34.